GEGE AKUTAMI

Hamburger!!!

GEGE AKUTAMI published a few short
works before starting *Jujutsu Kaisen*, which began
serialization in *Weekly Shonen Jump* in 2018.

JUJUTSU KAISEN

VOLUME 14
SHONEN JUMP MANGA EDITION

BY GEGE AKUTAMI

TRANSLATION **Stefan Koza**
TOUCH-UP ART & LETTERING **Snir Aharon**
DESIGN **Joy Zhang**
EDITOR **John Bae**
CONSULTING EDITOR **Erika Onabe**

JUJUTSU KAISEN © 2018 by Gege Akutami
All rights reserved.
First published in Japan in 2018 by SHUEISHA Inc., Tokyo.
English translation rights arranged by SHUEISHA Inc.

The stories, characters, and incidents mentioned
in this publication are entirely fictional.

No portion of this book may be reproduced
or transmitted in any form or by any means without
written permission from the copyright holders.

Printed in Italy

Published by VIZ Media, LLC
P.O. Box 77010
San Francisco, CA 94107

10 9 8 7 6 5
First printing, February 2022
Fifth printing, August 2024

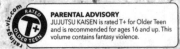

PARENTAL ADVISORY
JUJUTSU KAISEN is rated T+ for Older Teen
and is recommended for ages 16 and up. This
volume contains fantasy violence.

JUJUTSU KAISEN

14

THE SHIBUYA INCIDENT
—RIGHT AND WRONG—

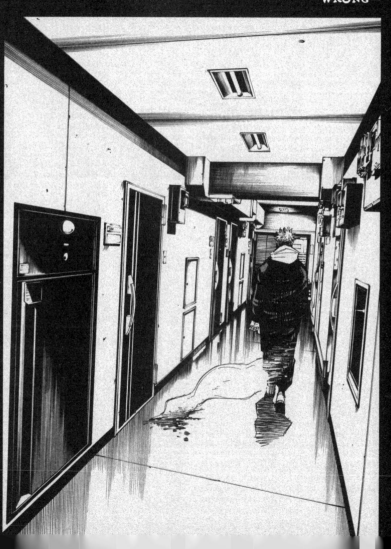

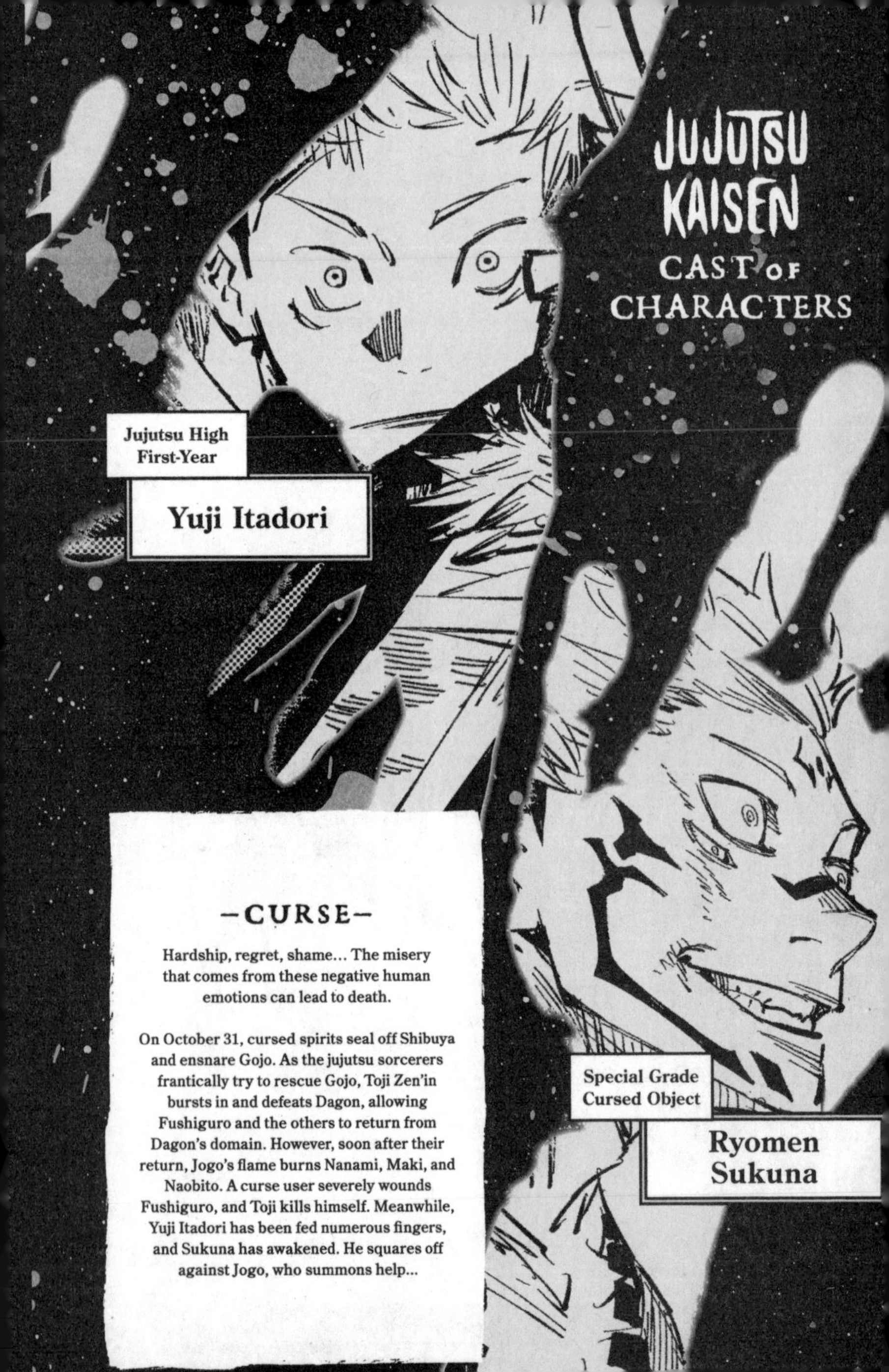
JUJUTSU KAISEN
CAST OF CHARACTERS
Jujutsu High First-Year
Yuji Itadori
Special Grade Cursed Object
Ryomen Sukuna

—CURSE—

Hardship, regret, shame… The misery that comes from these negative human emotions can lead to death.

On October 31, cursed spirits seal off Shibuya and ensnare Gojo. As the jujutsu sorcerers frantically try to rescue Gojo, Toji Zen'in bursts in and defeats Dagon, allowing Fushiguro and the others to return from Dagon's domain. However, soon after their return, Jogo's flame burns Nanami, Maki, and Naobito. A curse user severely wounds Fushiguro, and Toji kills himself. Meanwhile, Yuji Itadori has been fed numerous fingers, and Sukuna has awakened. He squares off against Jogo, who summons help...

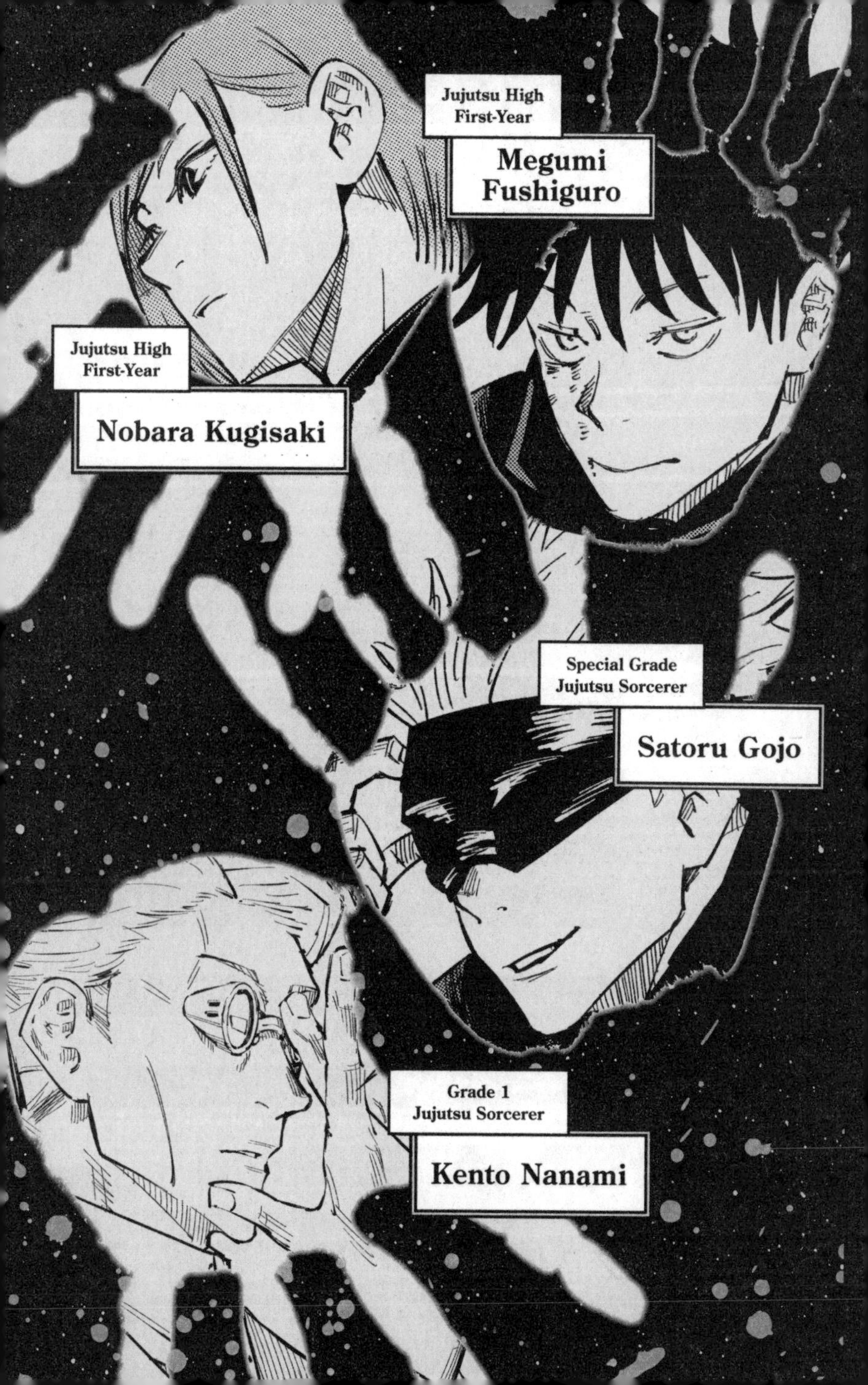
Jujutsu High
First-Year
Megumi
Fushiguro
Jujutsu High
First-Year
Nobara Kugisaki
Special Grade
Jujutsu Sorcerer
Satoru Gojo
Grade 1
Jujutsu Sorcerer
Kento Nanami

JUJUTSU KAISEN

14

THE SHIBUYA INCIDENT —RIGHT AND WRONG—

CHAPTER 116: THE SHIBUYA INCIDENT, PART 34

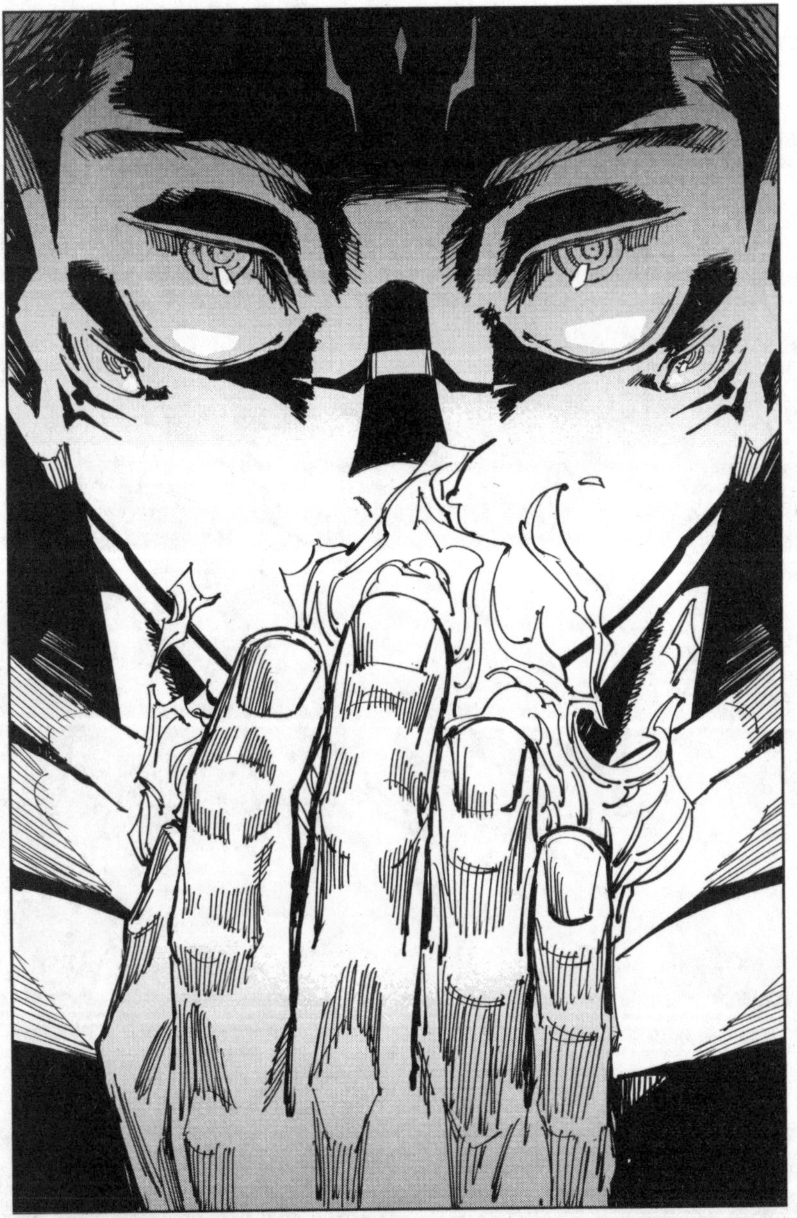

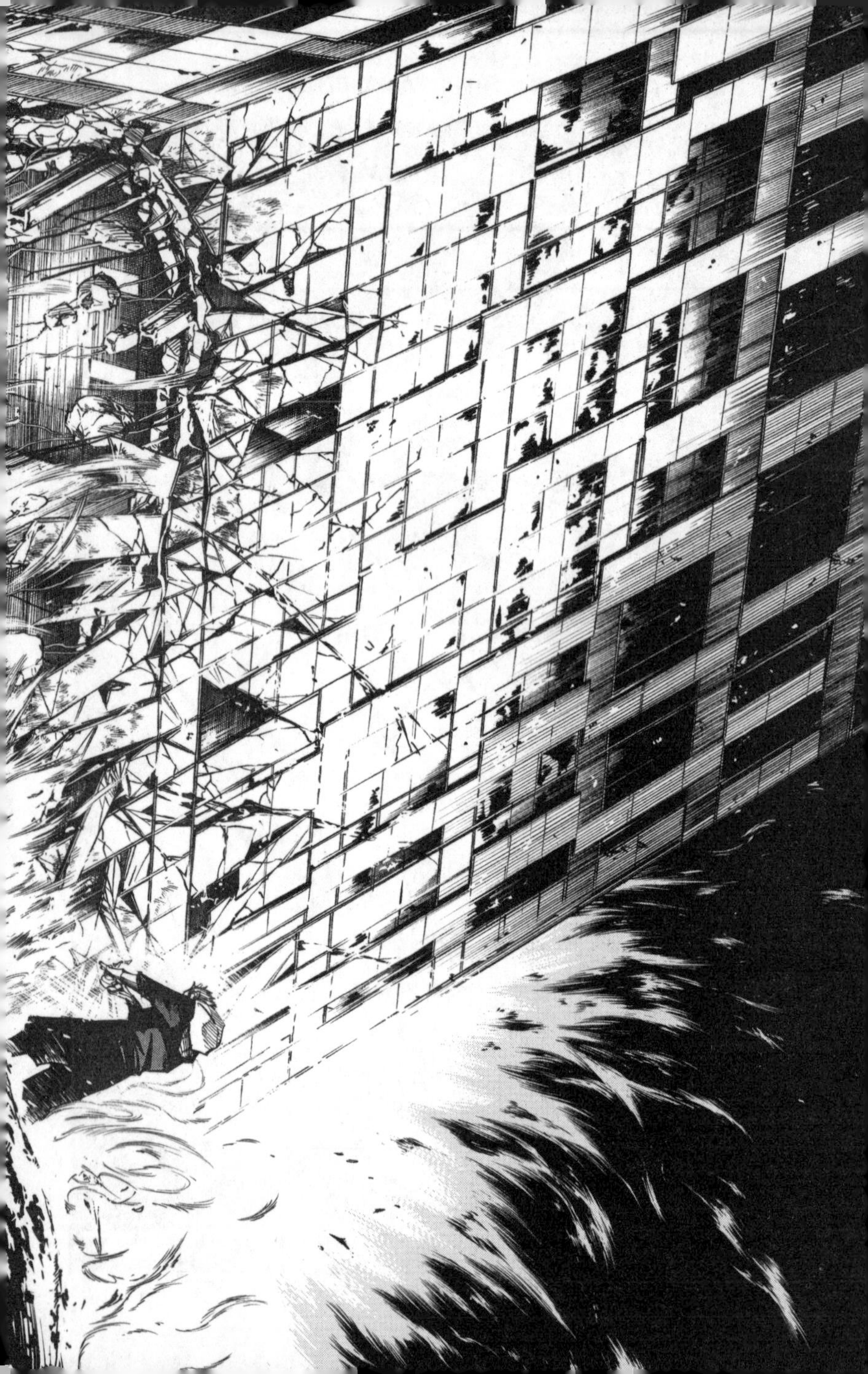

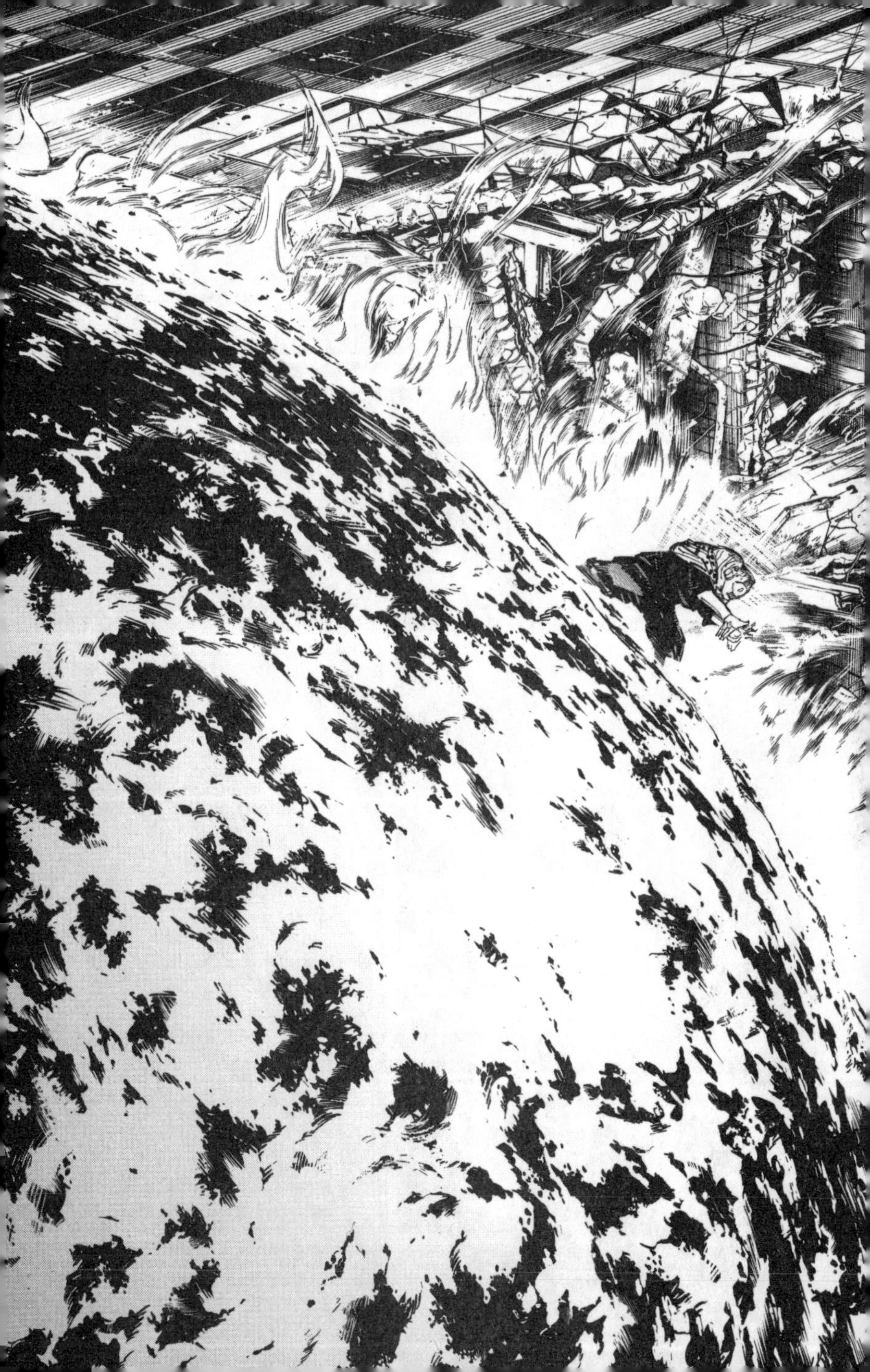

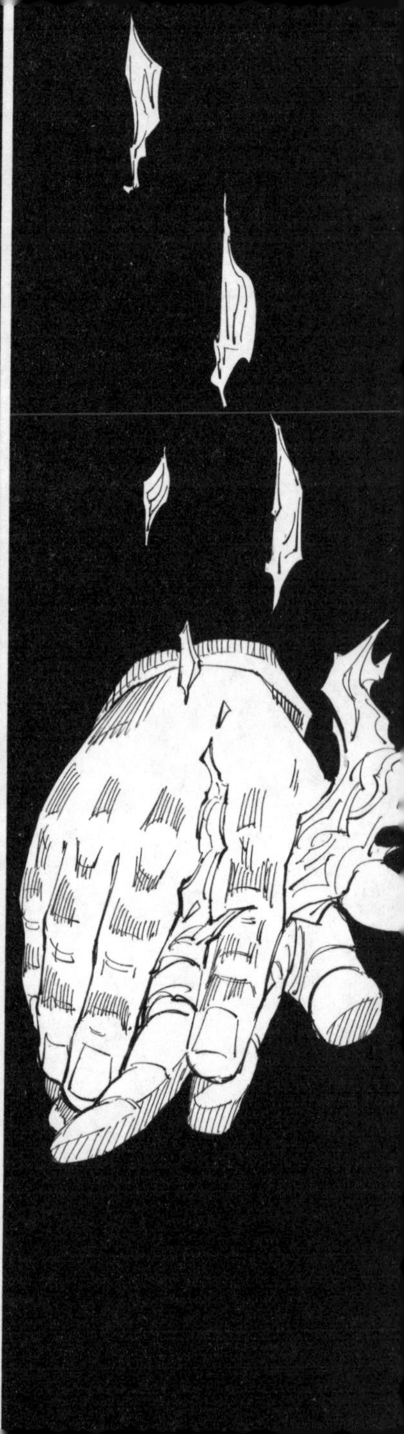
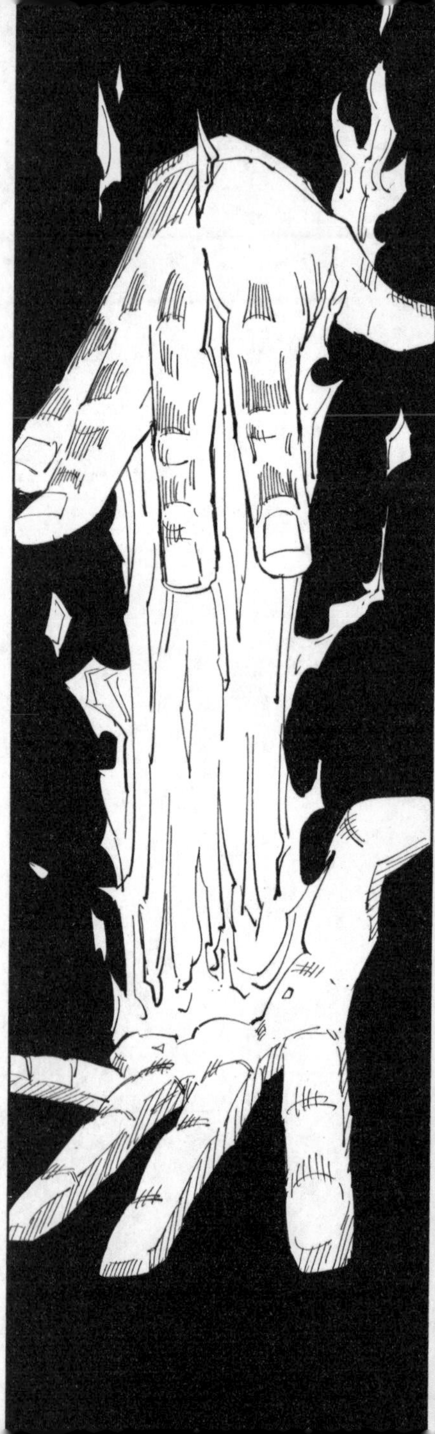

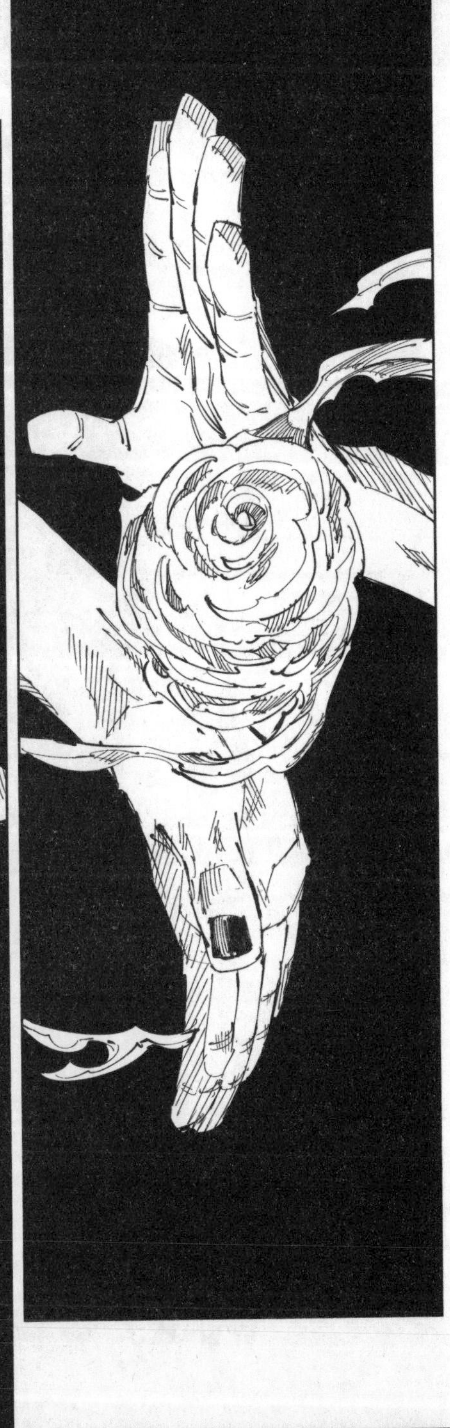
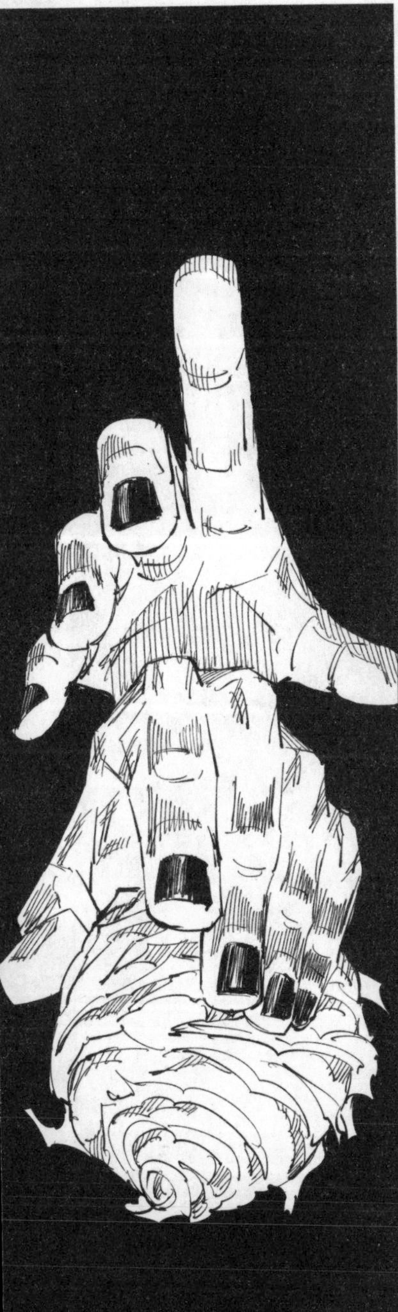

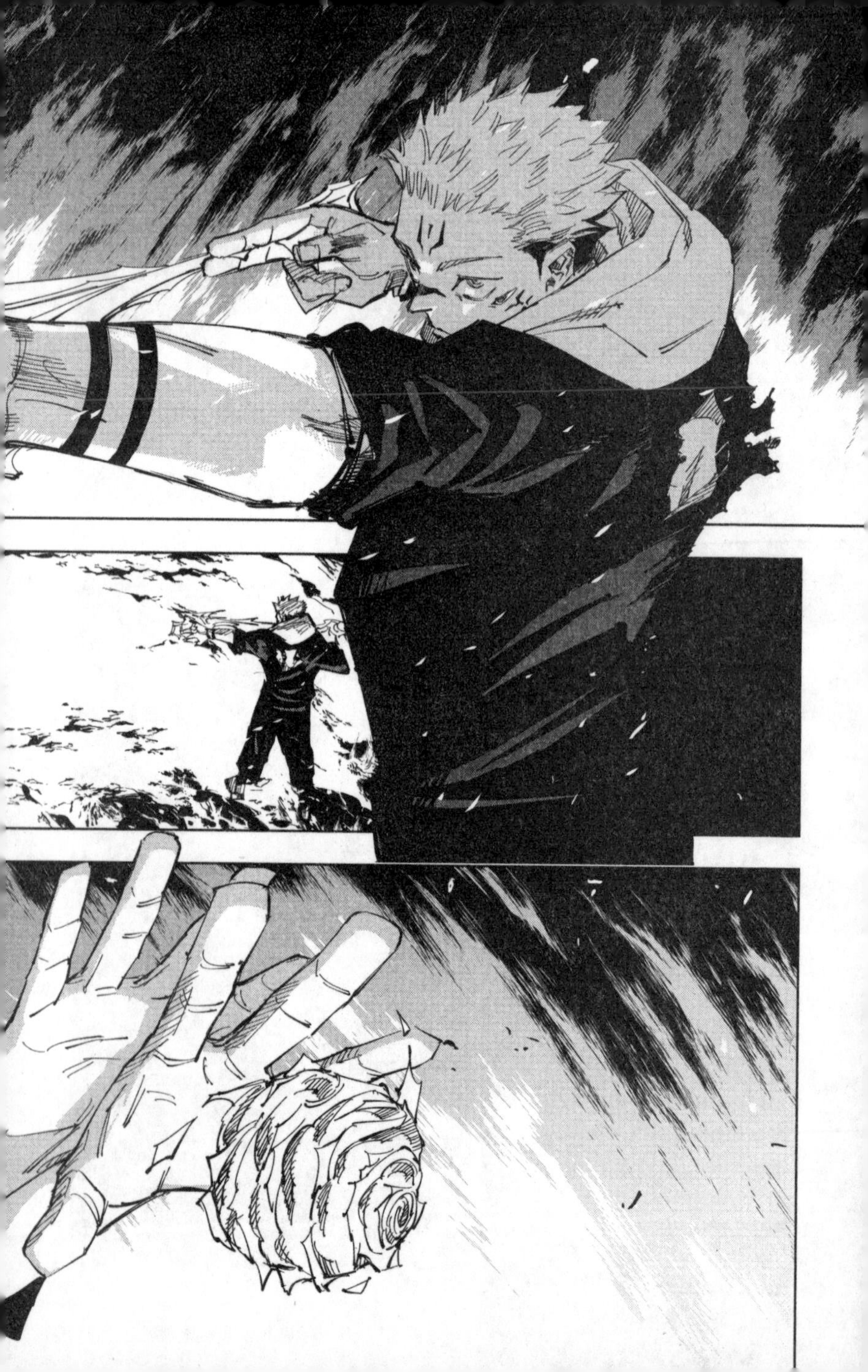

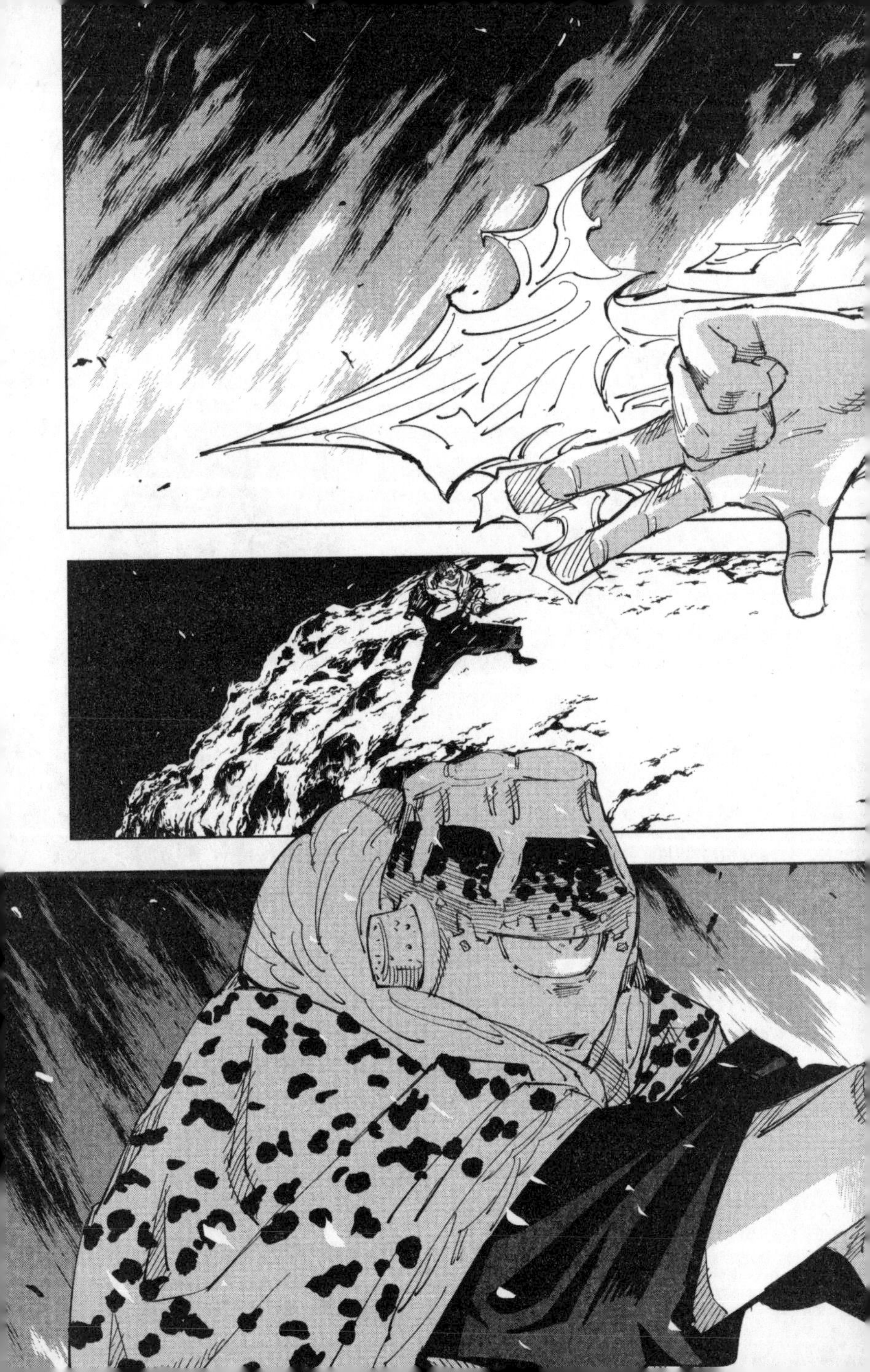

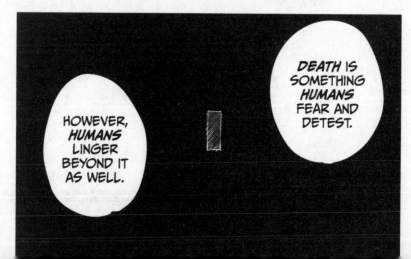

DEATH IS A MIRROR FOR *HUMANS*.

MAHITO IS THAT MIRROR.

MAHITO WILL CONTINUE TO GROW STRONGER.

THAT'S WHY YOU...

...PROPPED HIM UP AS THE LEADER.

...

WHEN WE'RE REBORN, WE WON'T BE THE SAME AS BEFORE.

EVEN SO, I'LL BE ANTICIPATING THE DAY WE MEET AGAIN.

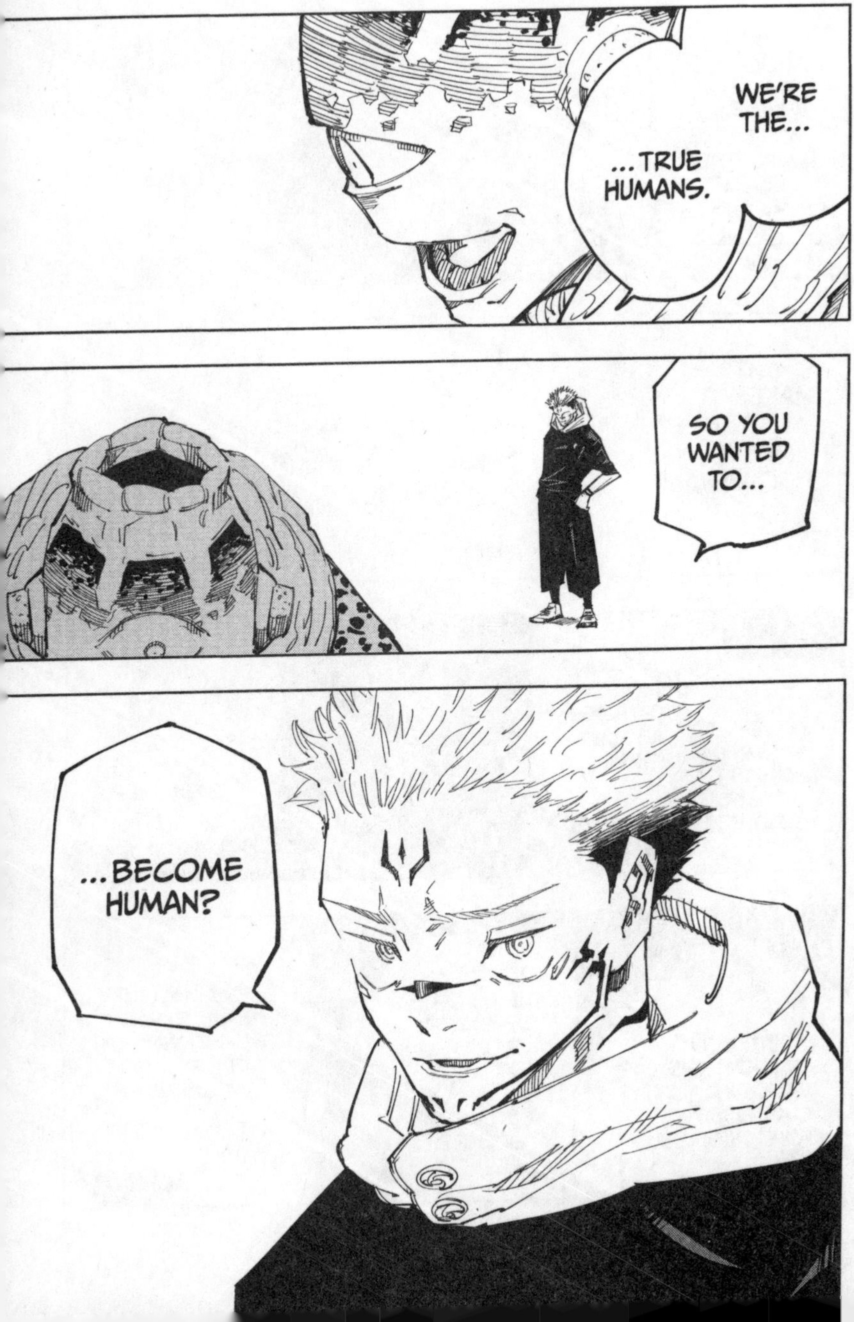
WE'RE THE...
...TRUE HUMANS.
SO YOU WANTED TO...
...BECOME HUMAN?

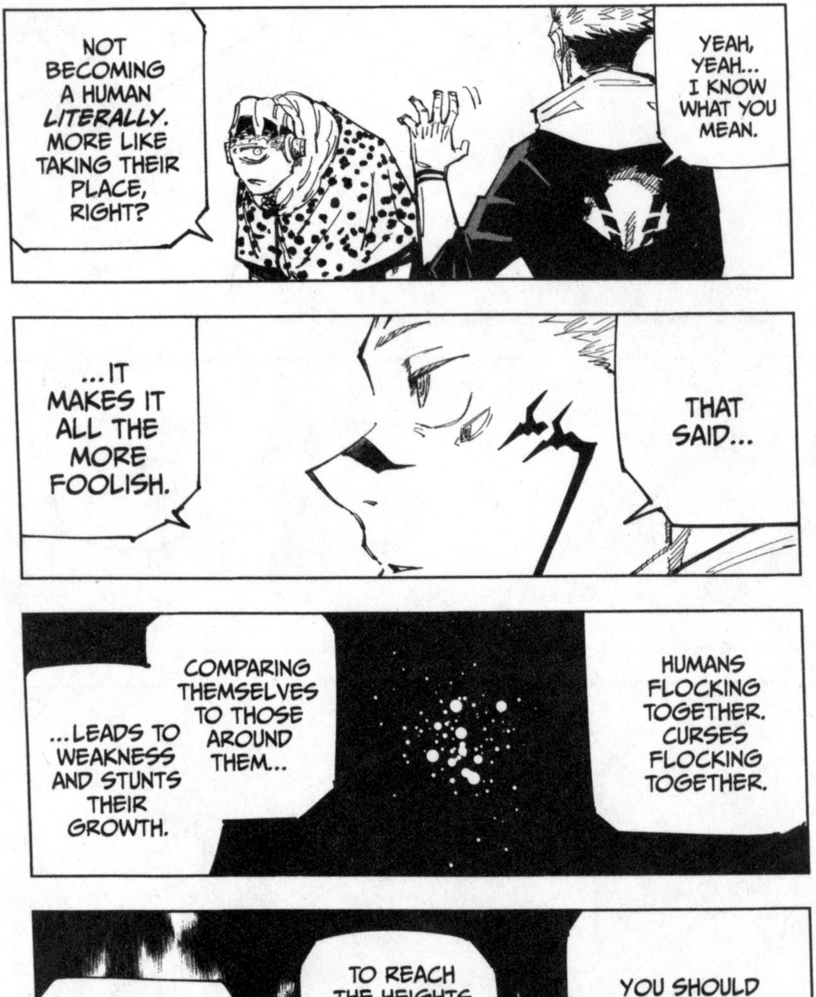
YEAH, YEAH... I KNOW WHAT YOU MEAN.
NOT BECOMING A HUMAN *LITERALLY*. MORE LIKE TAKING THEIR PLACE, RIGHT?
THAT SAID...
...IT MAKES IT ALL THE MORE FOOLISH.
HUMANS FLOCKING TOGETHER. CURSES FLOCKING TOGETHER.
COMPARING THEMSELVES TO THOSE AROUND THEM...
...LEADS TO WEAKNESS AND STUNTS THEIR GROWTH.
YOU SHOULD HAVE BURNT EVERYTHING YOU DESIRED TO A CINDER.
TO REACH THE HEIGHTS OF SATORU GOJO AND NOT WORRY ABOUT YOUR FUTURE OR IDENTITY.
BUT YOU LACKED THE *HUNGER* TO TAKE HOLD OF YOUR DESIRES.

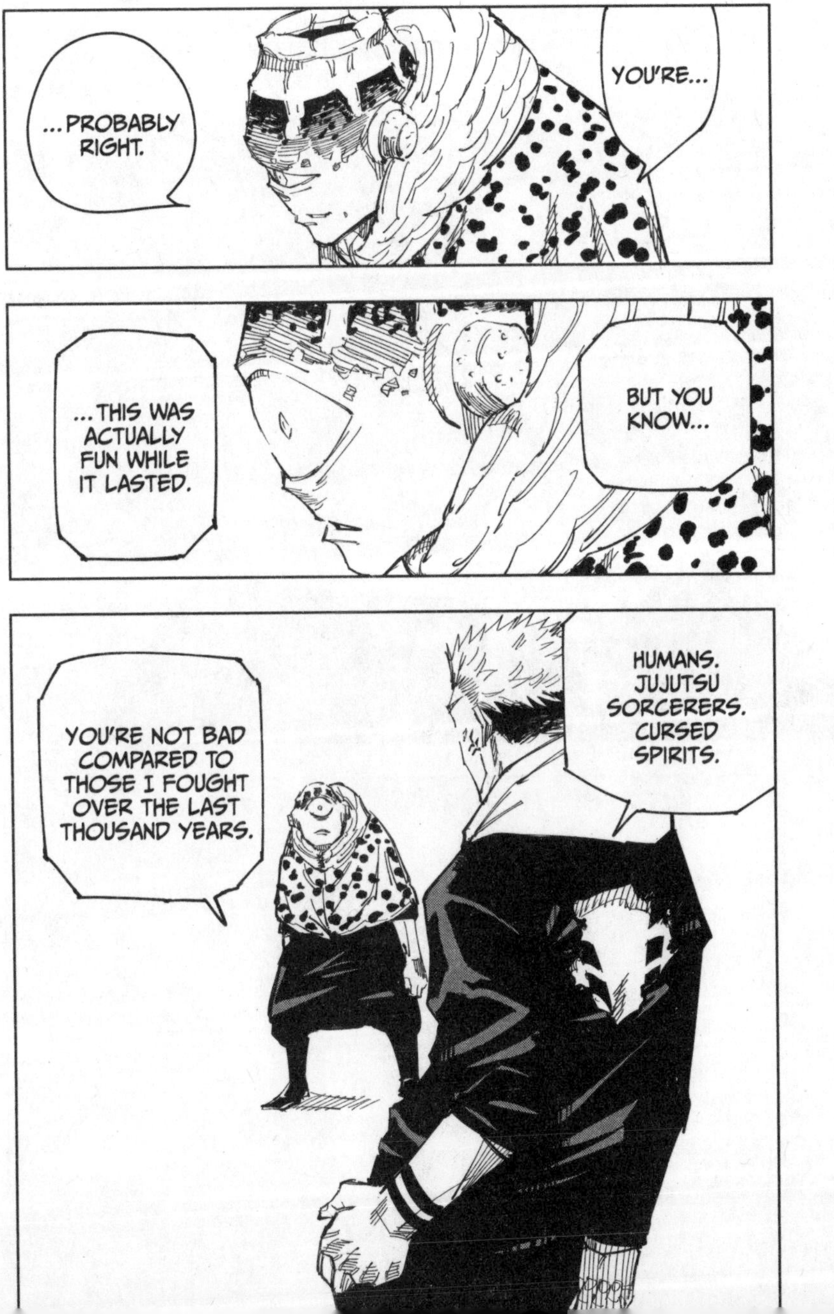
YOU'RE...
...PROBABLY RIGHT.
BUT YOU KNOW...
...THIS WAS ACTUALLY FUN WHILE IT LASTED.
HUMANS. JUJUTSU SORCERERS. CURSED SPIRITS.
YOU'RE NOT BAD COMPARED TO THOSE I FOUGHT OVER THE LAST THOUSAND YEARS.

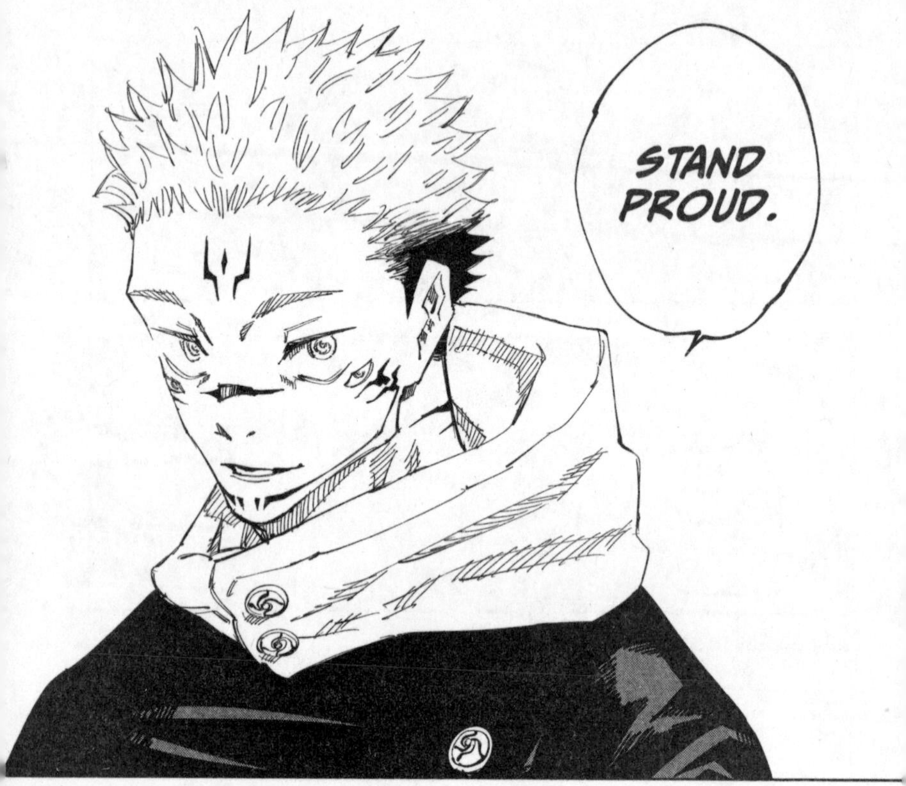
STAND PROUD.

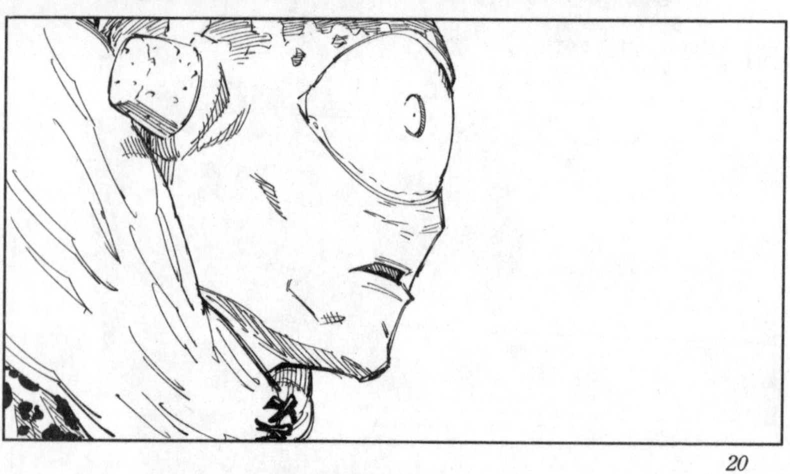

YOU'RE STRONG.

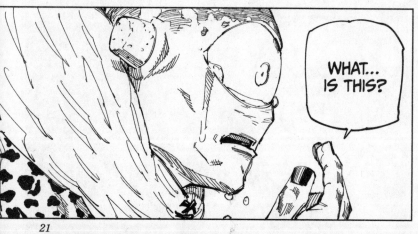

WHAT... IS THIS?

MASTER SUKUNA.

THMP

KRAKL
KRAKL

I'VE COME TO ESCORT YOU.

WHO ARE YOU?

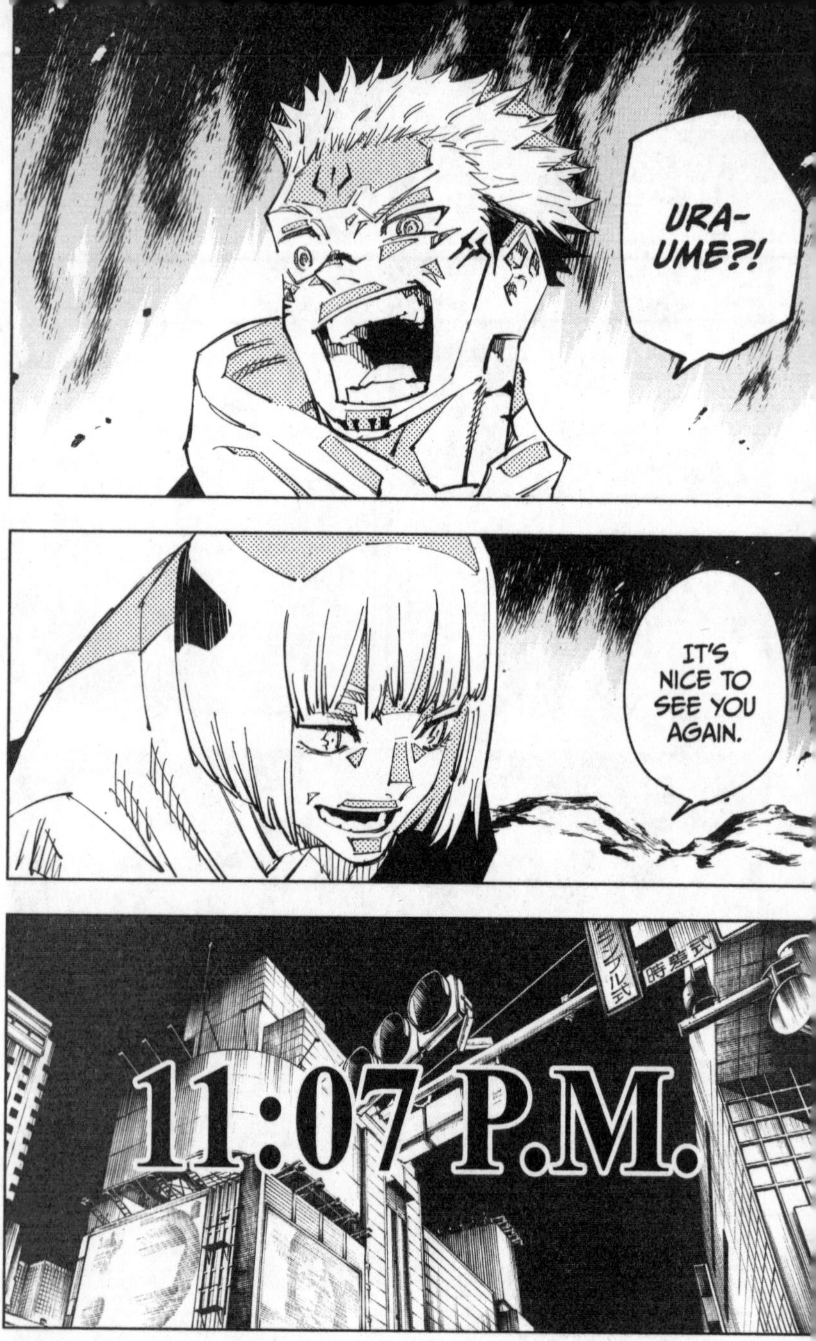
URA-
UME?!
IT'S NICE TO SEE YOU AGAIN.
11:07 P.M.

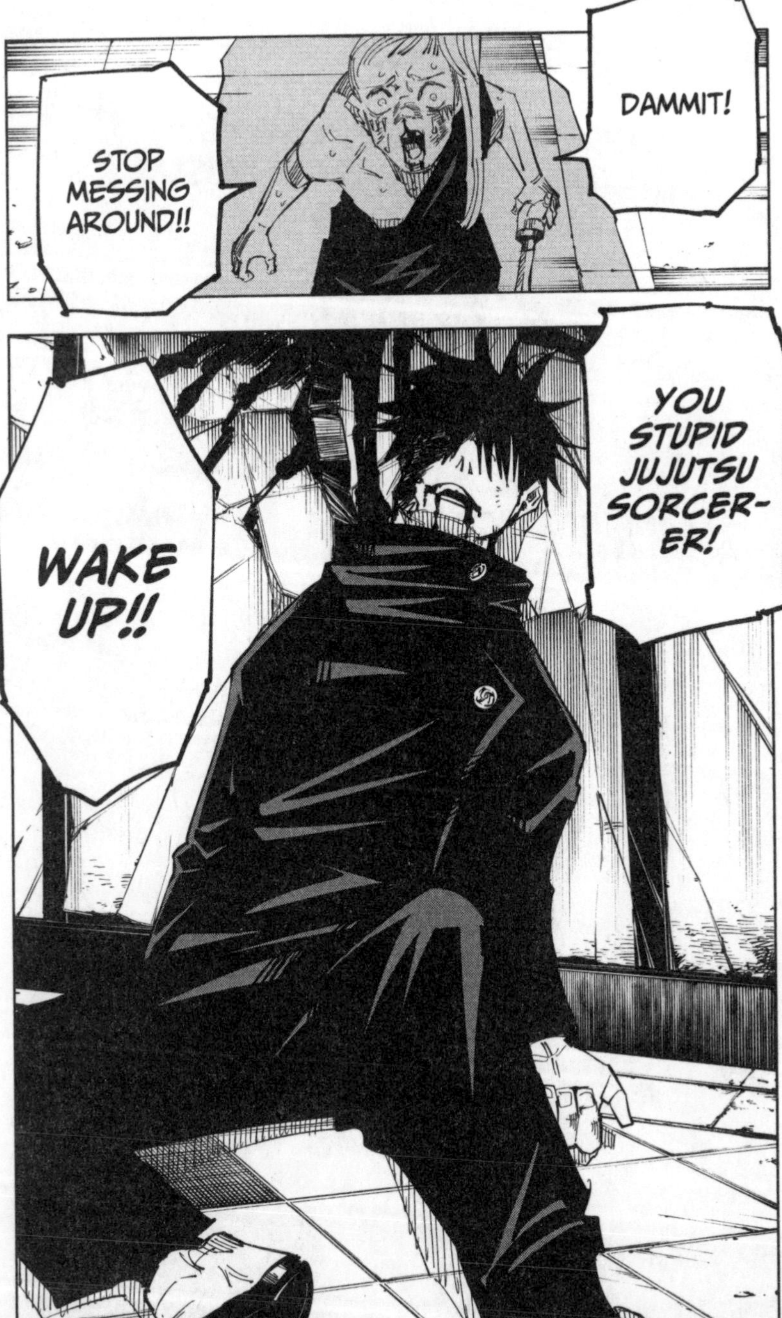
DAMMIT!
STOP MESSING AROUND!!
YOU STUPID JUJUTSU SORCERER!
WAKE UP!!

THE 2020 VALENTINES RANKINGS THAT I SERIOUSLY ALMOST FORGOT

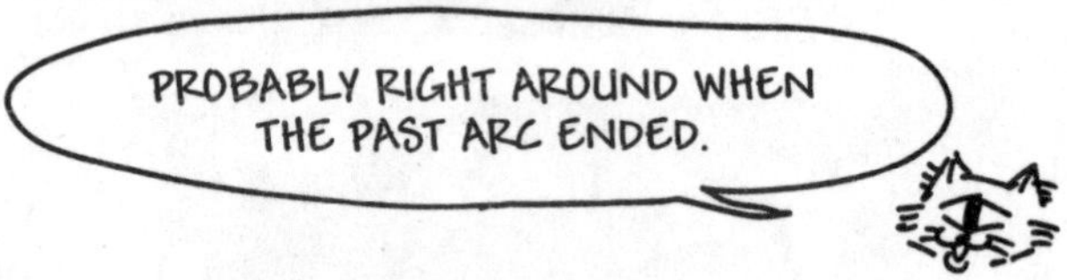
PROBABLY RIGHT AROUND WHEN THE PAST ARC ENDED.

RANKINGS (VALENTINES RECEIVED)	CHARACTER	AKUTAMI'S COMMENT
1 (54)	GOJO	OKAY, I GET IT ALREADY...
2 (30)	GETO	NOT TOO BAD.
3 (23)	FUSHIGURO	YOU NEED TO TRY A LITTLE HARDER.
4 (22)	ITADORI	SQUEAKING BY AS THE MAIN CHARACTER.

CHAPTER 117: THE SHIBUYA INCIDENT, PART 35

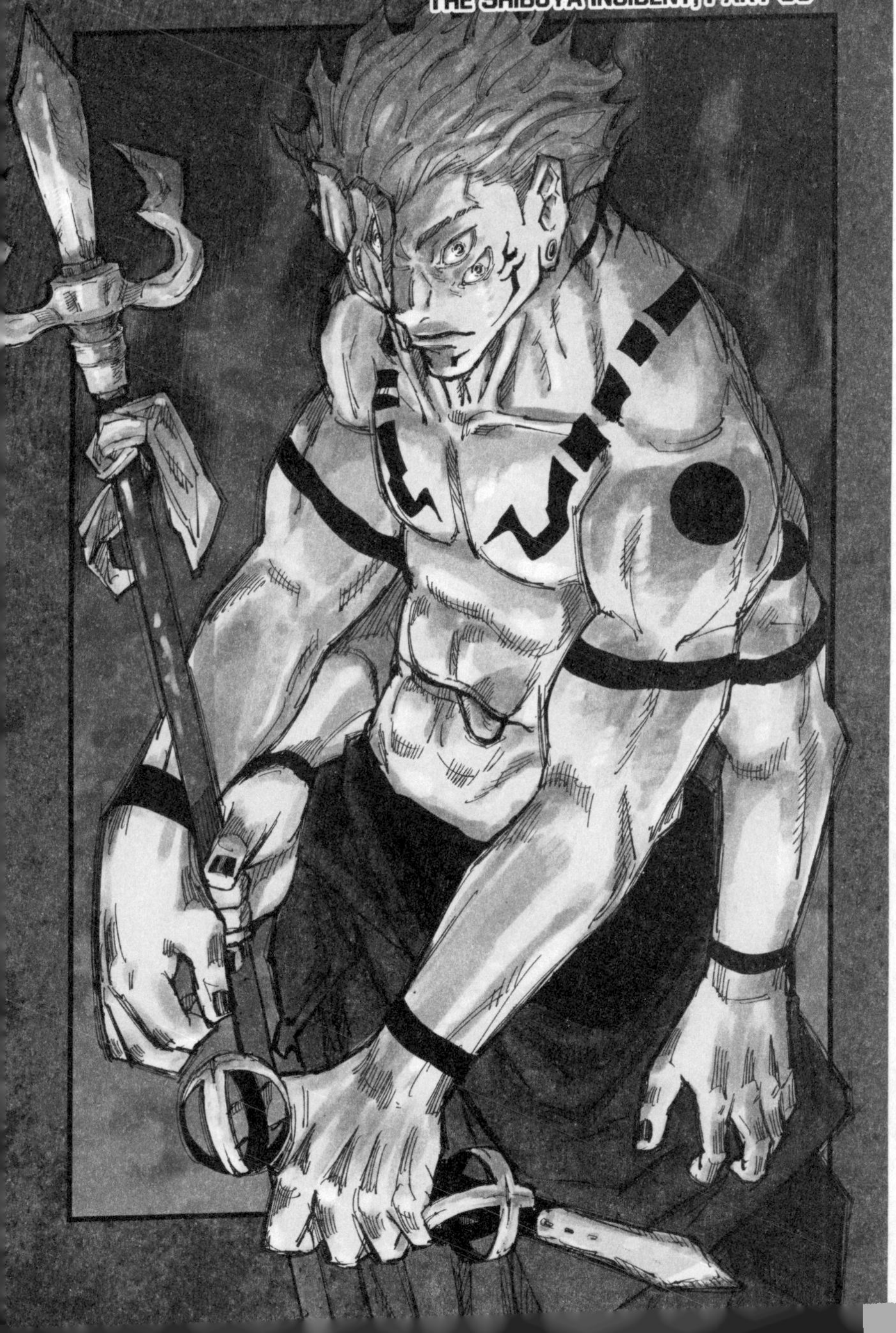

JUJUTSU KAISEN

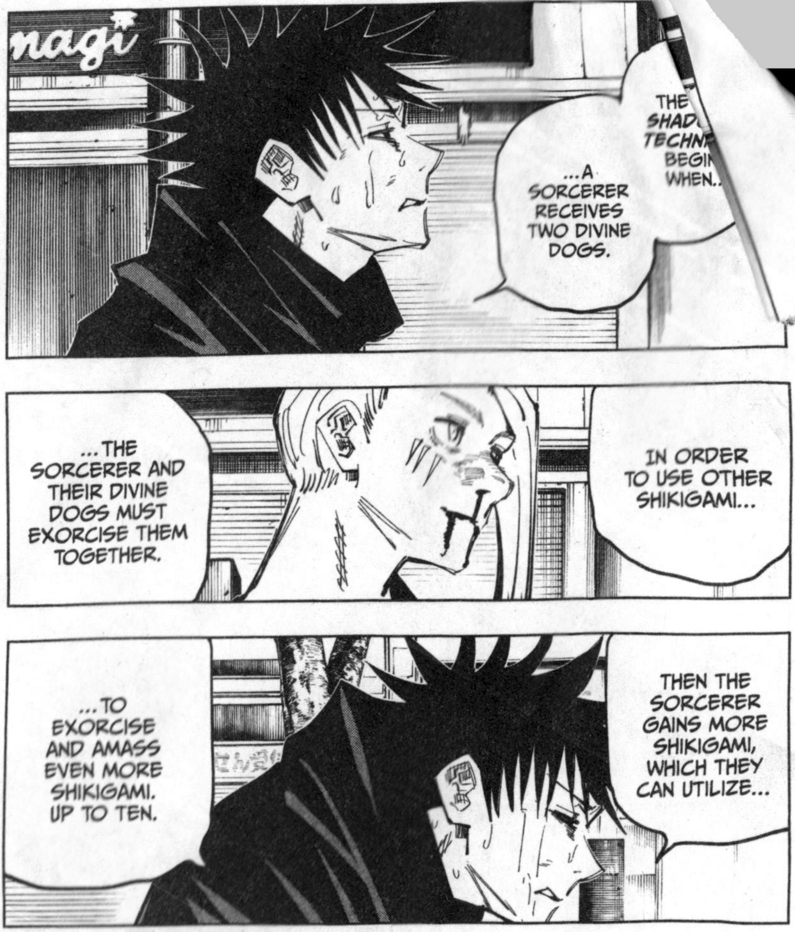
nagi
THE SHAD TECHN BEGI WHEN..
...A SORCERER RECEIVES TWO DIVINE DOGS.
IN ORDER TO USE OTHER SHIKIGAMI...
...THE SORCERER AND THEIR DIVINE DOGS MUST EXORCISE THEM TOGETHER.
THEN THE SORCERER GAINS MORE SHIKIGAMI, WHICH THEY CAN UTILIZE...
...TO EXORCISE AND AMASS EVEN MORE SHIKIGAMI. UP TO TEN.
...
ARE YOU FINISHED YET?

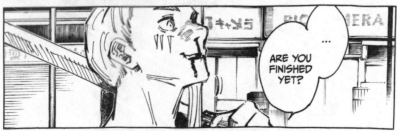

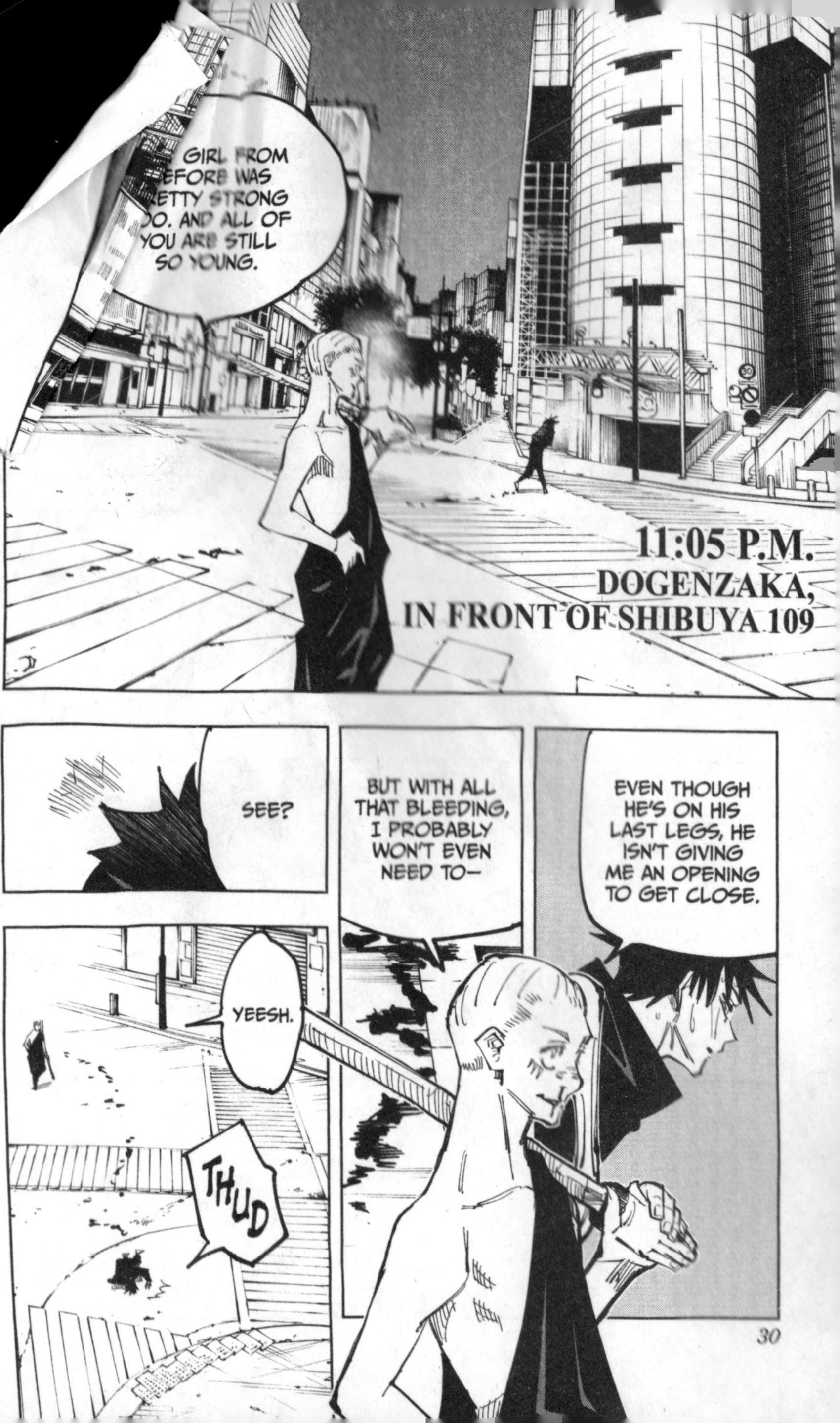
GIRL FROM EFORE WAS ETTY STRONG OO. AND ALL OF YOU ARE STILL SO YOUNG.
11:05 P.M.
DOGENZAKA, IN FRONT OF SHIBUYA 109
EVEN THOUGH HE'S ON HIS LAST LEGS, HE ISN'T GIVING ME AN OPENING TO GET CLOSE.
BUT WITH ALL THAT BLEEDING, I PROBABLY WON'T EVEN NEED TO—
SEE?
YEESH.
THUD

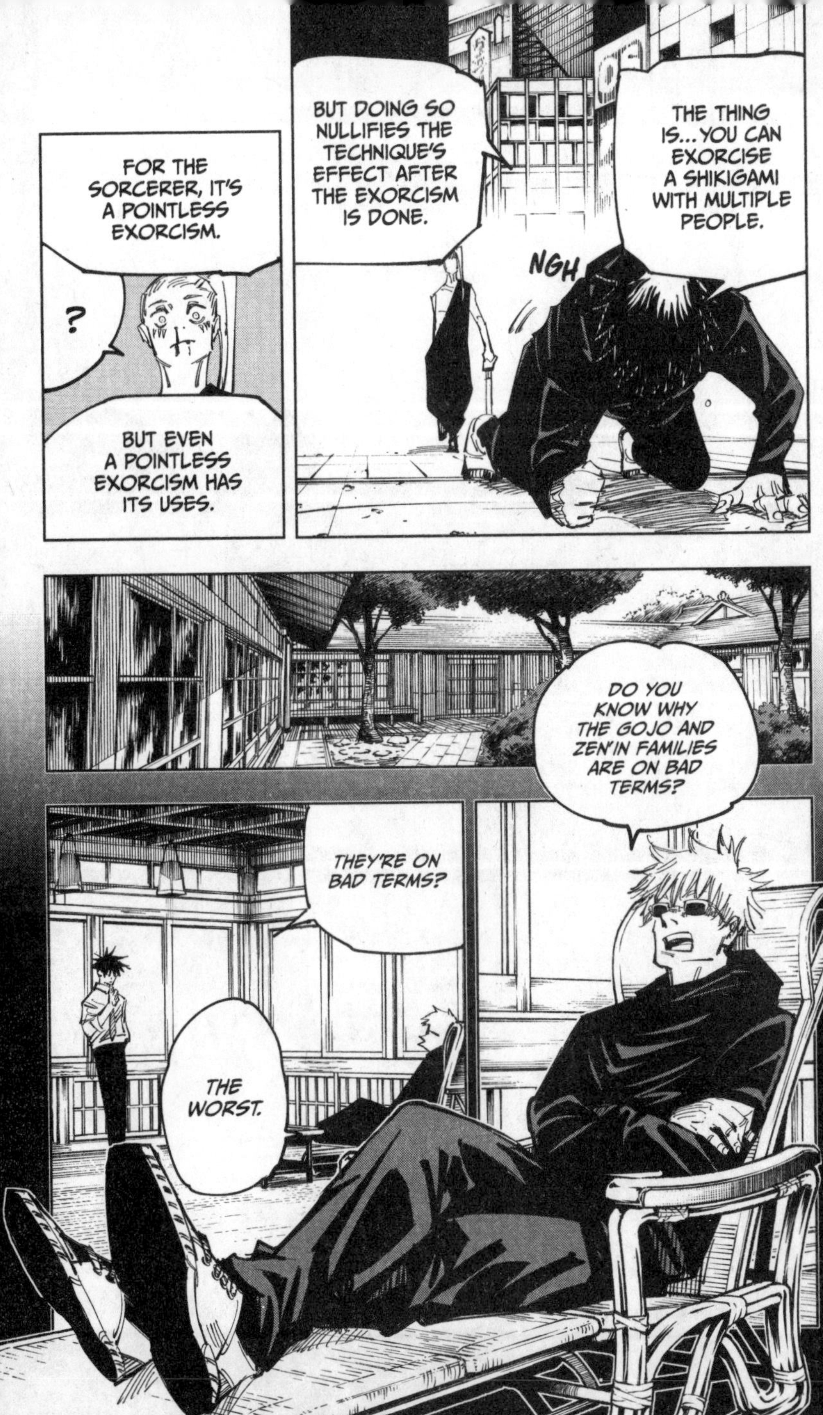
THE THING IS...YOU CAN EXORCISE A SHIKIGAMI WITH MULTIPLE PEOPLE.
BUT DOING SO NULLIFIES THE TECHNIQUE'S EFFECT AFTER THE EXORCISM IS DONE.
NGH
FOR THE SORCERER, IT'S A POINTLESS EXORCISM.
?
BUT EVEN A POINTLESS EXORCISM HAS ITS USES.
DO YOU KNOW WHY THE GOJO AND ZEN'IN FAMILIES ARE ON BAD TERMS?
THEY'RE ON BAD TERMS?
THE WORST.

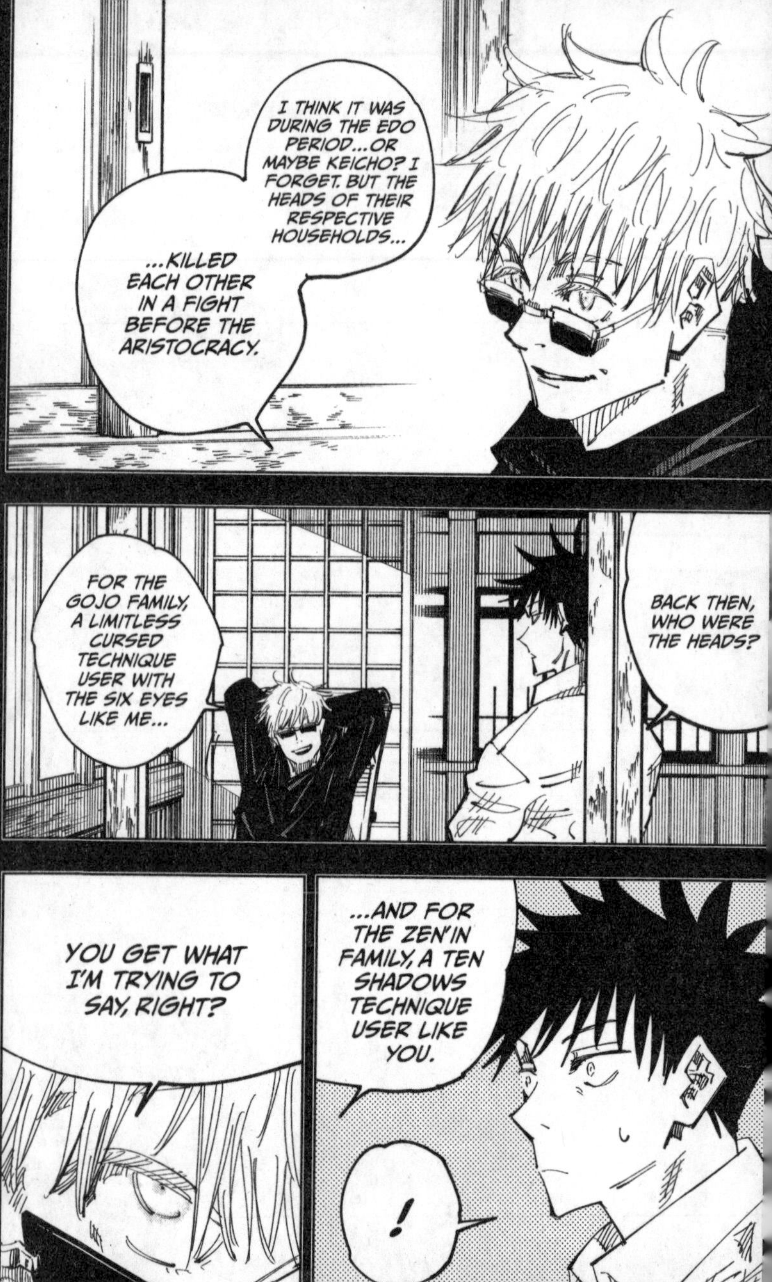
I THINK IT WAS DURING THE EDO PERIOD...OR MAYBE KEICHO? I FORGET. BUT THE HEADS OF THEIR RESPECTIVE HOUSEHOLDS...
...KILLED EACH OTHER IN A FIGHT BEFORE THE ARISTOCRACY.
BACK THEN, WHO WERE THE HEADS?
FOR THE GOJO FAMILY, A LIMITLESS CURSED TECHNIQUE USER WITH THE SIX EYES LIKE ME...
...AND FOR THE ZEN'IN FAMILY, A TEN SHADOWS TECHNIQUE USER LIKE YOU.
!
YOU GET WHAT I'M TRYING TO SAY, RIGHT?

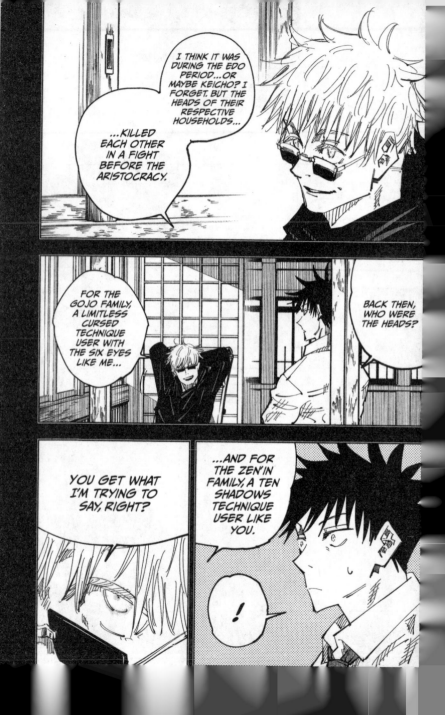

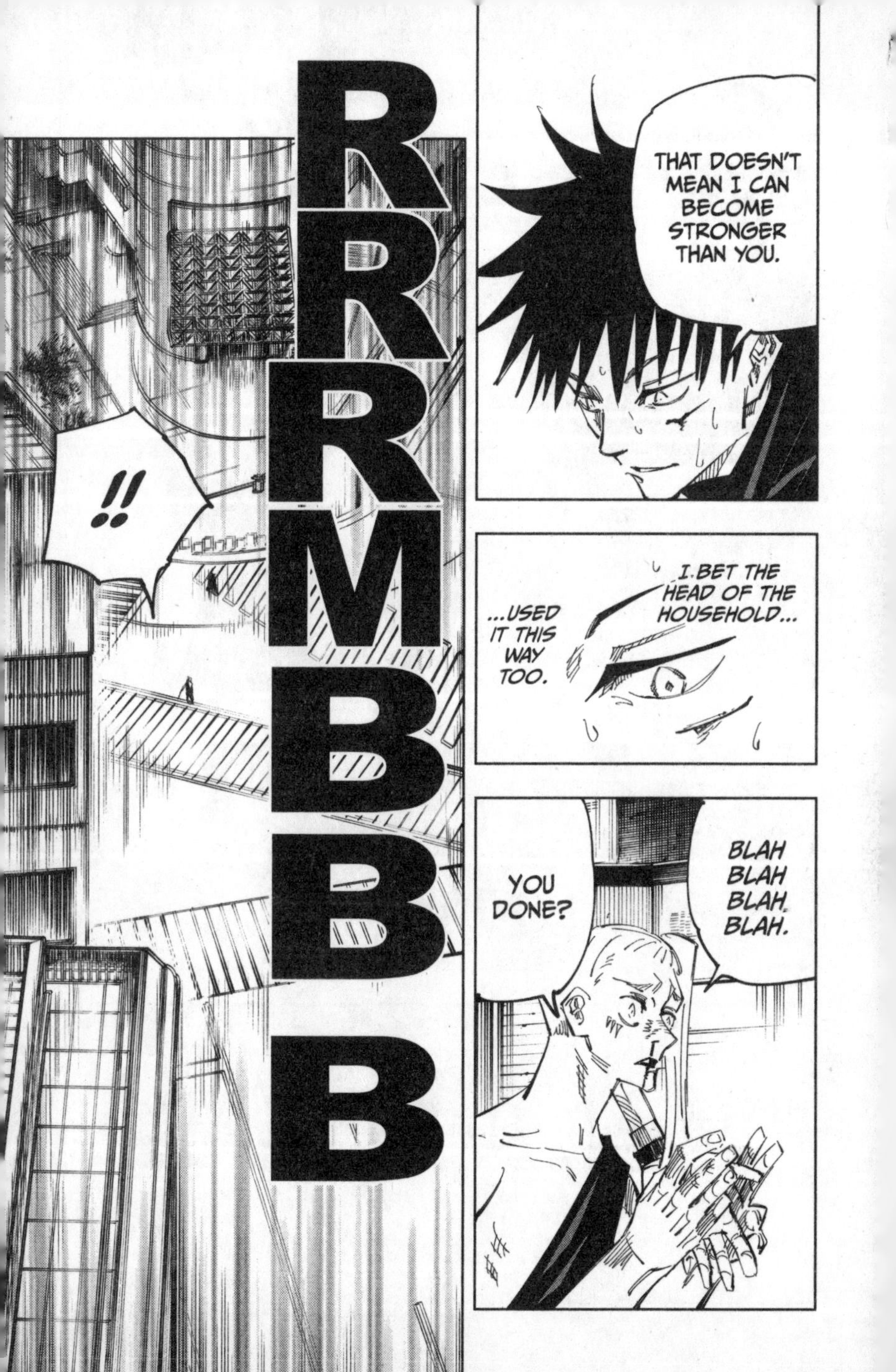
THAT DOESN'T MEAN I CAN BECOME STRONGER THAN YOU.
I BET THE HEAD OF THE HOUSEHOLD...
...USED IT THIS WAY TOO.
BLAH BLAH BLAH, BLAH.
YOU DONE?
RRRMBBB
!!

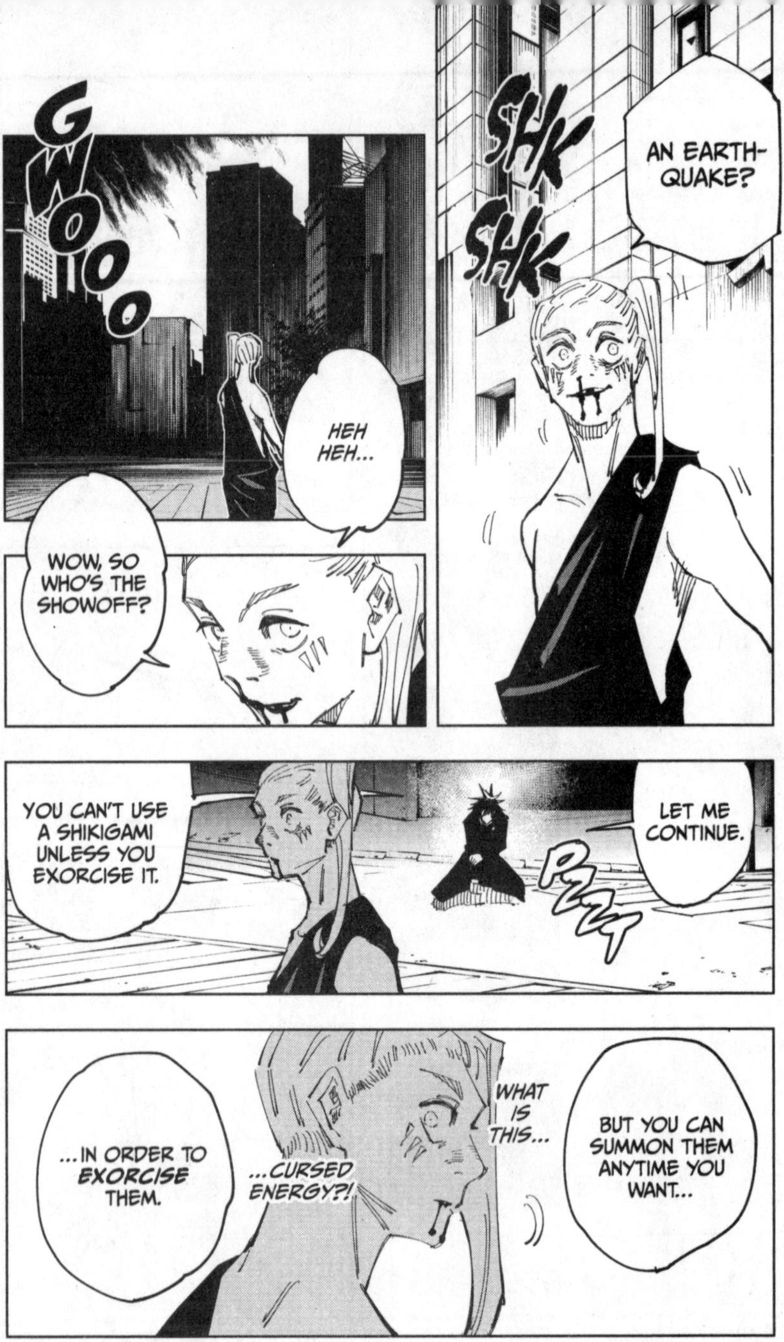
SHK SHK
AN EARTH-QUAKE?
GWOOO
HEH HEH...
WOW, SO WHO'S THE SHOWOFF?
LET ME CONTINUE.
PZZT
YOU CAN'T USE A SHIKIGAMI UNLESS YOU EXORCISE IT.
BUT YOU CAN SUMMON THEM ANYTIME YOU WANT...
WHAT IS THIS...
...CURSED ENERGY?!
...IN ORDER TO **EXORCISE** THEM.

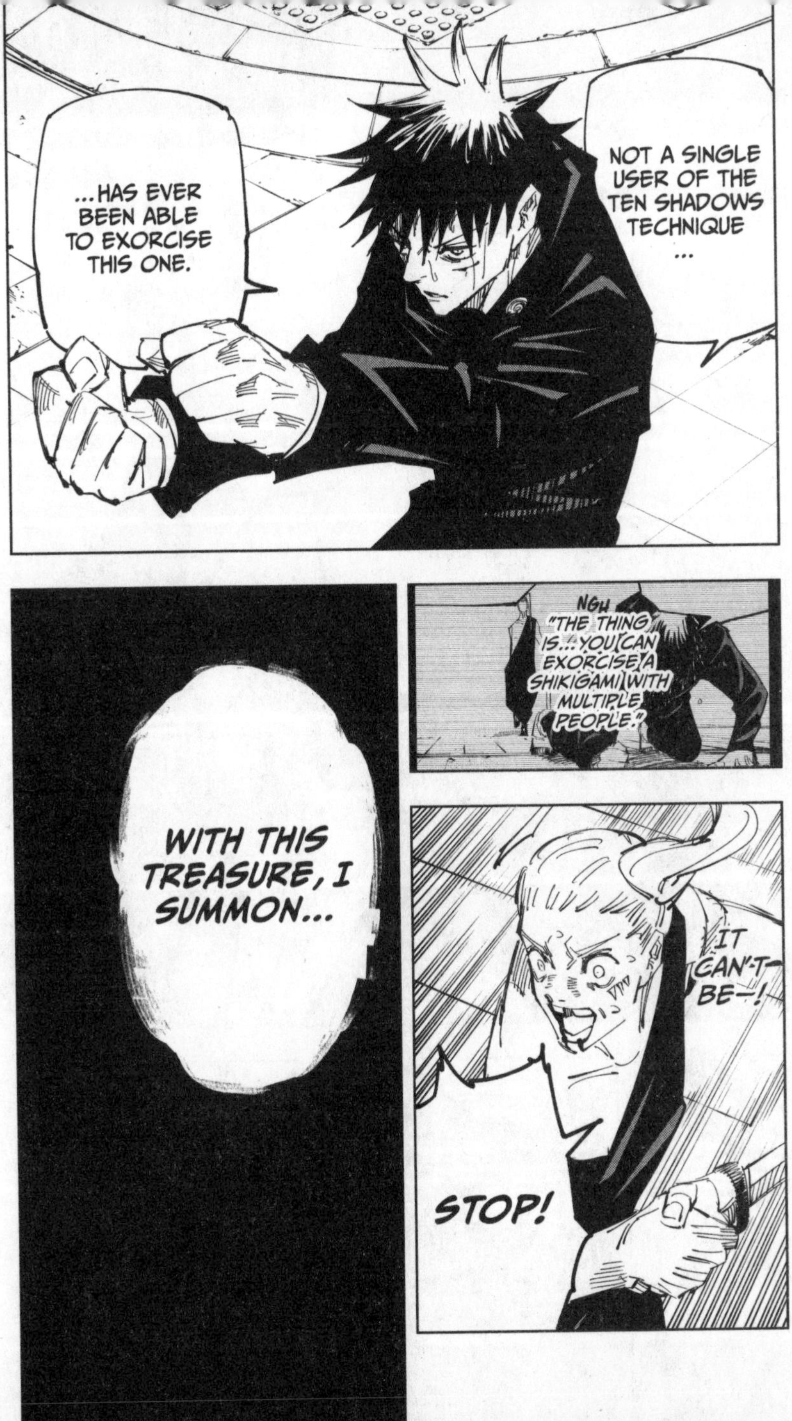
NOT A SINGLE USER OF THE TEN SHADOWS TECHNIQUE ...
...HAS EVER BEEN ABLE TO EXORCISE THIS ONE.
NGH
"THE THING IS... YOU CAN EXORCISE A SHIKIGAMI WITH MULTIPLE PEOPLE."
IT CAN'T BE—!
STOP!
WITH THIS TREASURE, I SUMMON...

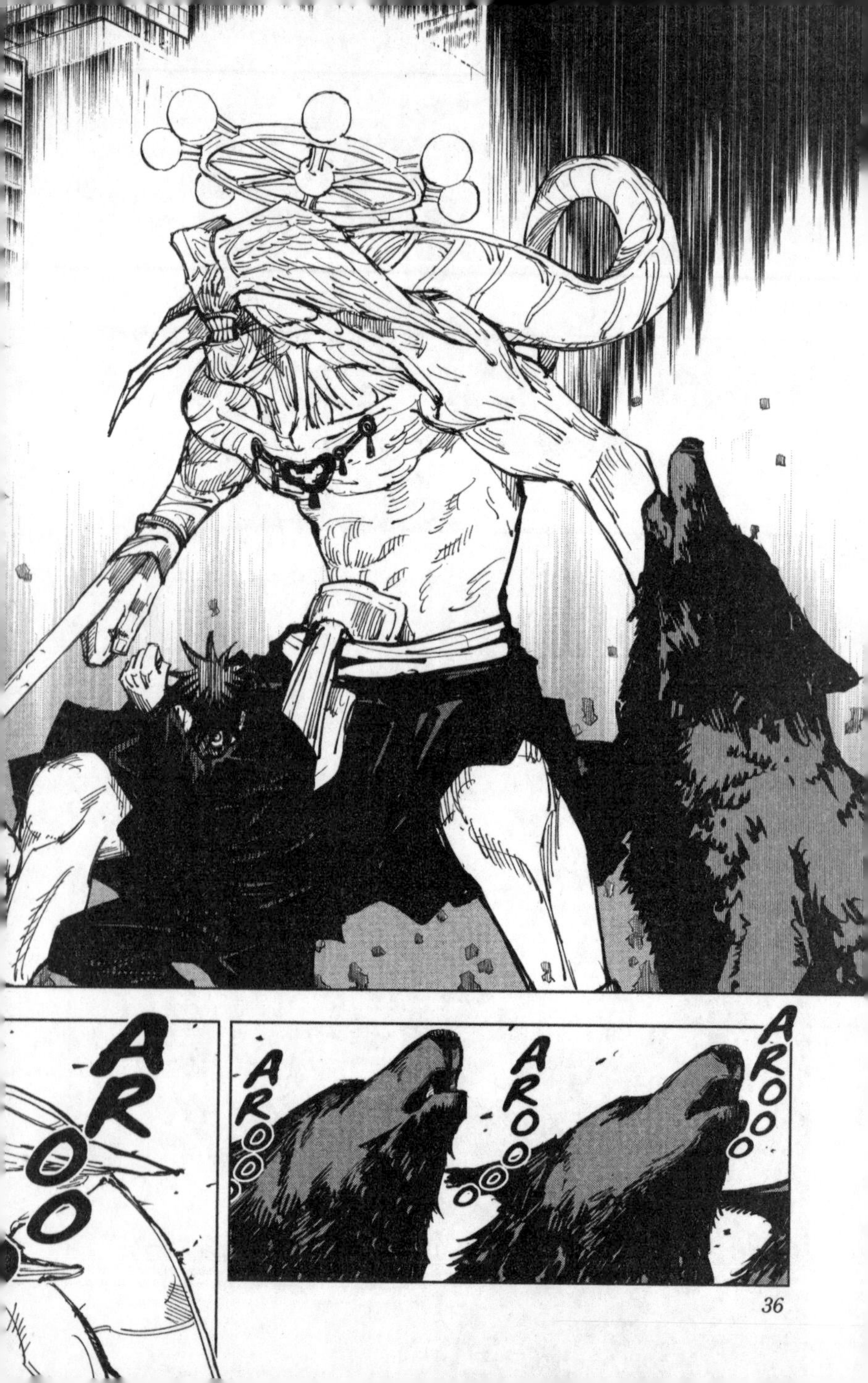
AROOOO
AROOOO
AROOOO
AROO

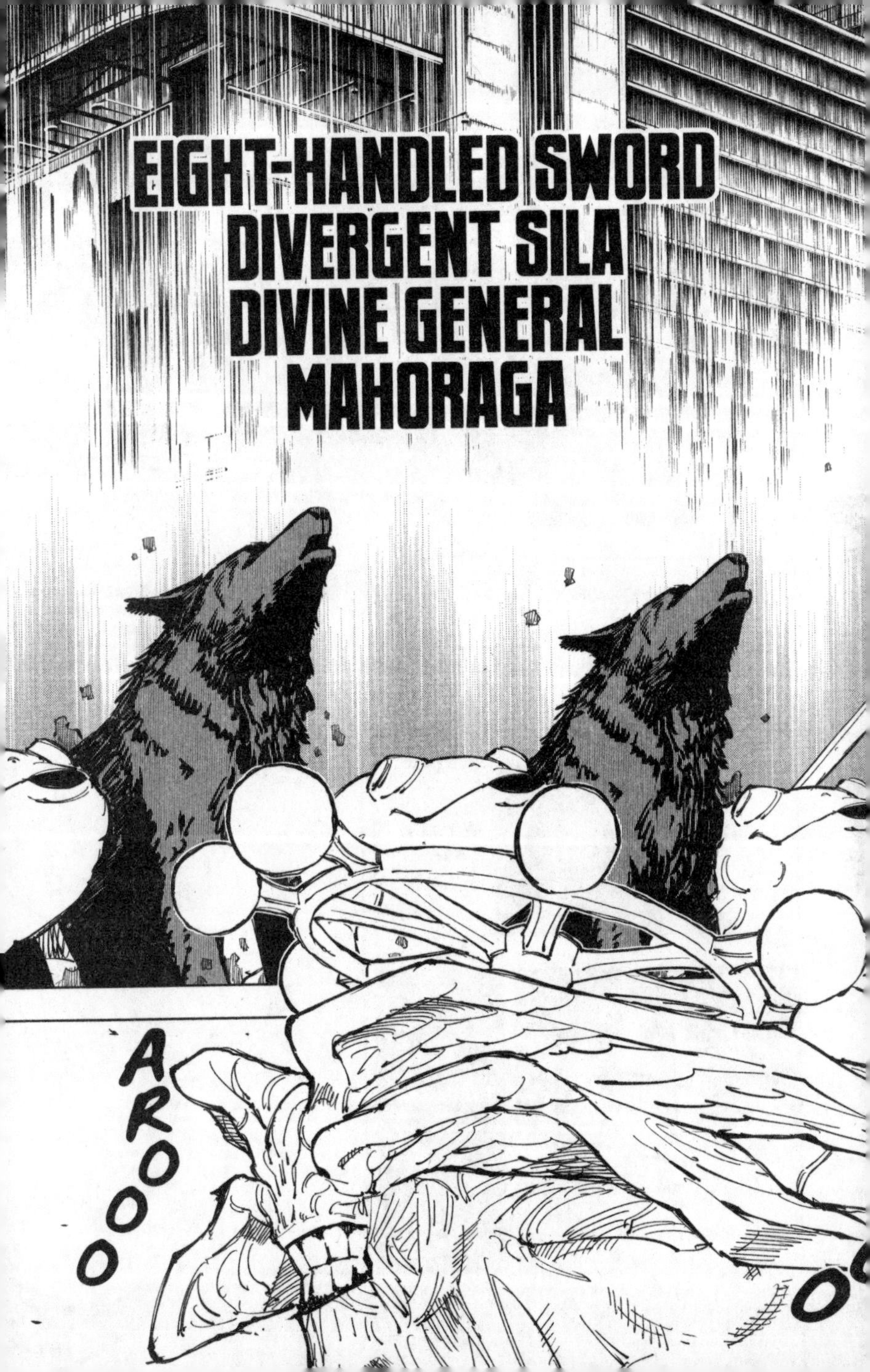
EIGHT-HANDLED SWORD
DIVERGENT SILA
DIVINE GENERAL
MAHORAGA
AROOOO
OO

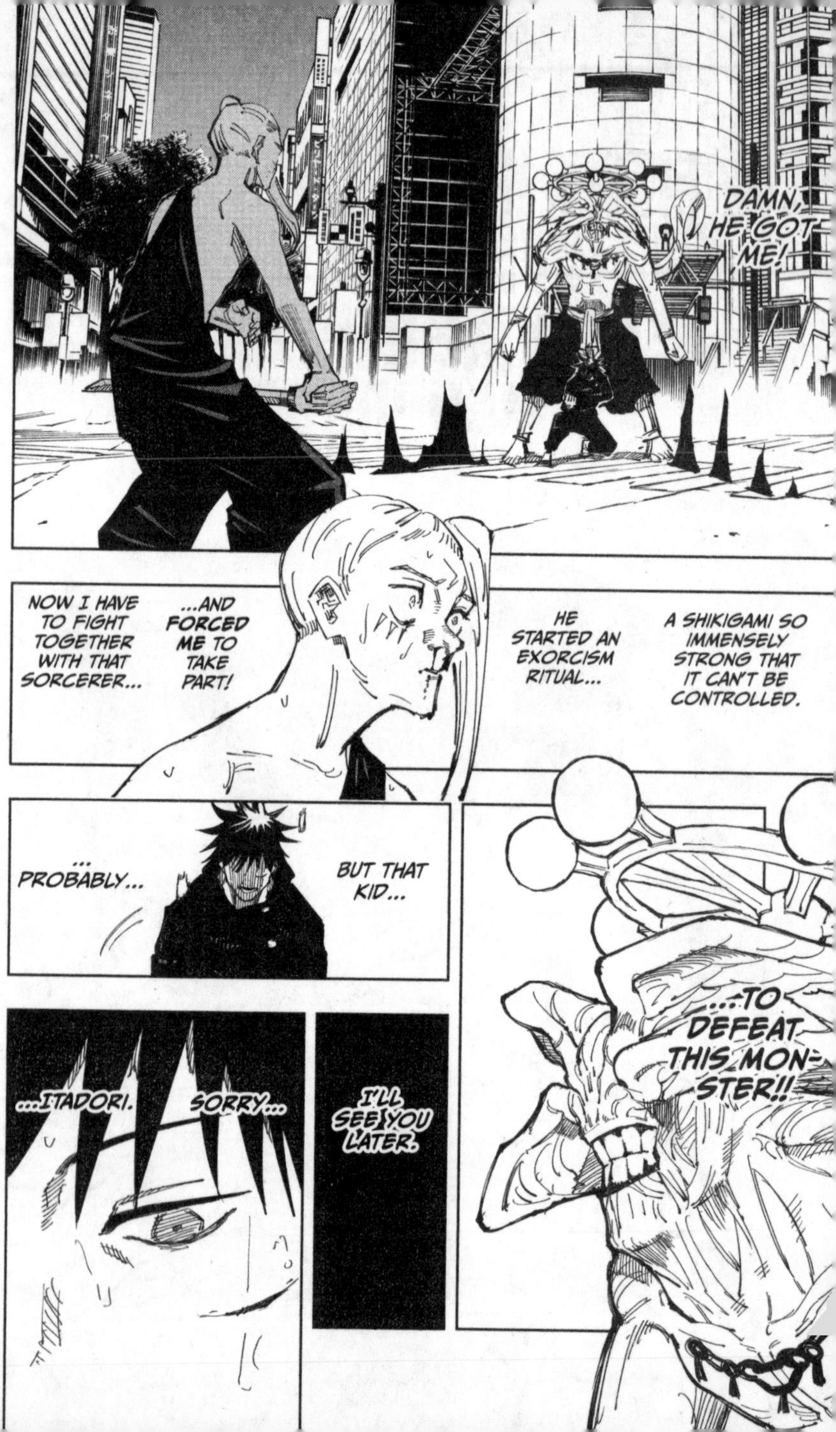
DAMN, HE GOT ME!
A SHIKIGAMI SO IMMENSELY STRONG THAT IT CAN'T BE CONTROLLED.
HE STARTED AN EXORCISM RITUAL...
...AND FORCED ME TO TAKE PART!
NOW I HAVE TO FIGHT TOGETHER WITH THAT SORCERER...
...TO DEFEAT THIS MON-STER!!
BUT THAT KID...
...PROBABLY...
I'LL SEE YOU LATER.
SORRY...
...ITADORI.

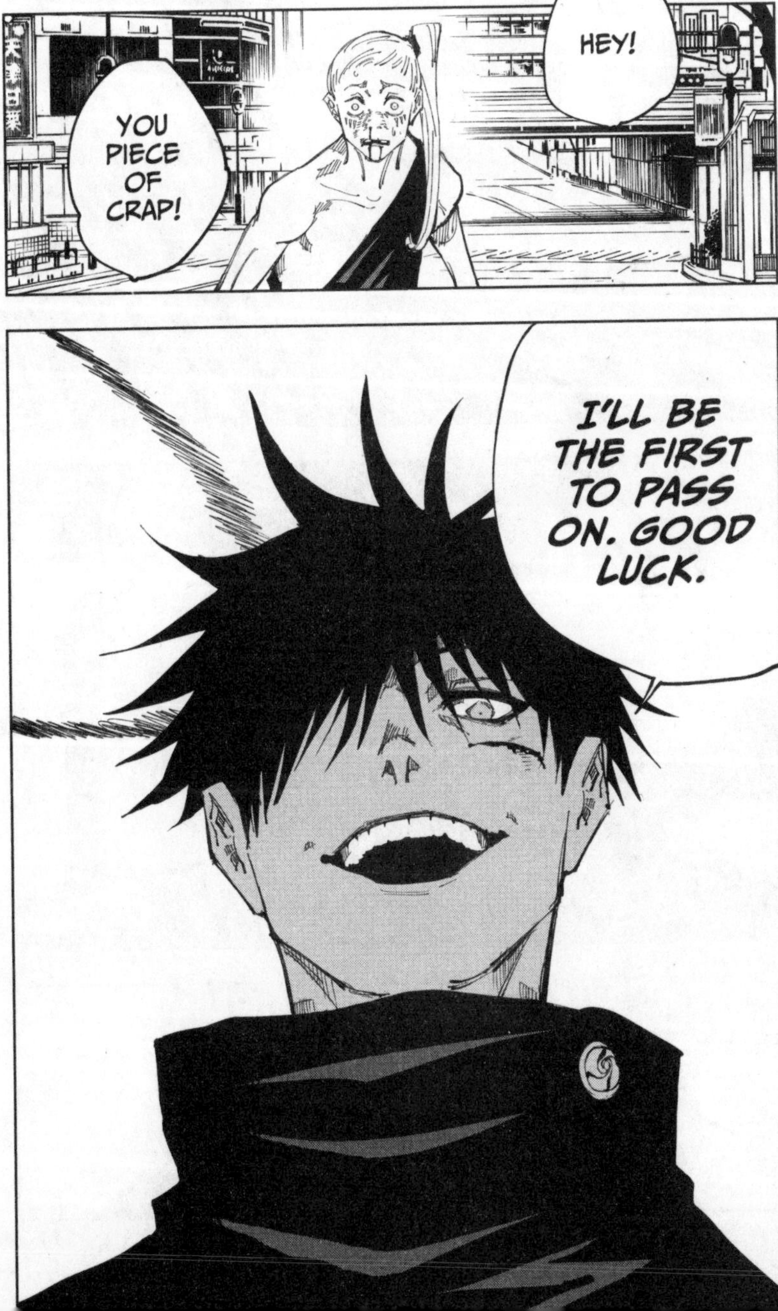
HEY!
YOU PIECE OF CRAP!
I'LL BE THE FIRST TO PASS ON. GOOD LUCK.

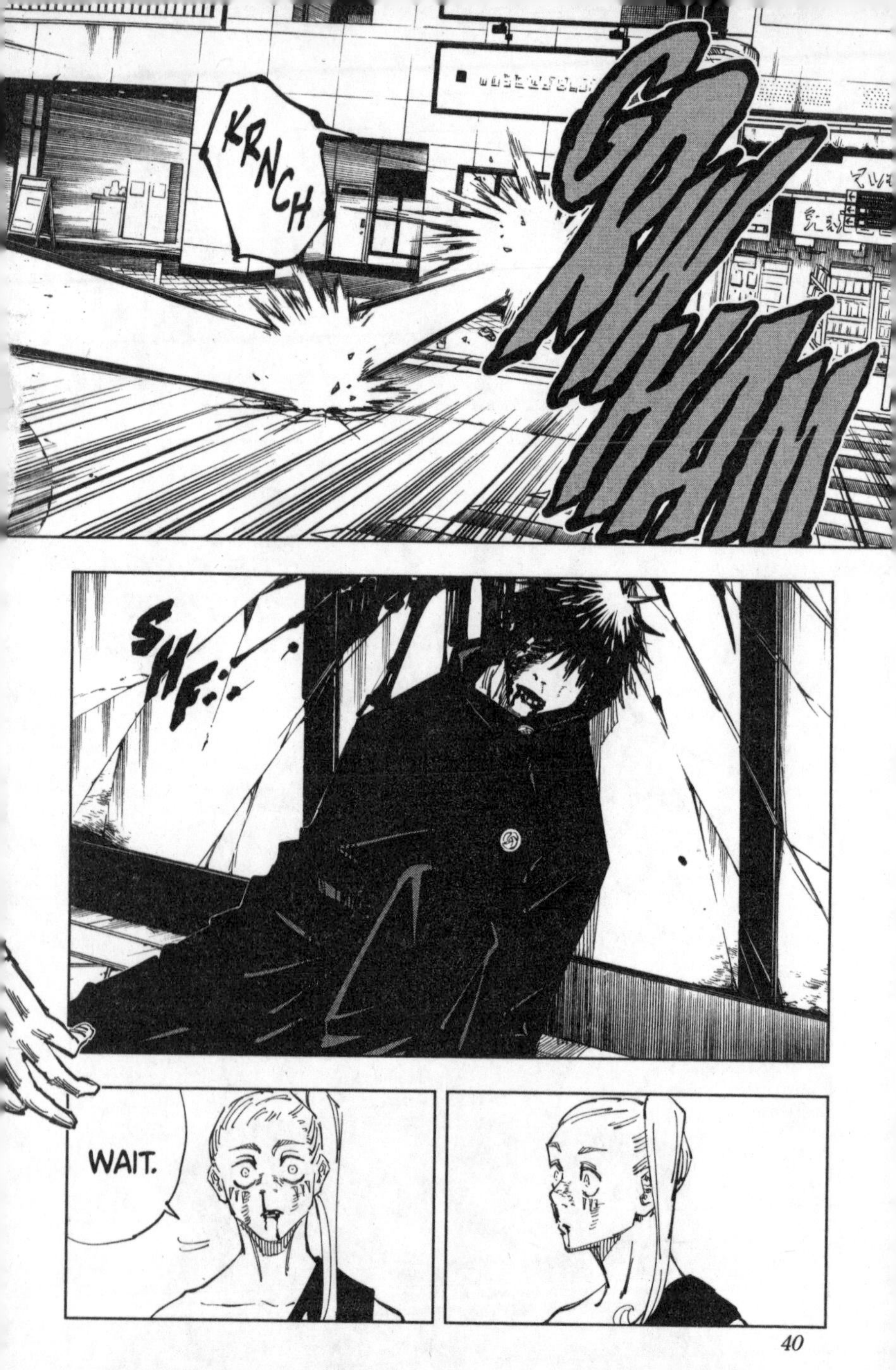
KRNCH
SHF...
WAIT.

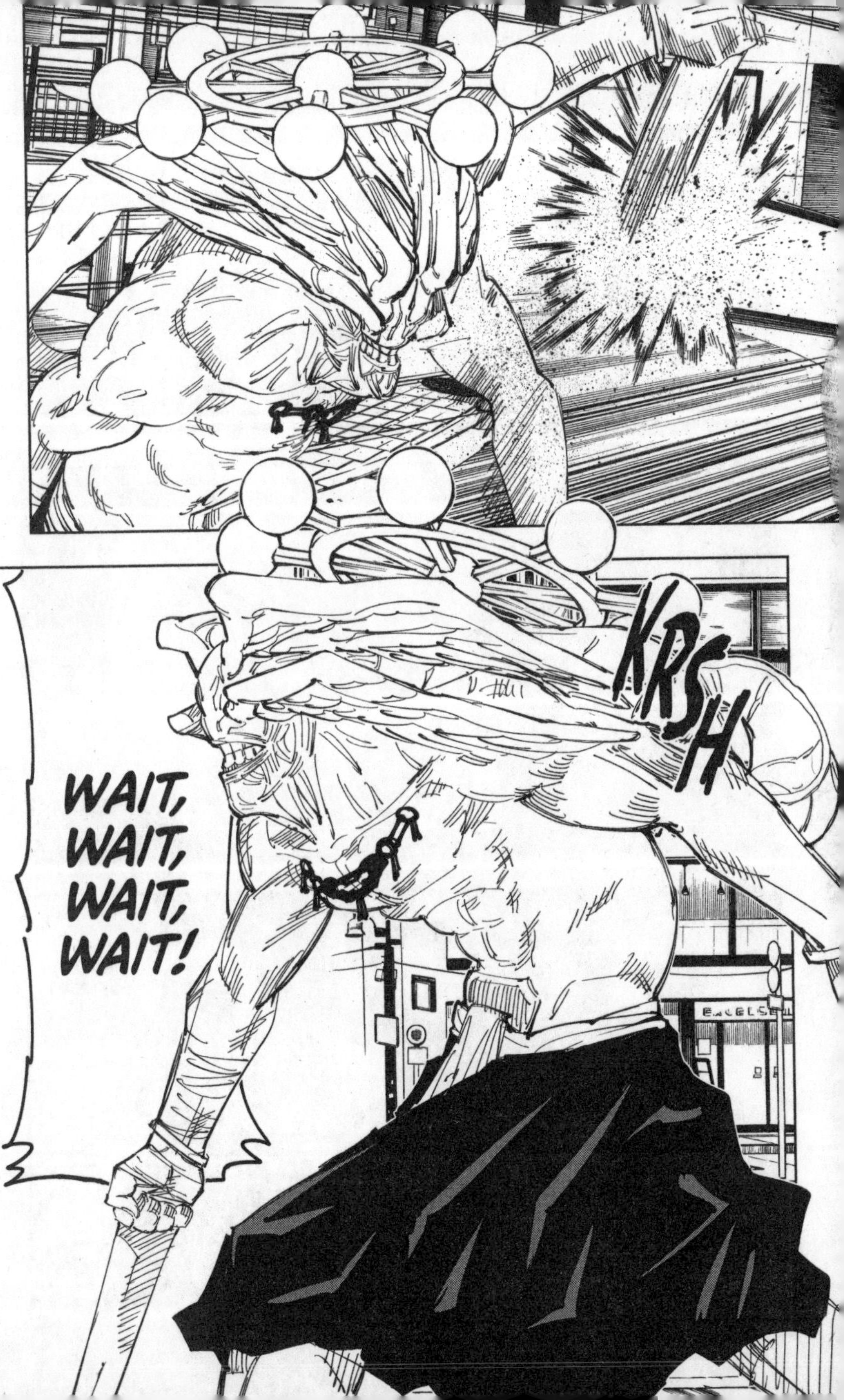
KRSH
WAIT, WAIT, WAIT, WAIT!

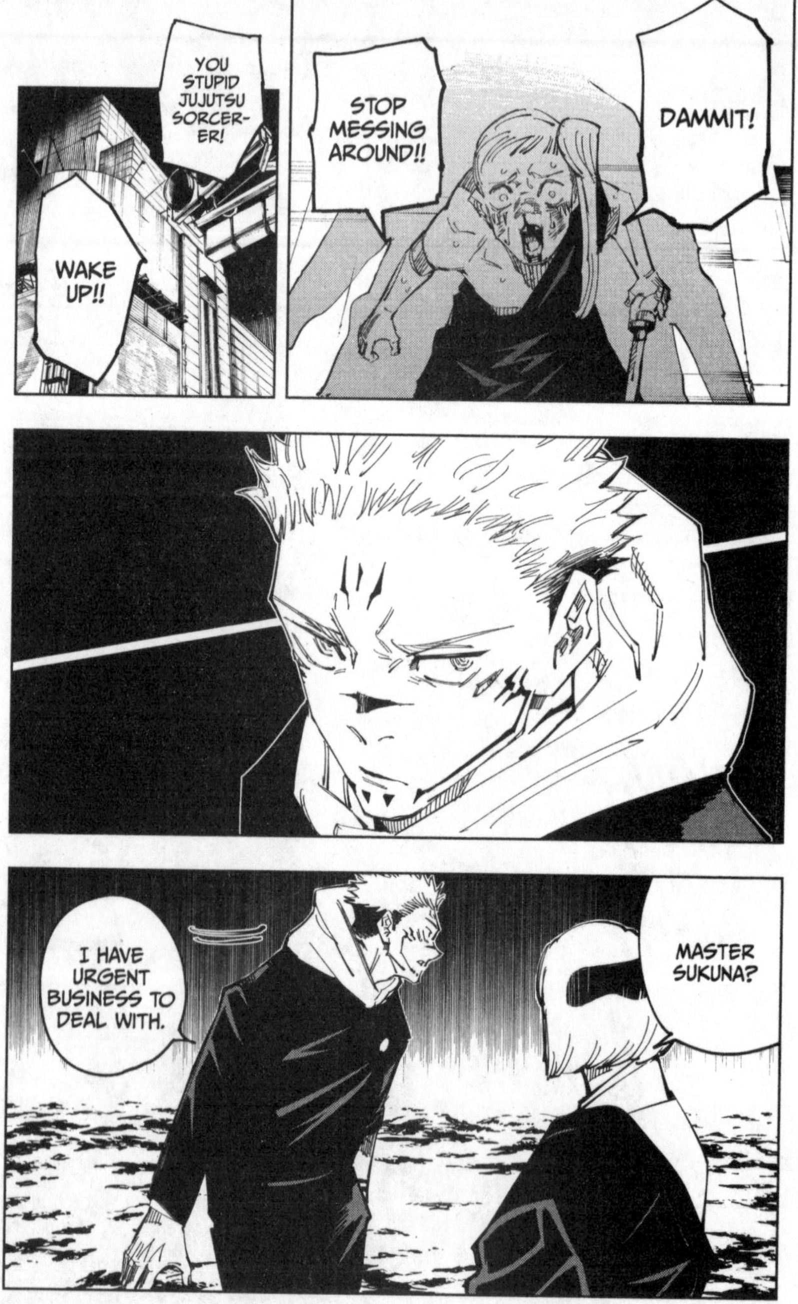
DAMMIT!
STOP MESSING AROUND!!
YOU STUPID JUJUTSU SORCER-ER!
WAKE UP!!
MASTER SUKUNA?
I HAVE URGENT BUSINESS TO DEAL WITH.

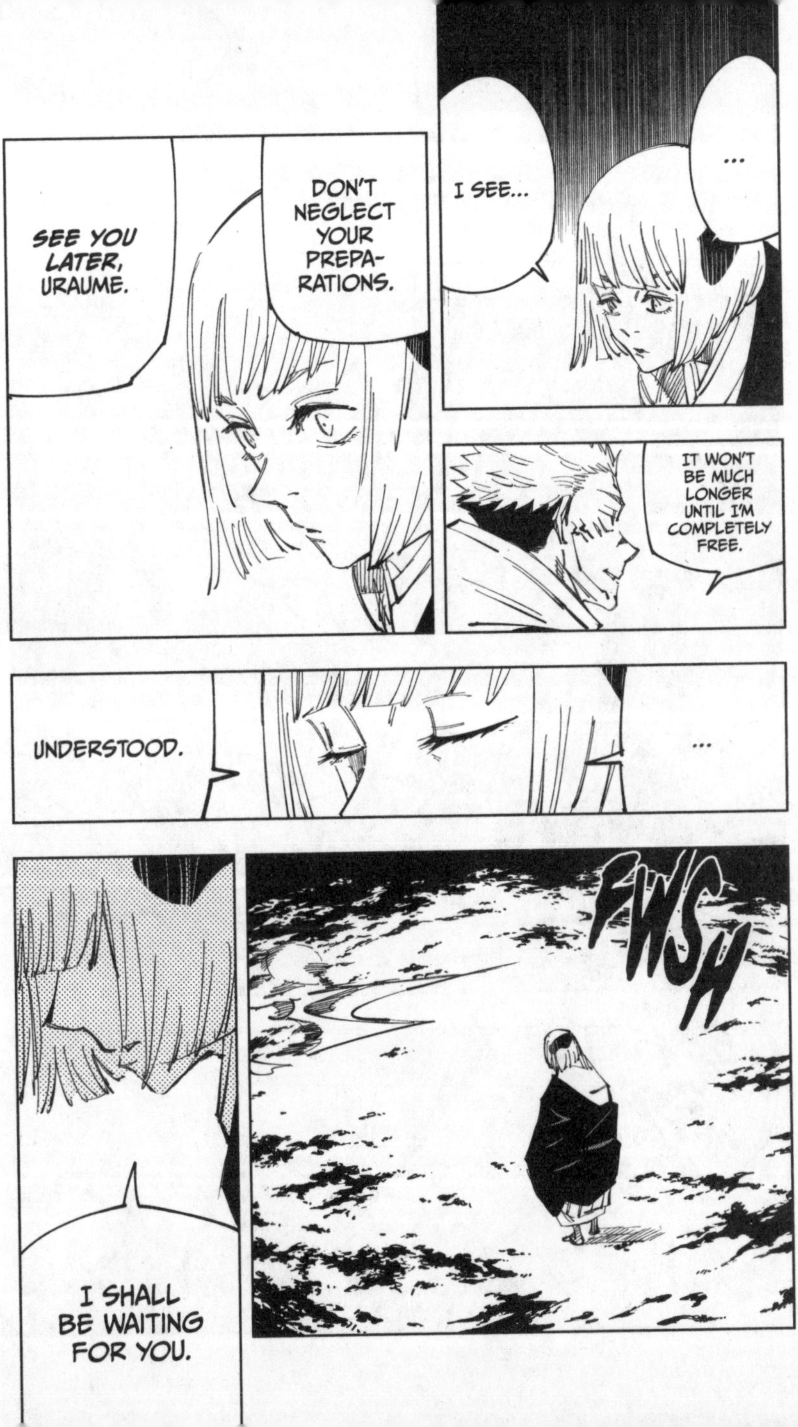
...
I SEE...
IT WON'T BE MUCH LONGER UNTIL I'M COMPLETELY FREE.
DON'T NEGLECT YOUR PREPA-RATIONS.
SEE YOU LATER, URAUME.
...
UNDERSTOOD.
FWSH
I SHALL BE WAITING FOR YOU.

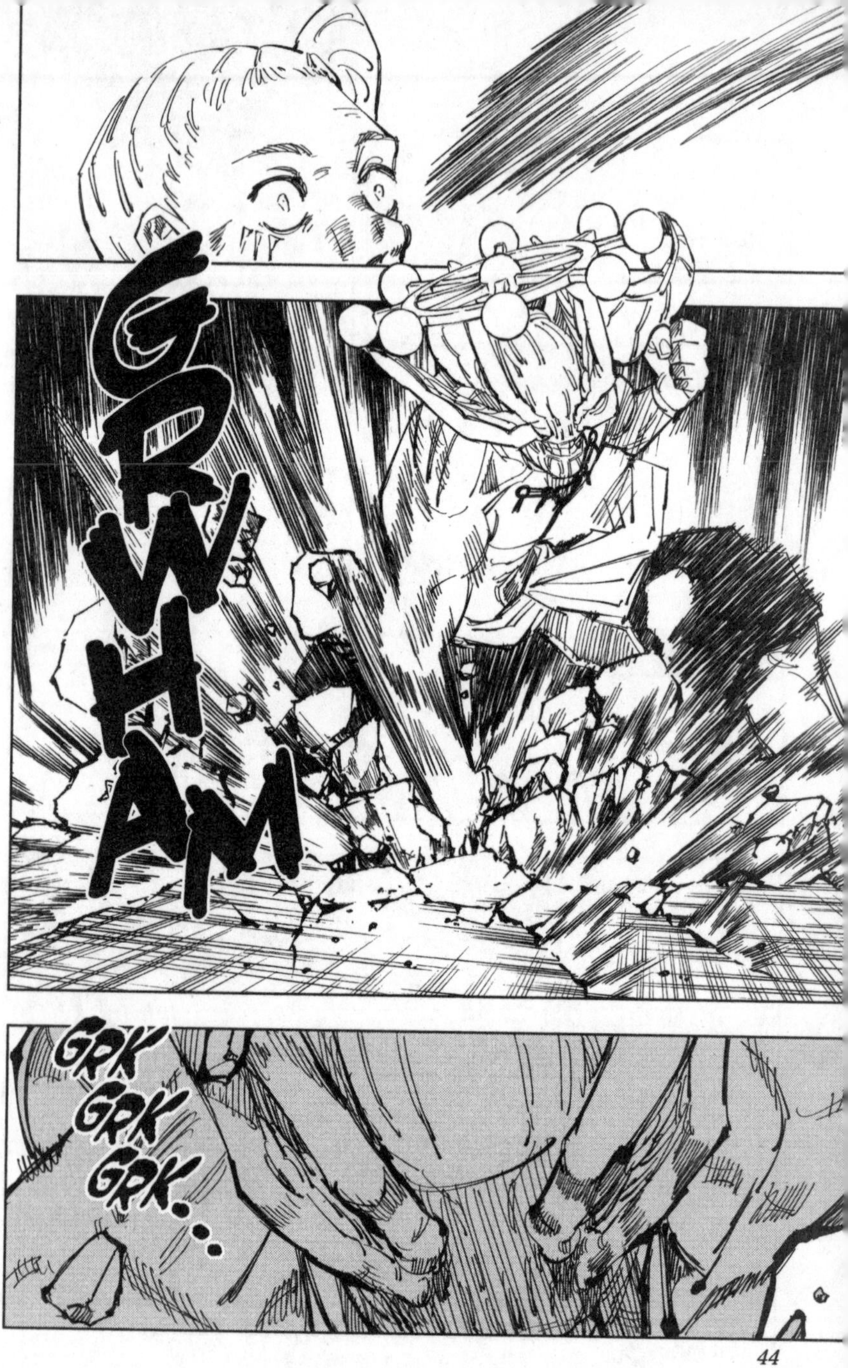
GRWHAM
GRK GRK GRK...

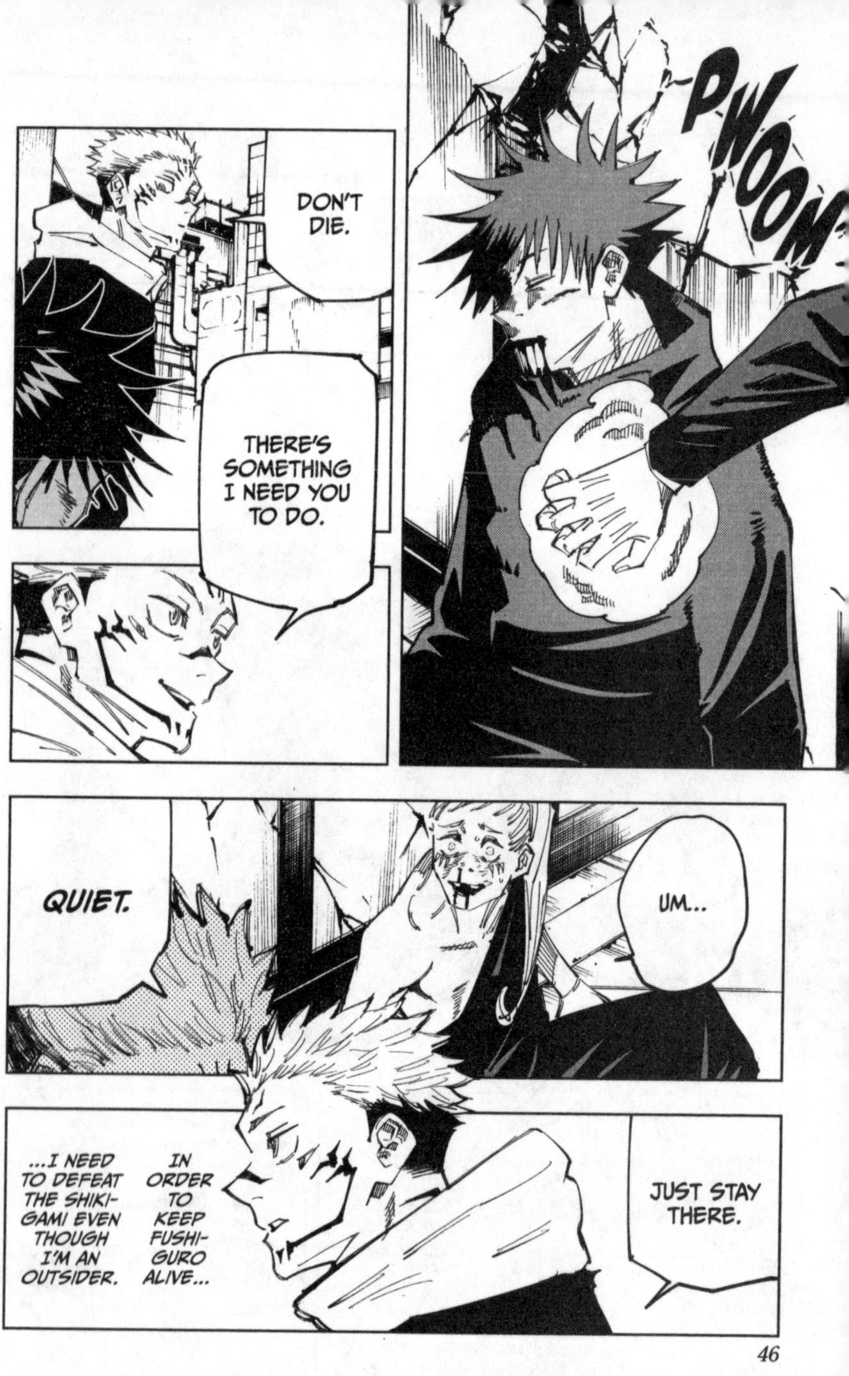
PWOOM
DON'T DIE.
THERE'S SOMETHING I NEED YOU TO DO.
UM...
QUIET.
JUST STAY THERE.
IN ORDER TO KEEP FUSHIGURO ALIVE...
...I NEED TO DEFEAT THE SHIKIGAMI EVEN THOUGH I'M AN OUTSIDER.

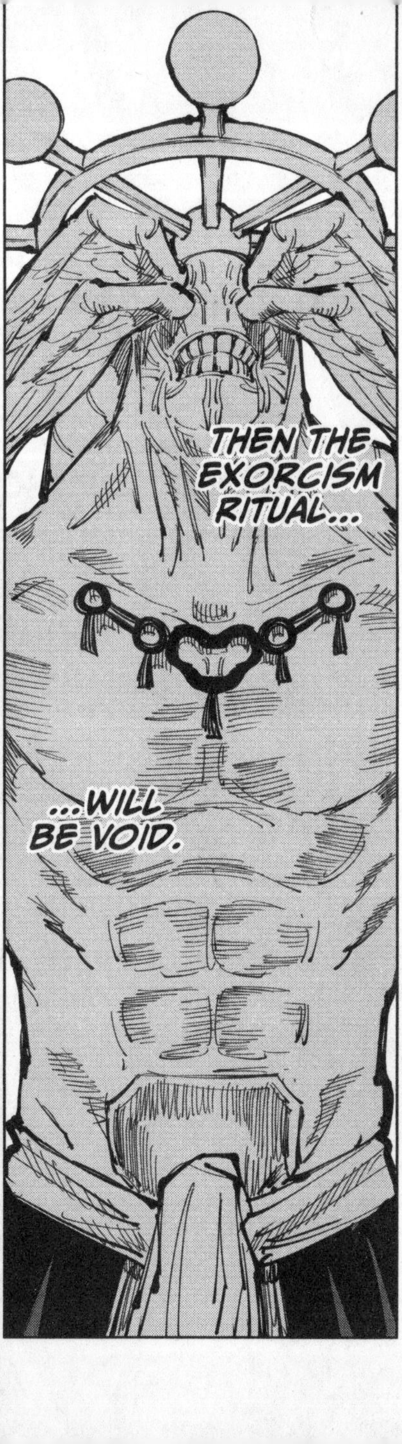
THEN THE EXORCISM RITUAL...
...WILL BE VOID.
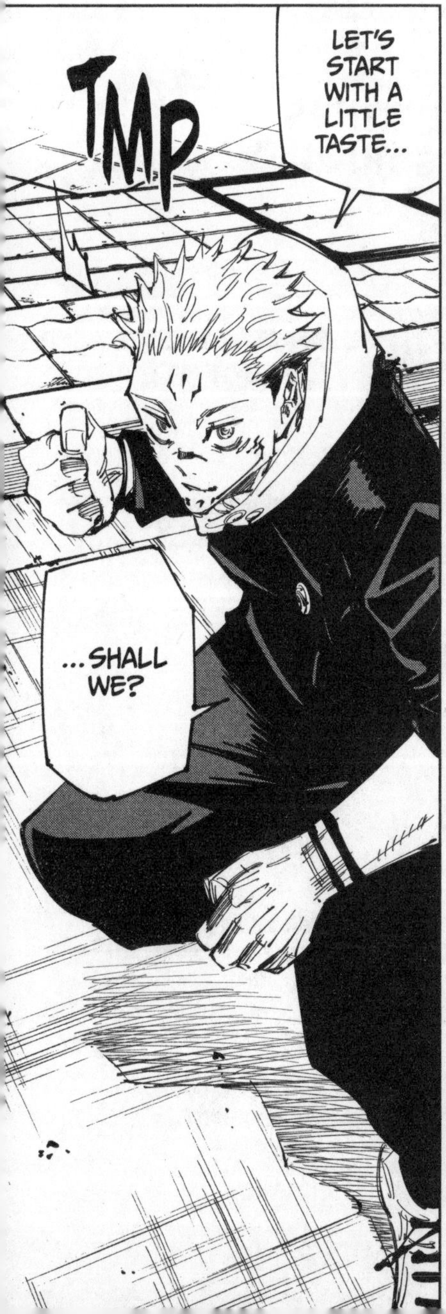
LET'S START WITH A LITTLE TASTE...
TMP
...SHALL WE?

THE 2020 VALENTINES RANKINGS THAT I SERIOUSLY ALMOST FORGOT

RANKINGS (VALENTINES RECEIVED)	CHARACTER	AKUTAMI'S COMMENT
5 (19)	NANAMI	FIFTH IS FIRST.
6 (13)	KUGISAKI	NICE!
7 (7)	CHOSO	HE HASN'T BEEN SHOWING UP MUCH, HAS HE?
8 (6)	INUMAKI	EVEN THOUGH I'VE BARELY EXPLORED HIM...
9 (5)	MAKI	MAYBE I'LL CHANGE HER HAIRSTYLE...

Chapter 118: The Shibuya Incident, Part 36

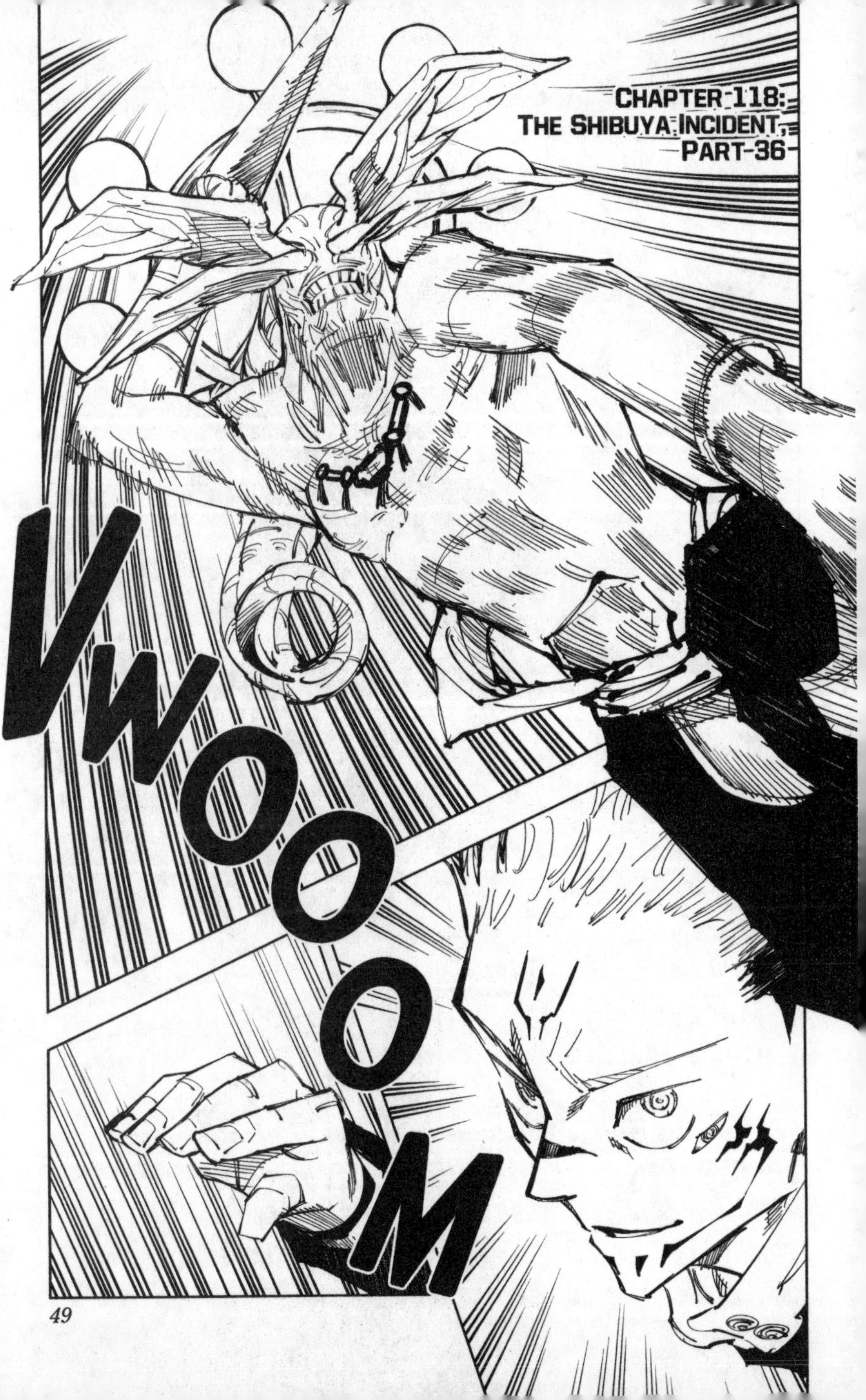
VWOOOOM

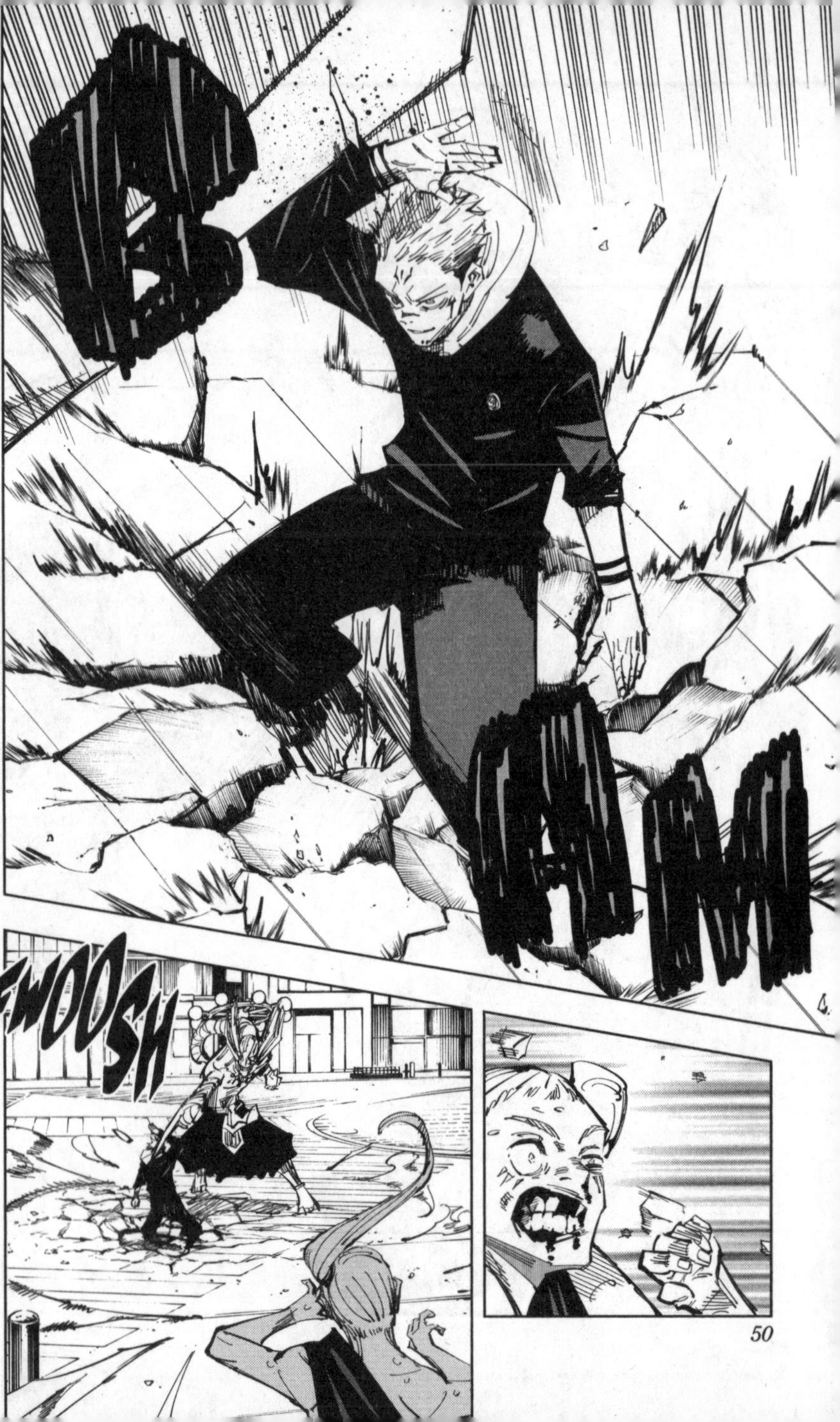
BAM
FWOOSH

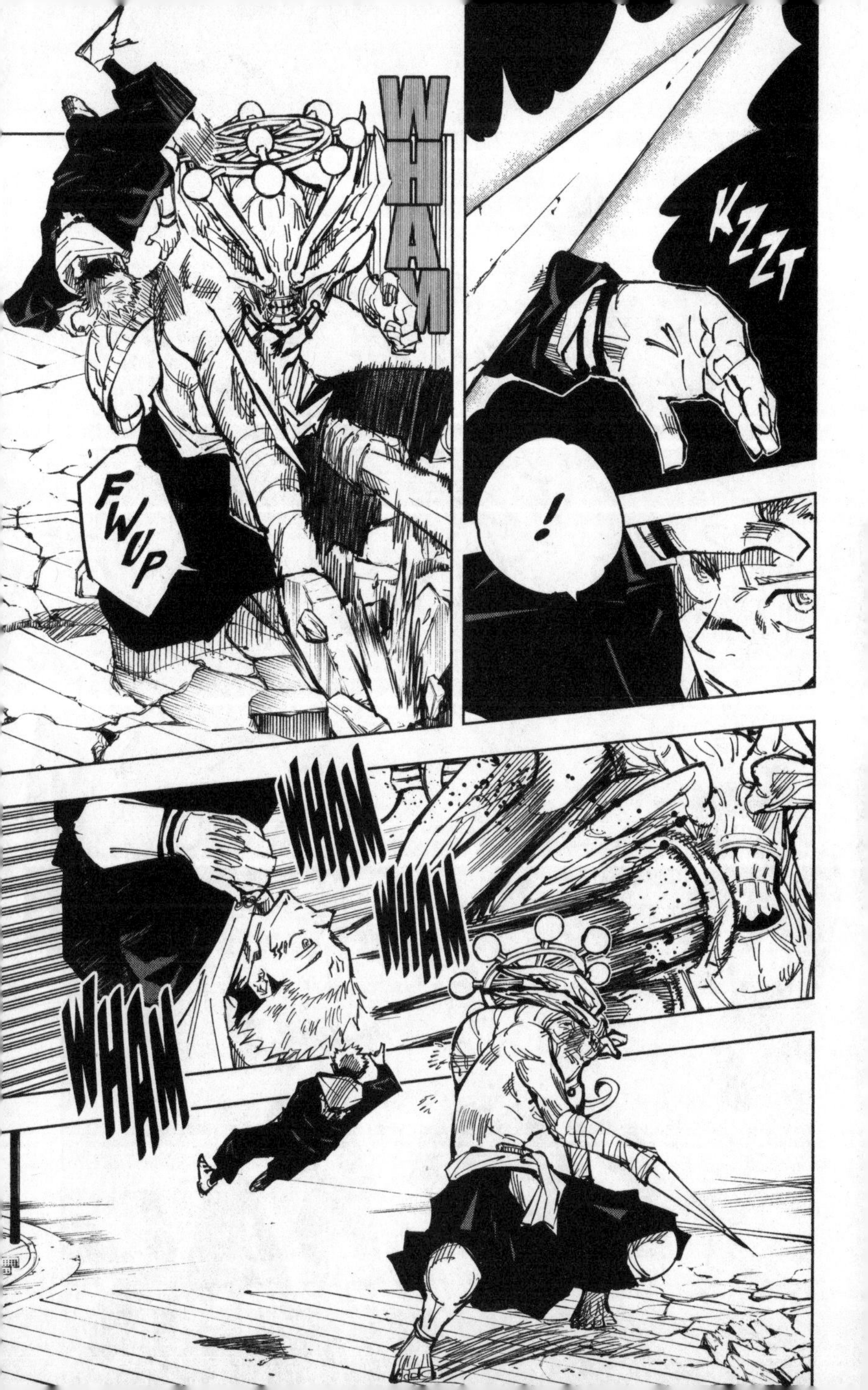
KZZT
!
WHAM
FWUP
WHAM
WHAM
WHAM

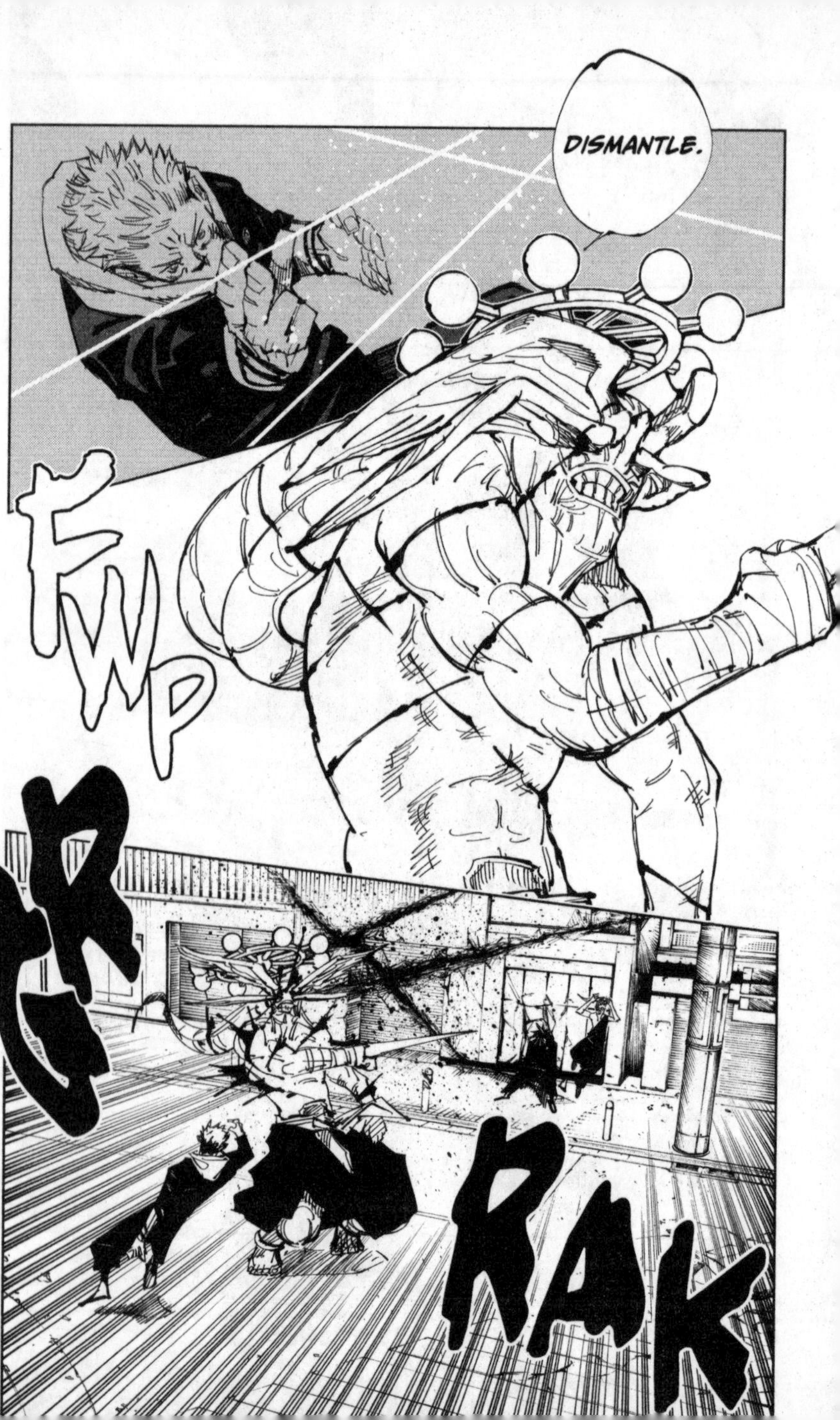
DISMANTLE.
FWP
CRAK

THAT'S A SPECIALIZED BLADE FOR CURSED SPIRITS. THE SWORD OF EXTERMINATION.

IT'S ENVELOPED IN POSITIVE ENERGY, THAT IS SIMILAR TO REVERSE CURSED ENERGY.

KZZT

IF I WAS A CURSED SPIRIT, I'D BE A GONER.

TH U N K

KTNK

GRK GRK GRK...

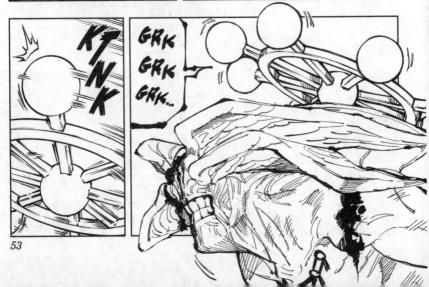

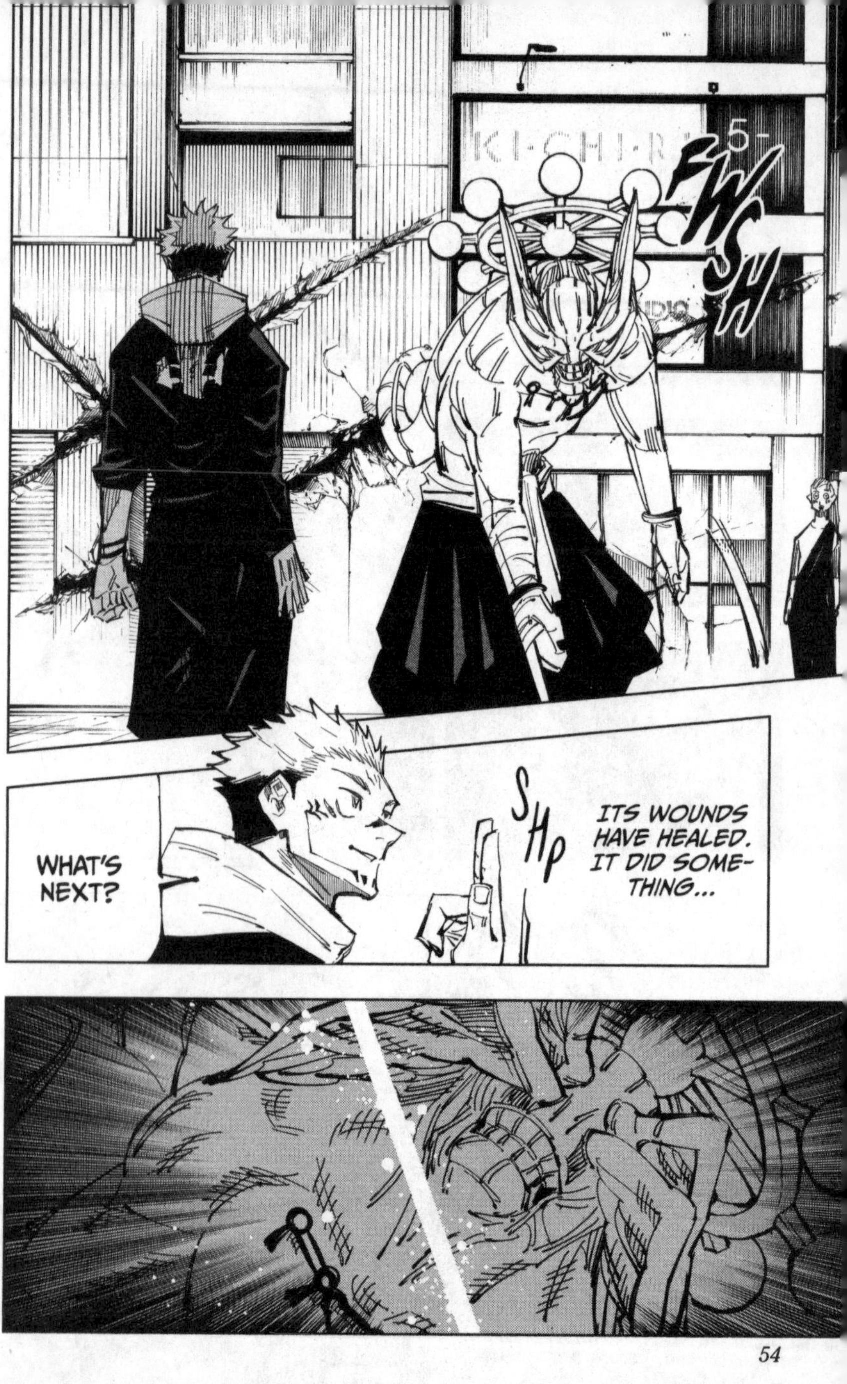
FWSH
SHP
ITS WOUNDS HAVE HEALED. IT DID SOMETHING...
WHAT'S NEXT?

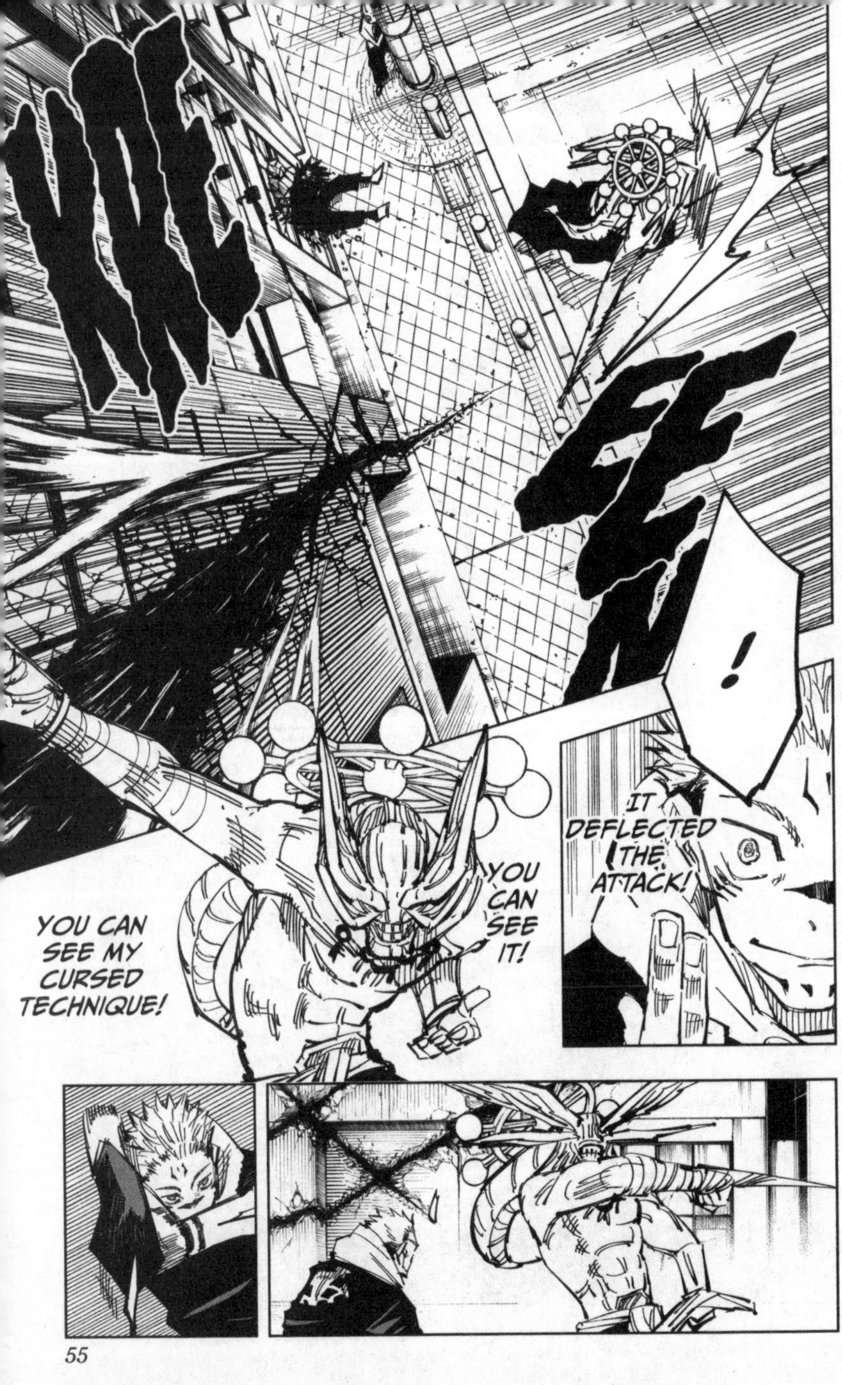
!
IT DEFLECTED THE ATTACK!
YOU CAN SEE IT!
YOU CAN SEE MY CURSED TECHNIQUE!

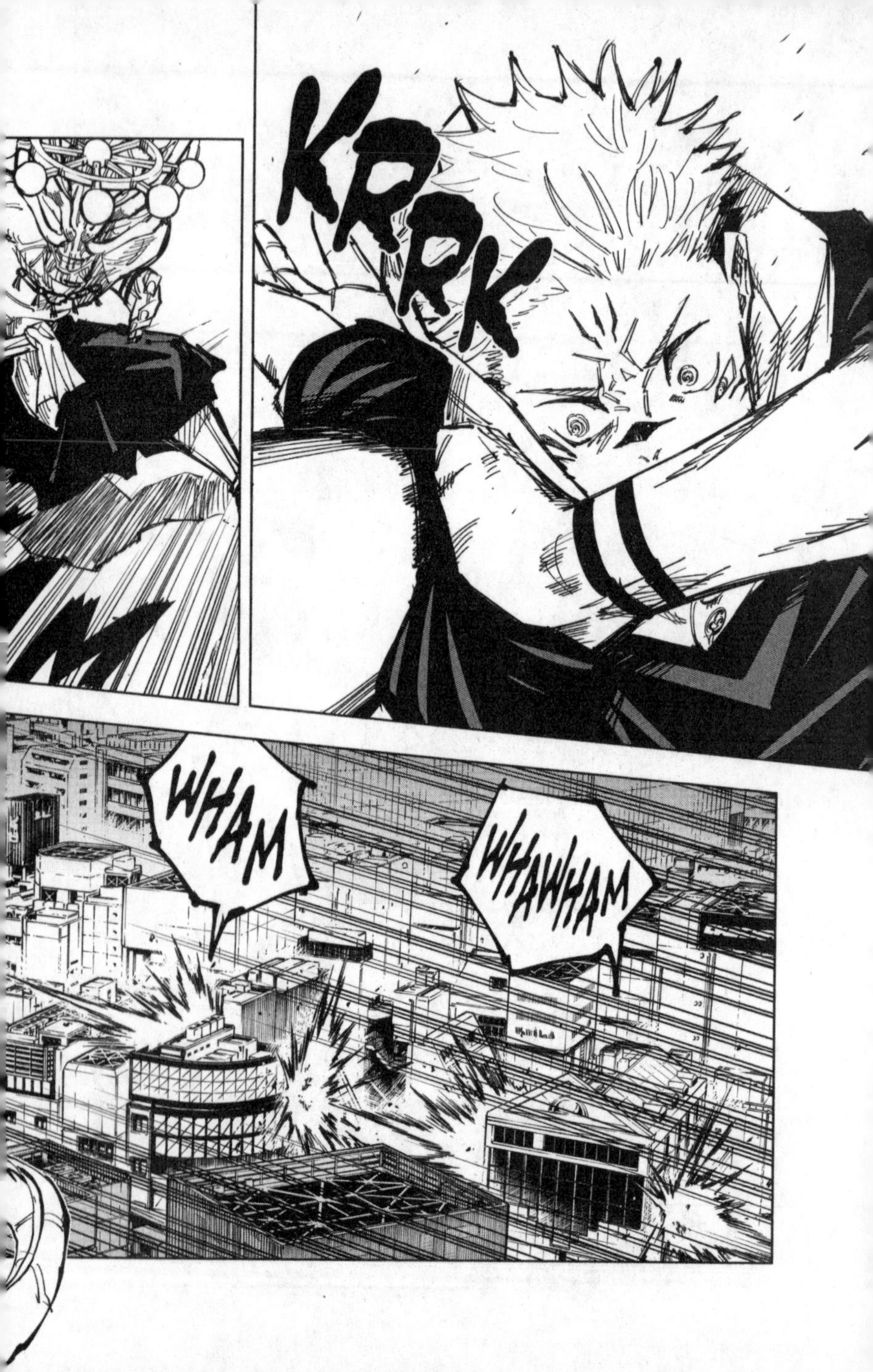
KRRK
WHAM
WHAWHAM

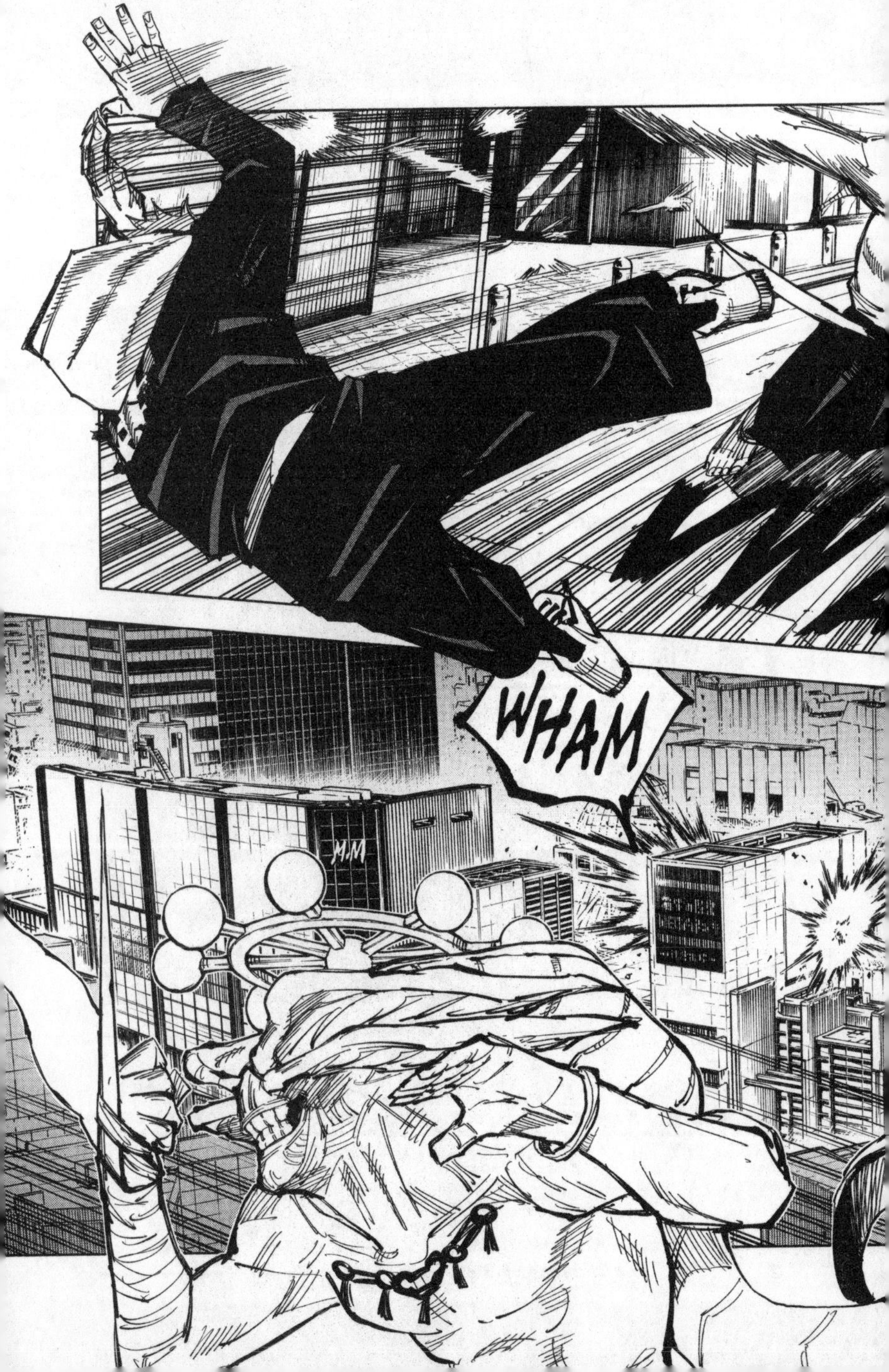
WHAM

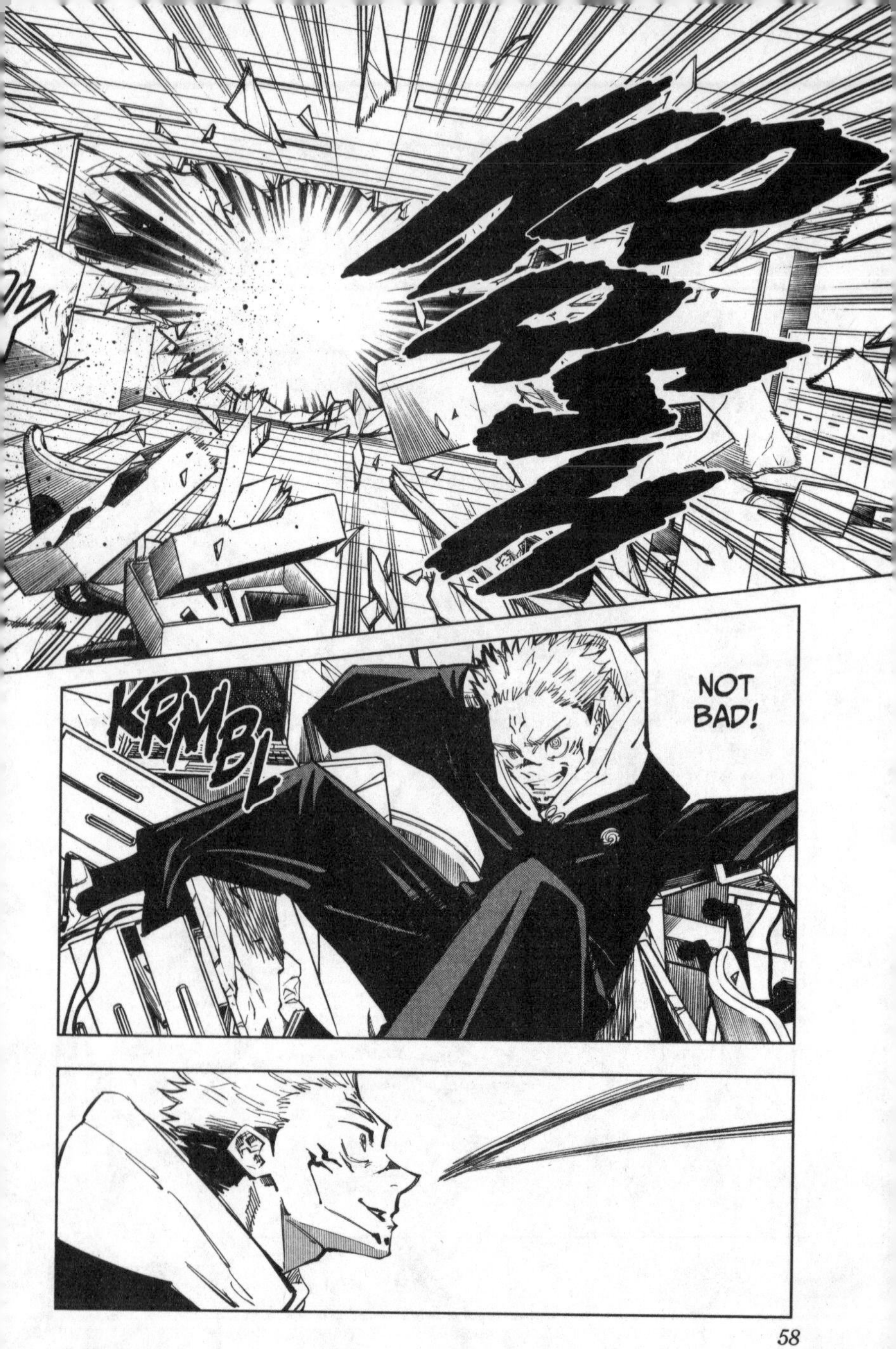
NOT BAD!
KRMBL

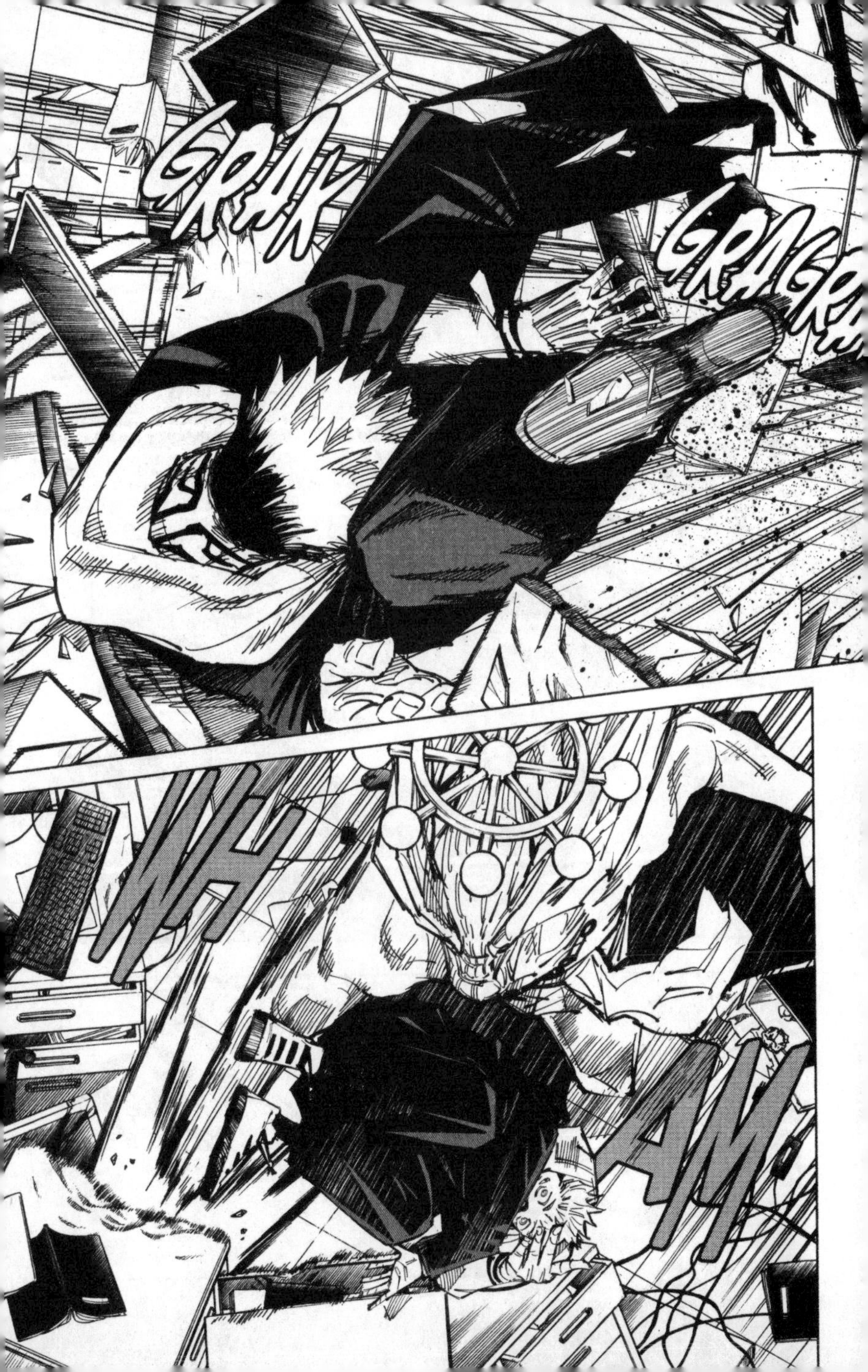
GRAK
WHAM

KRK

FWM

MY TURN.

FZZT...

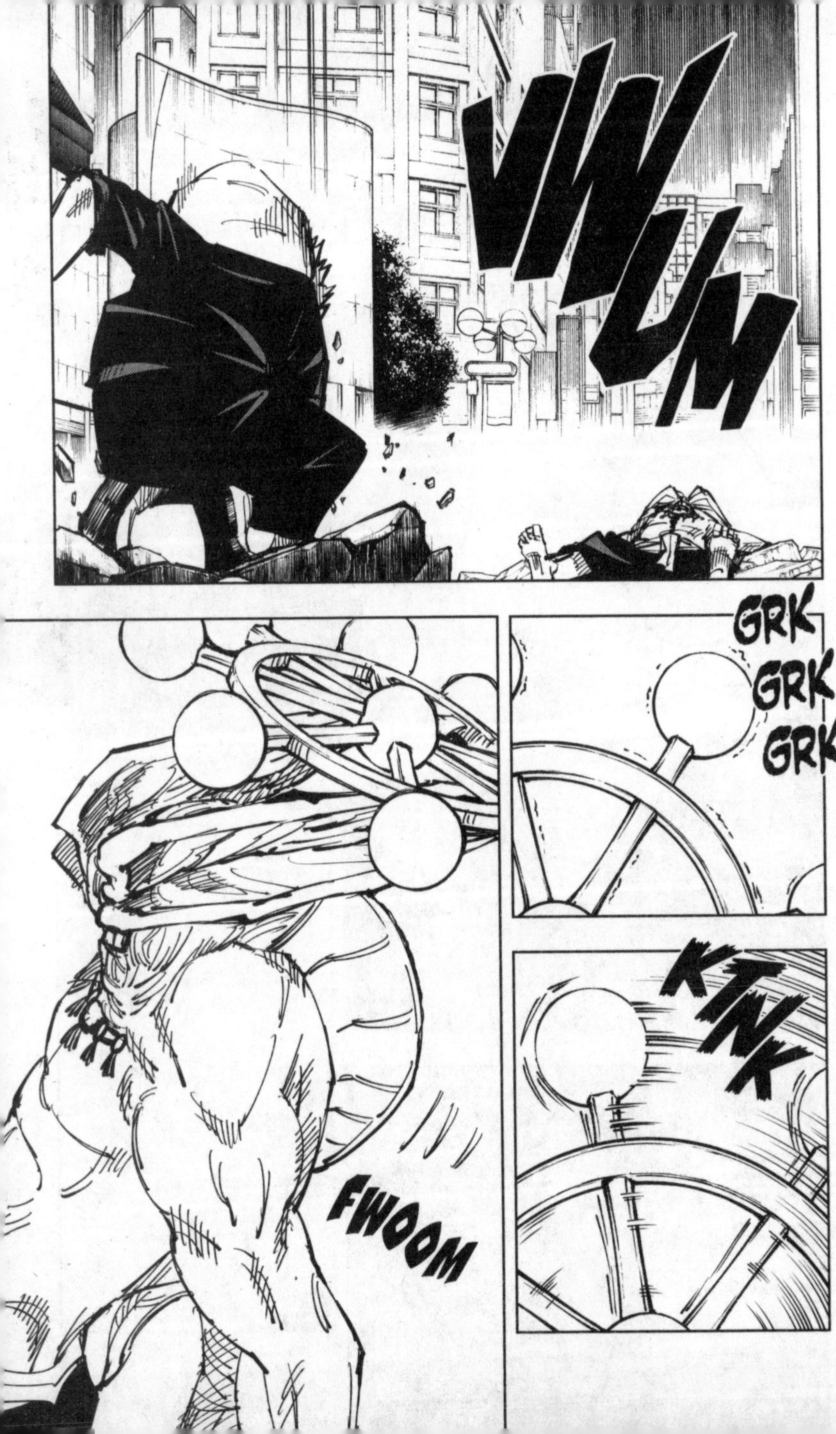
VWUM
GRK
GRK
GRK
KTINK
FWOOM

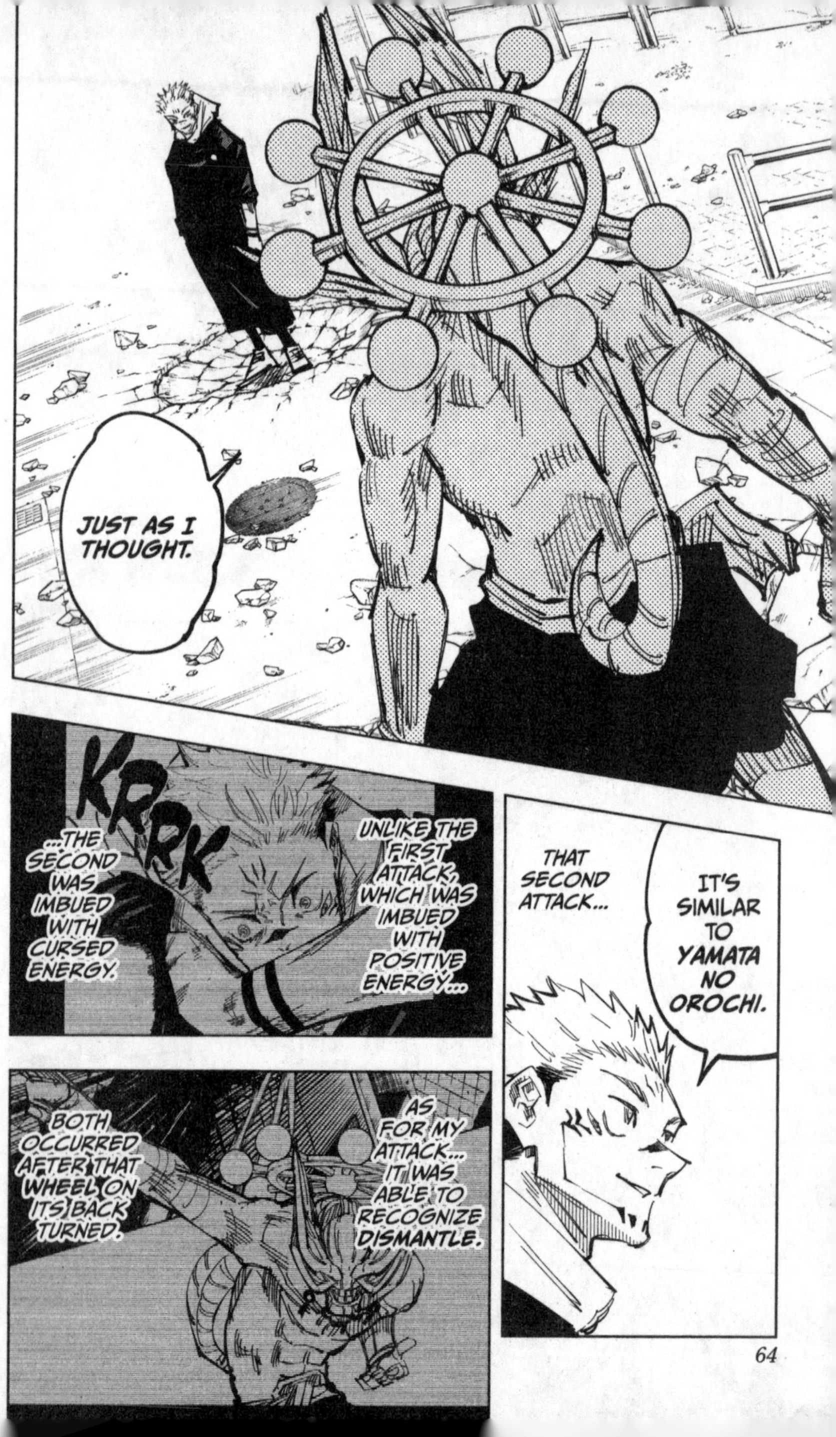
JUST AS I THOUGHT.
THAT SECOND ATTACK...
IT'S SIMILAR TO YAMATA NO OROCHI.
KRRK
UNLIKE THE FIRST ATTACK, WHICH WAS IMBUED WITH POSITIVE ENERGY...
...THE SECOND WAS IMBUED WITH CURSED ENERGY.
AS FOR MY ATTACK... IT WAS ABLE TO RECOGNIZE DISMANTLE.
BOTH OCCURRED AFTER THAT WHEEL ON ITS BACK TURNED.

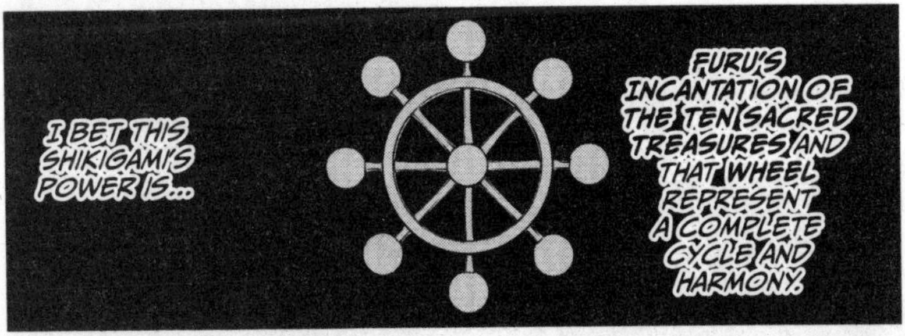
FURU'S INCANTATION OF THE TEN SACRED TREASURES AND THAT WHEEL REPRESENT A COMPLETE CYCLE AND HARMONY.
I BET THIS SHIKIGAMI'S POWER IS...

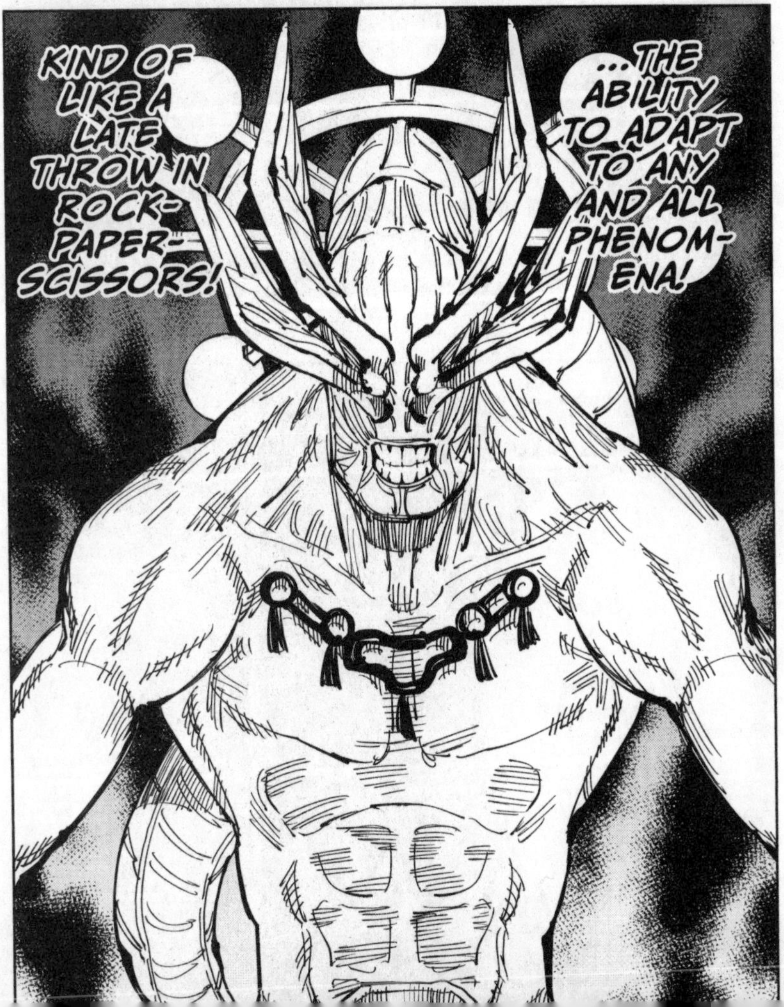
...THE ABILITY TO ADAPT TO ANY AND ALL PHENOM-ENA!
KIND OF LIKE A LATE THROW IN ROCK-PAPER-SCISSORS!

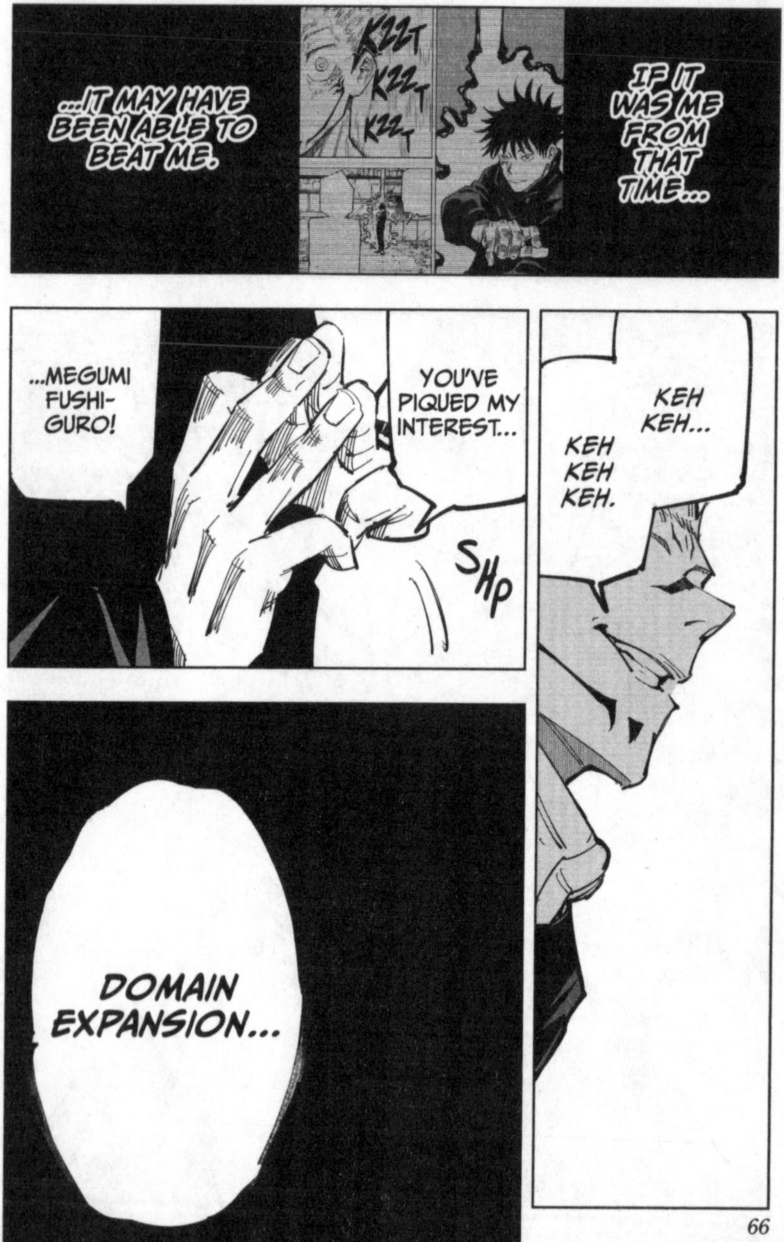
IF IT WAS ME FROM THAT TIME...
KZZT KZZT KZZT
...IT MAY HAVE BEEN ABLE TO BEAT ME.
KEH KEH...
KEH KEH KEH.
YOU'VE PIQUED MY INTEREST...
...MEGUMI FUSHI-GURO!
SHP
DOMAIN EXPANSION...

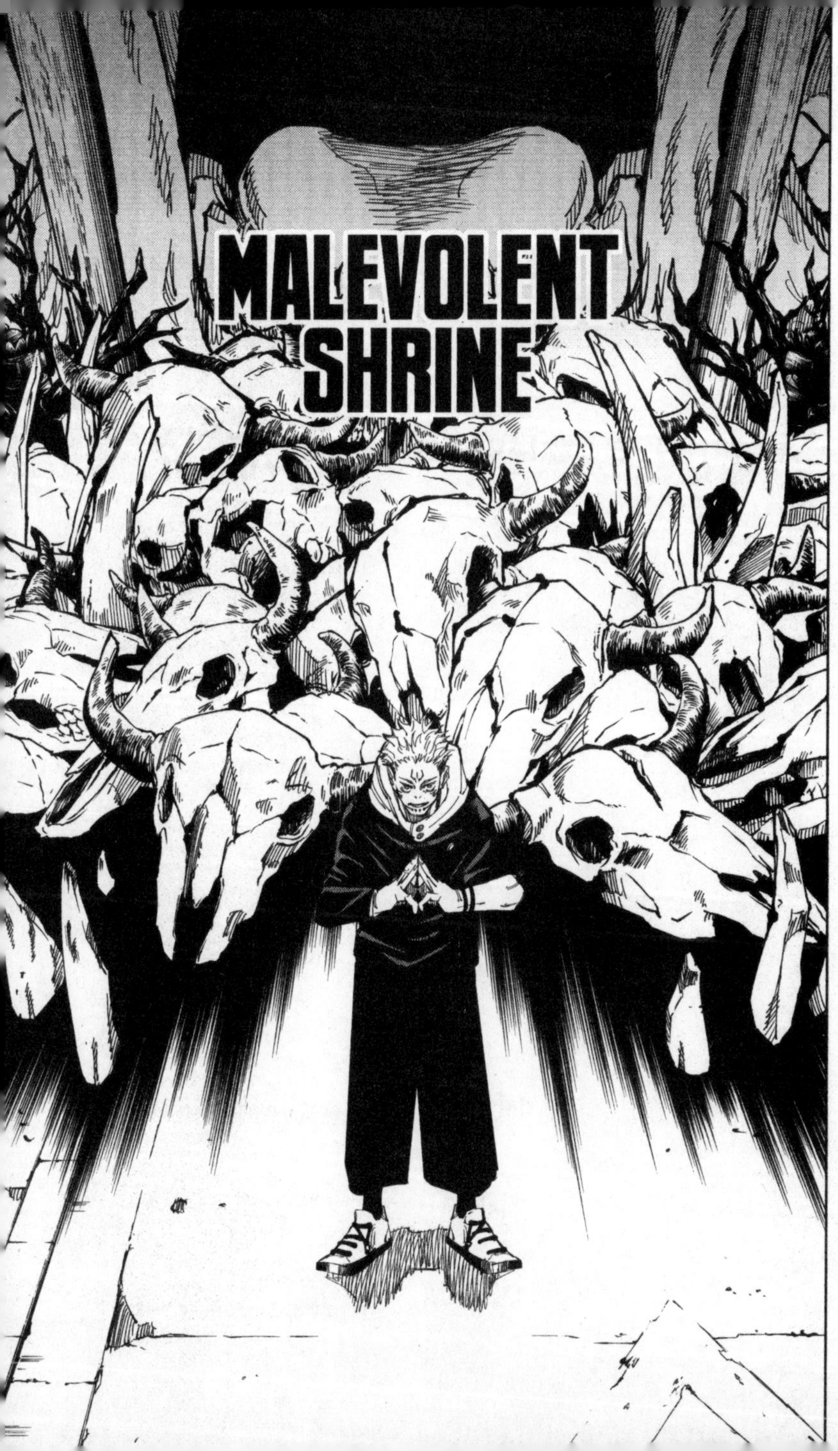
MALEVOLENT SHRINE

THE 2020 VALENTINES RANKINGS THAT I SERIOUSLY ALMOST FORGOT

RANKINGS (VALENTINES RECEIVED)	CHARACTER	AKUTAMI'S COMMENT
10 (4)	INO	MAYBE THE INCIDENT WAS STARTING ABOUT THAT TIME?
11 (3)	IEIRI	MACROSS F IN A SET WITH GOJO.
	IJICHI	COME ON, TETSUO!
	KAMO	HE LOST TO CHOSO... HA HA!
14 (2)	MEI MEI	AGE INDETERMINATE.
	MIWA	AFTER ALL, SHE'S CUTE!
	OZAWA	EVEN THOUGH SHE JUST BRIEFLY POPPED IN?

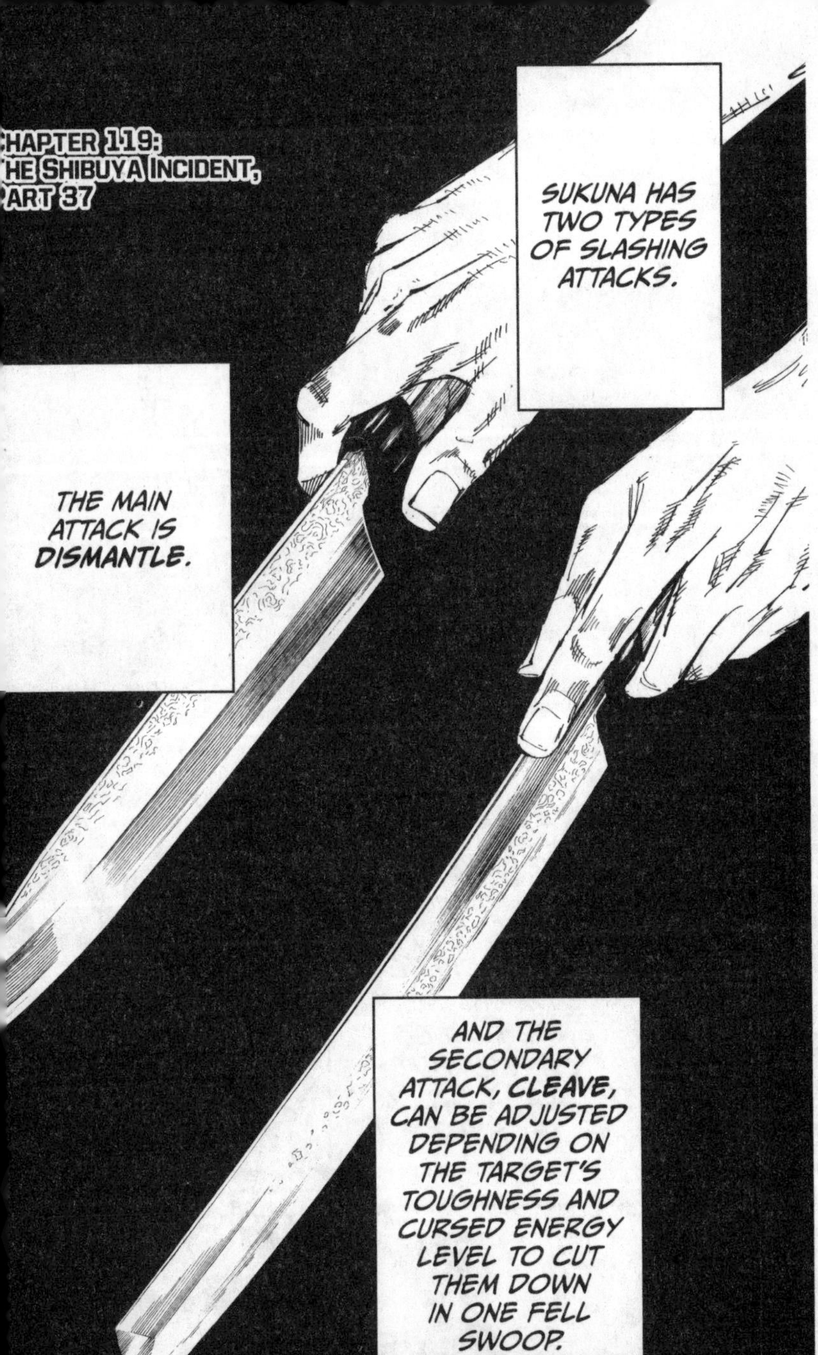
CHAPTER 119:
THE SHIBUYA INCIDENT,
PART 37
SUKUNA HAS TWO TYPES OF SLASHING ATTACKS.
THE MAIN ATTACK IS DISMANTLE.
AND THE SECONDARY ATTACK, CLEAVE, CAN BE ADJUSTED DEPENDING ON THE TARGET'S TOUGHNESS AND CURSED ENERGY LEVEL TO CUT THEM DOWN IN ONE FELL SWOOP.

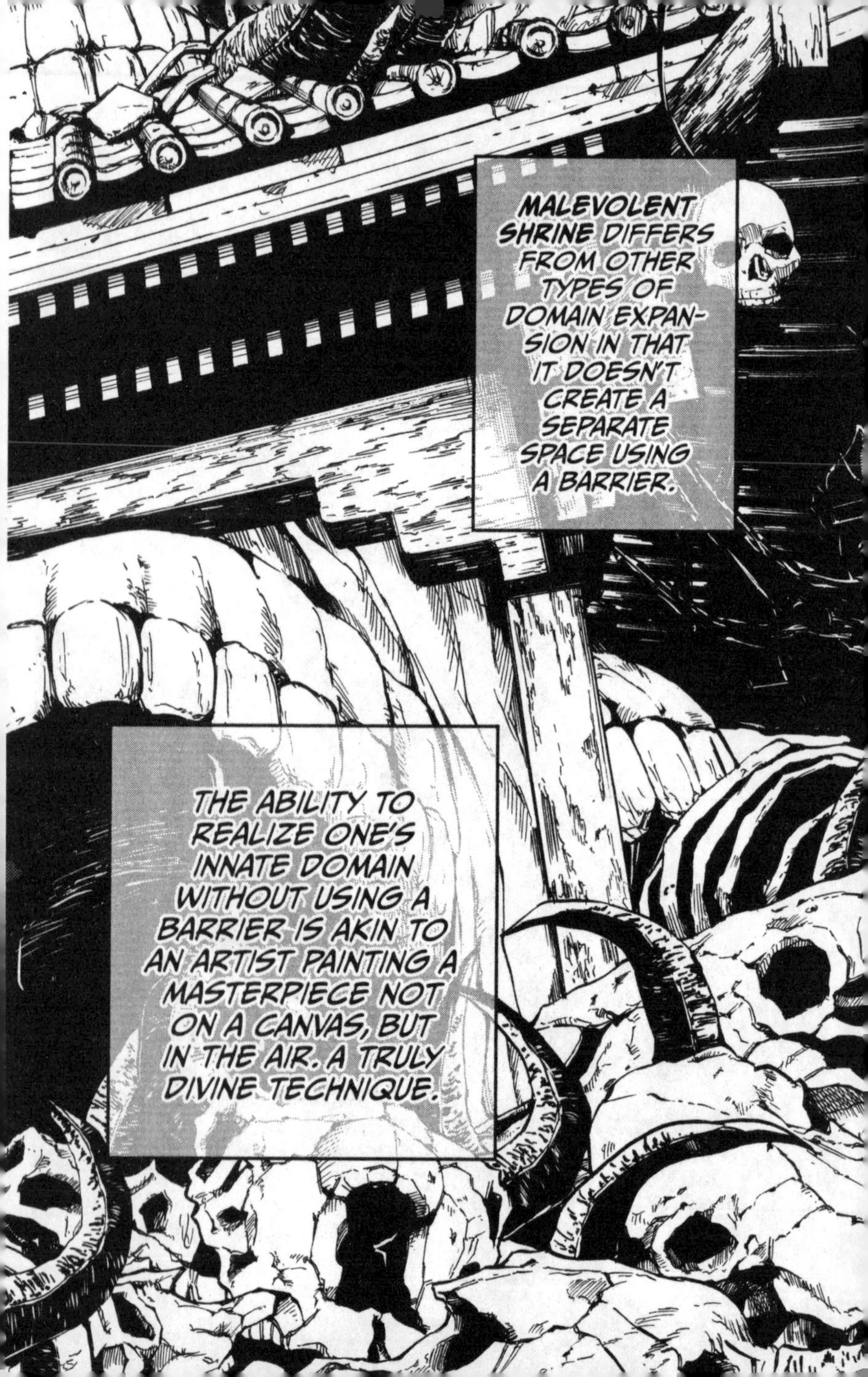
MALEVOLENT SHRINE DIFFERS FROM OTHER TYPES OF DOMAIN EXPANSION IN THAT IT DOESN'T CREATE A SEPARATE SPACE USING A BARRIER.
THE ABILITY TO REALIZE ONE'S INNATE DOMAIN WITHOUT USING A BARRIER IS AKIN TO AN ARTIST PAINTING A MASTERPIECE NOT ON A CANVAS, BUT IN THE AIR. A TRULY DIVINE TECHNIQUE.

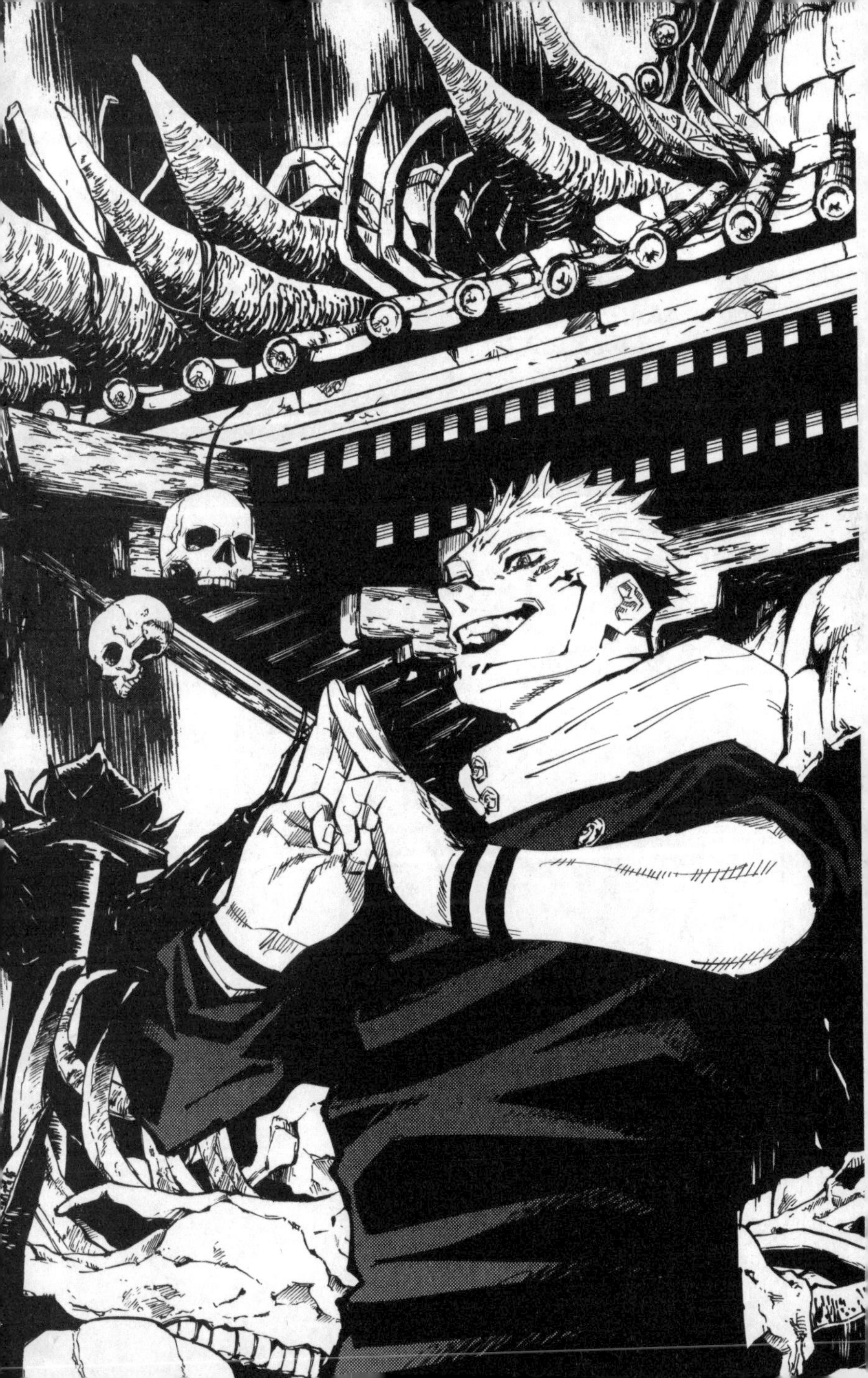

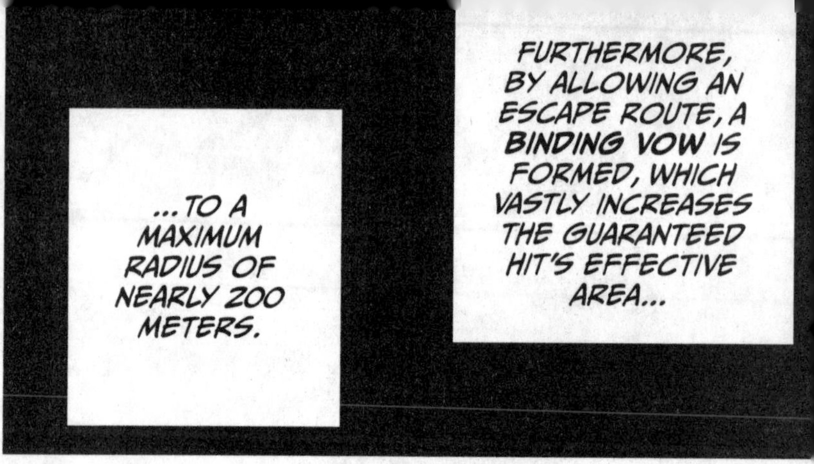
FURTHERMORE, BY ALLOWING AN ESCAPE ROUTE, A BINDING VOW IS FORMED, WHICH VASTLY INCREASES THE GUARANTEED HIT'S EFFECTIVE AREA...
...TO A MAXIMUM RADIUS OF NEARLY 200 METERS.

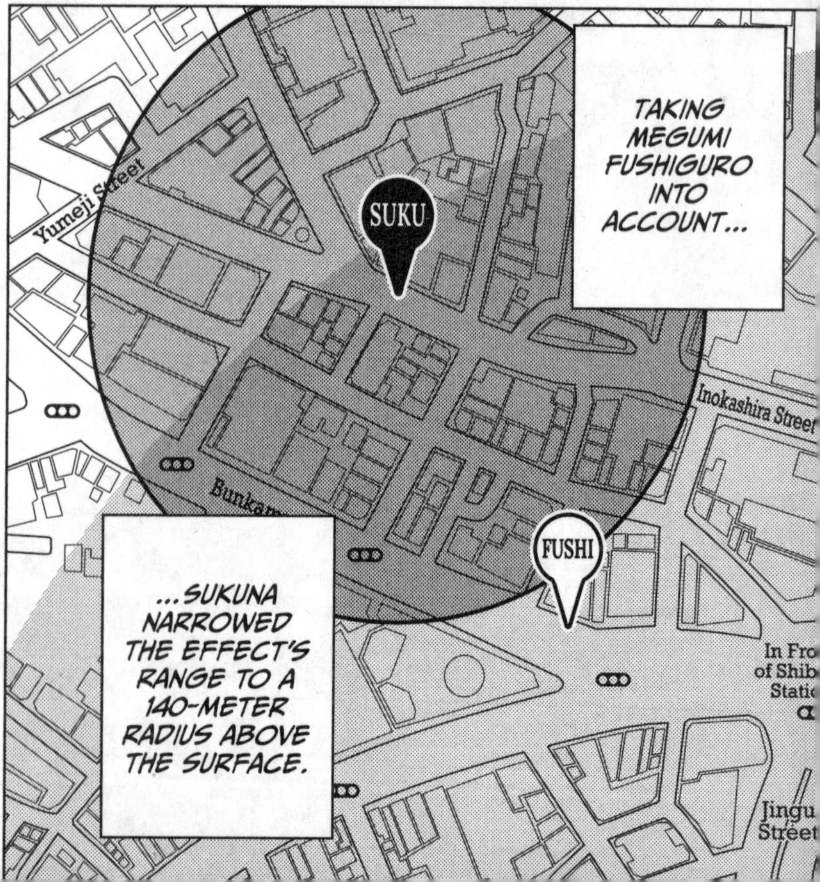
TAKING MEGUMI FUSHIGURO INTO ACCOUNT...
SUKU
Yumeji Street
Inokashira Street
FUSHI
...SUKUNA NARROWED THE EFFECT'S RANGE TO A 140-METER RADIUS ABOVE THE SURFACE.
Jingu Street

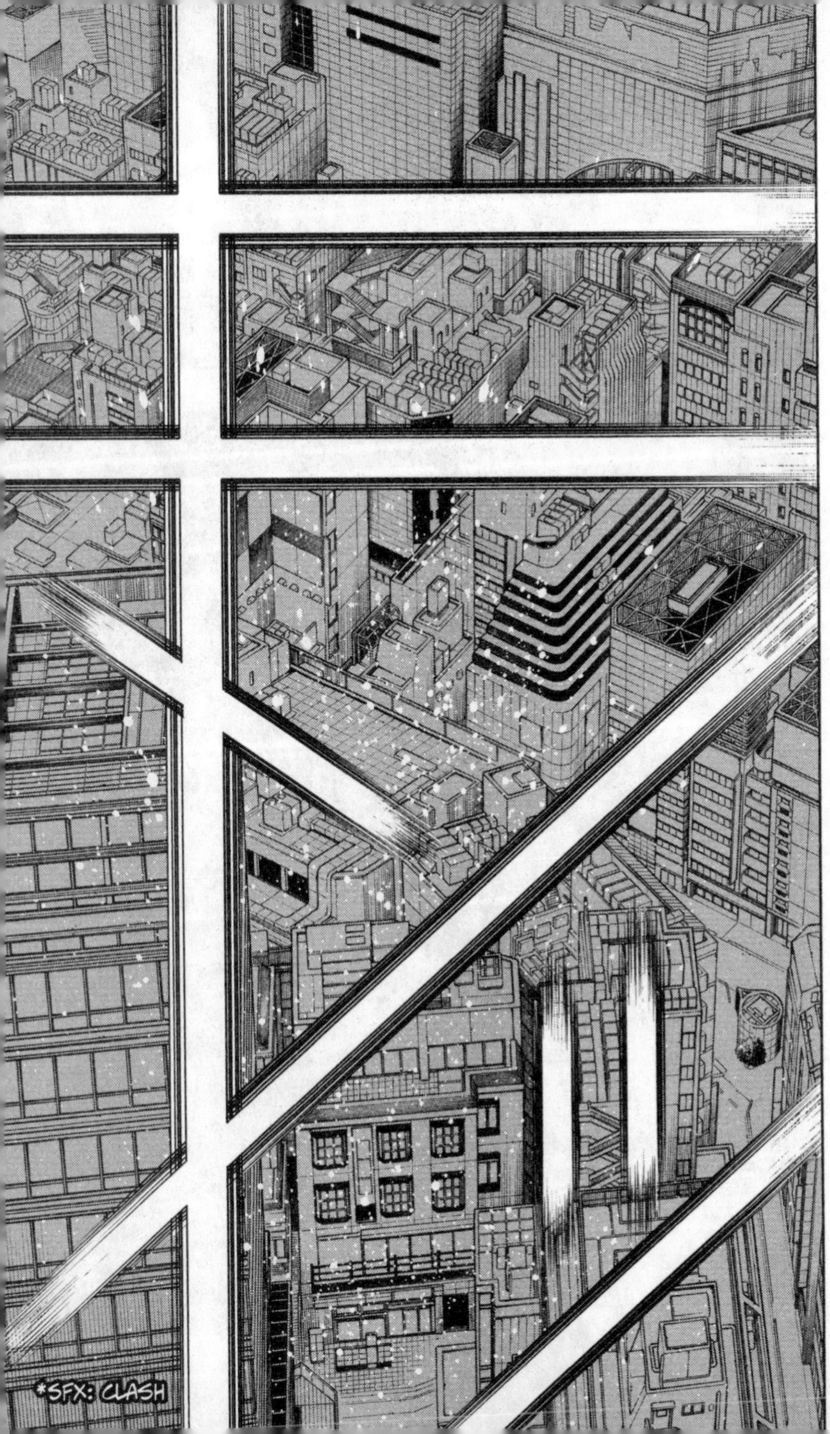
*SFX: CLASH

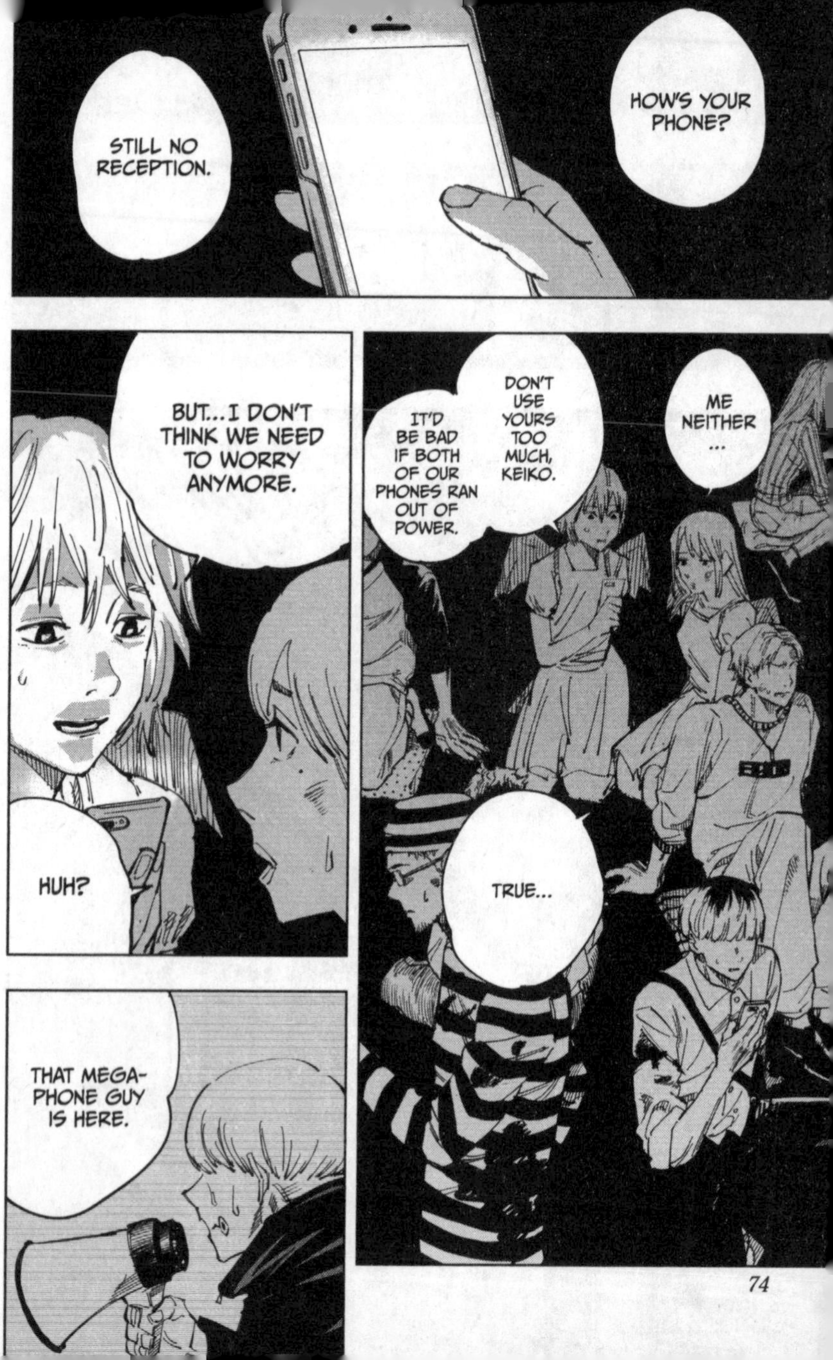
HOW'S YOUR PHONE?
STILL NO RECEPTION.
ME NEITHER...
DON'T USE YOURS TOO MUCH, KEIKO.
IT'D BE BAD IF BOTH OF OUR PHONES RAN OUT OF POWER.
TRUE...
BUT...I DON'T THINK WE NEED TO WORRY ANYMORE.
HUH?
THAT MEGA-PHONE GUY IS HERE.

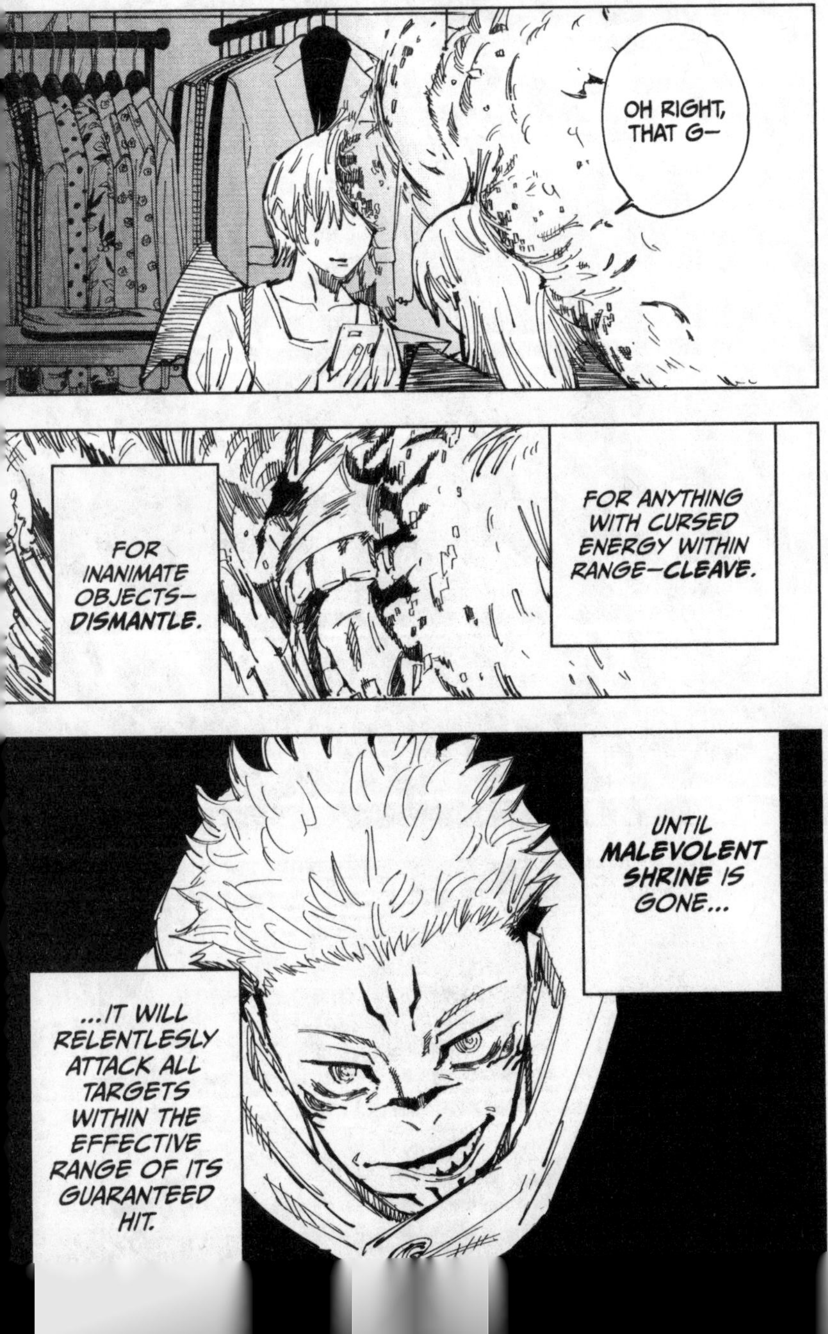
OH RIGHT, THAT G—
FOR ANYTHING WITH CURSED ENERGY WITHIN RANGE—CLEAVE.
FOR INANIMATE OBJECTS—DISMANTLE.
UNTIL MALEVOLENT SHRINE IS GONE...
...IT WILL RELENTLESLY ATTACK ALL TARGETS WITHIN THE EFFECTIVE RANGE OF ITS GUARANTEED HIT.

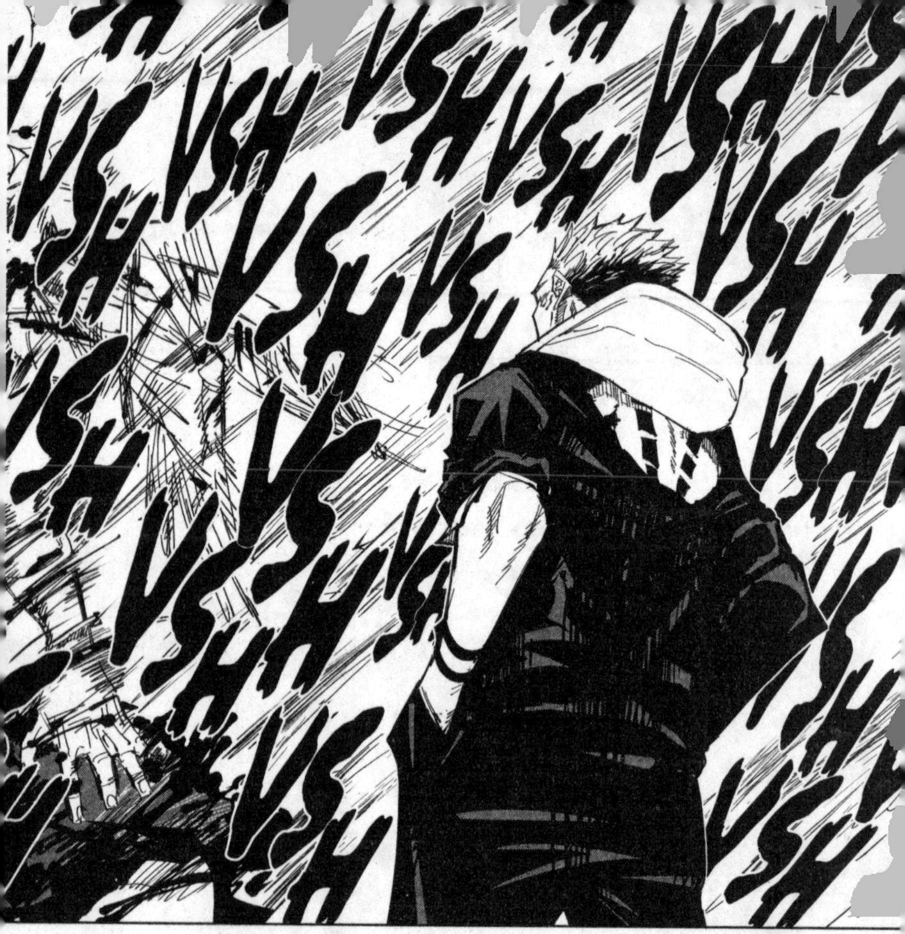
VSH VSH VSH VSH VSH VSH VSH VSH VSH VSH VSH VSH VSH VSH VSH VSH VSH VSH
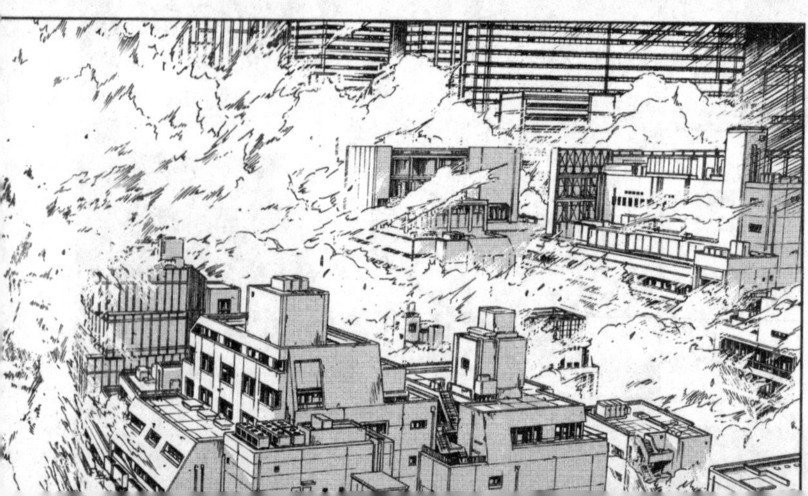

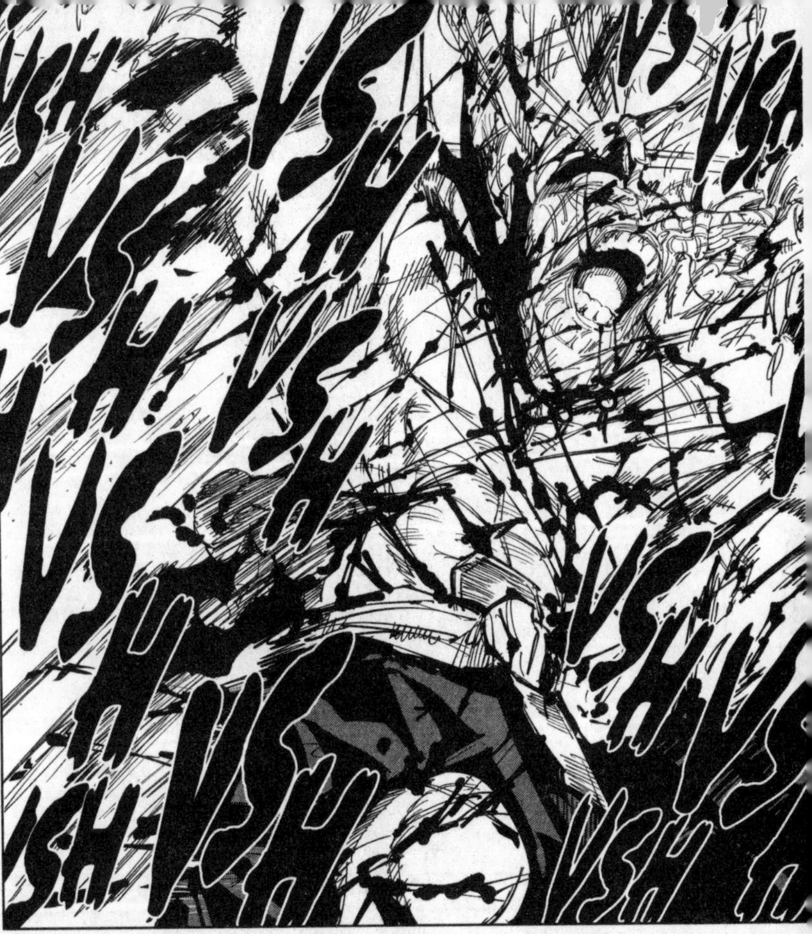
VSH VSH VSH
VSH VSH VSH
VSH VSH VSH
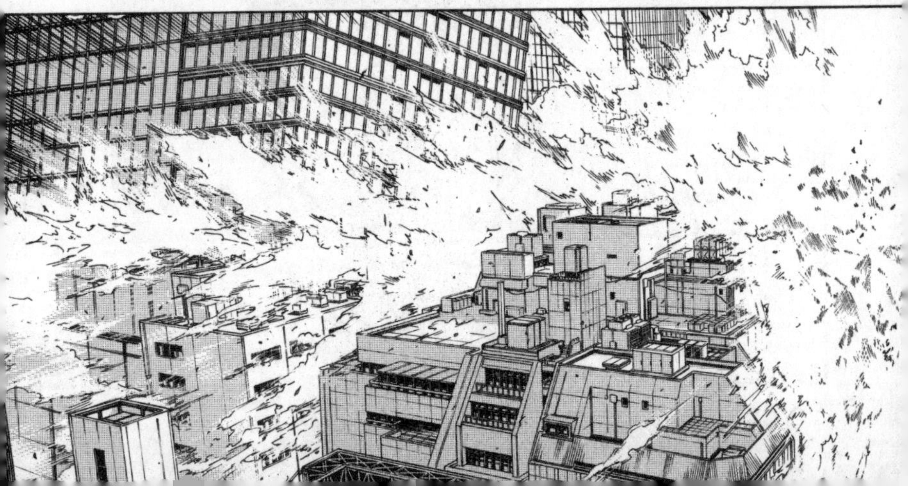

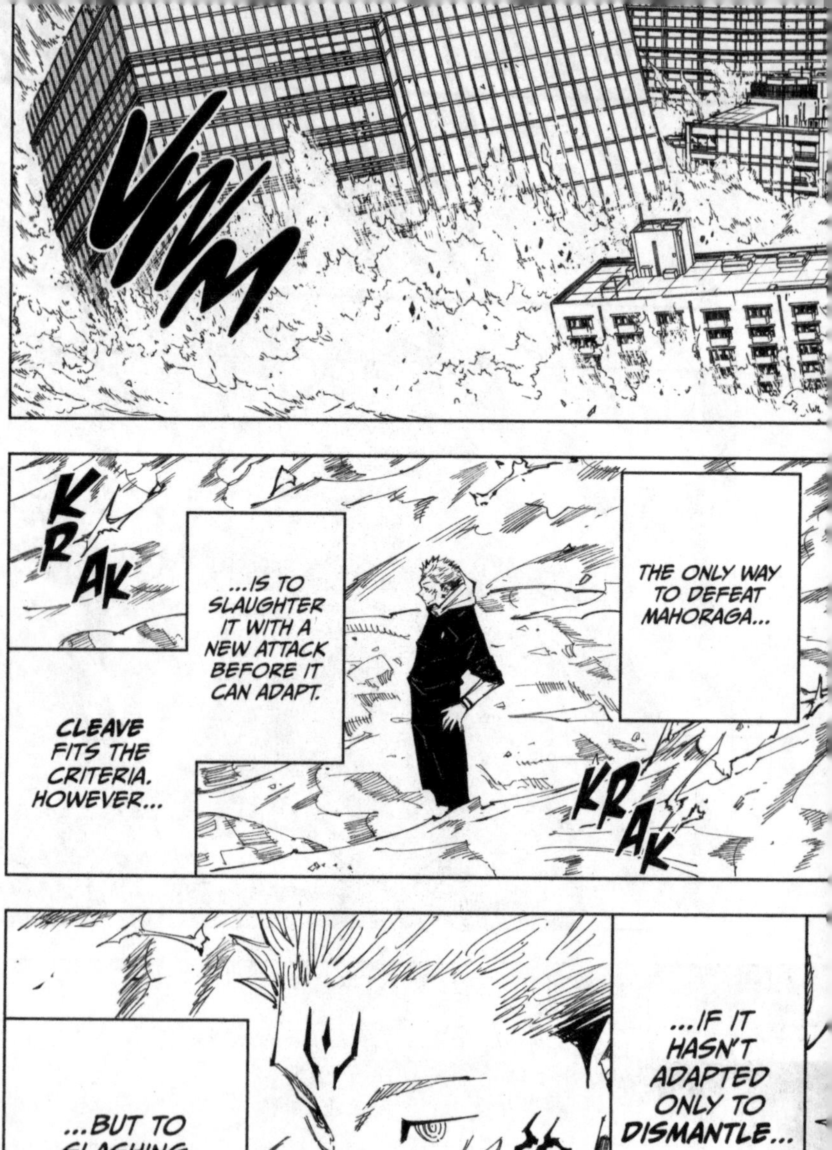
VMM
THE ONLY WAY TO DEFEAT MAHORAGA...
KRAK
...IS TO SLAUGHTER IT WITH A NEW ATTACK BEFORE IT CAN ADAPT.
KRAK
CLEAVE FITS THE CRITERIA. HOWEVER...
...IF IT HASN'T ADAPTED ONLY TO DISMANTLE...
...BUT TO SLASHING ATTACKS IN GENERAL, THEN...

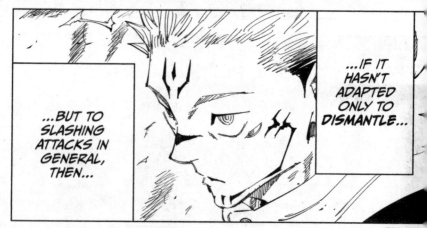

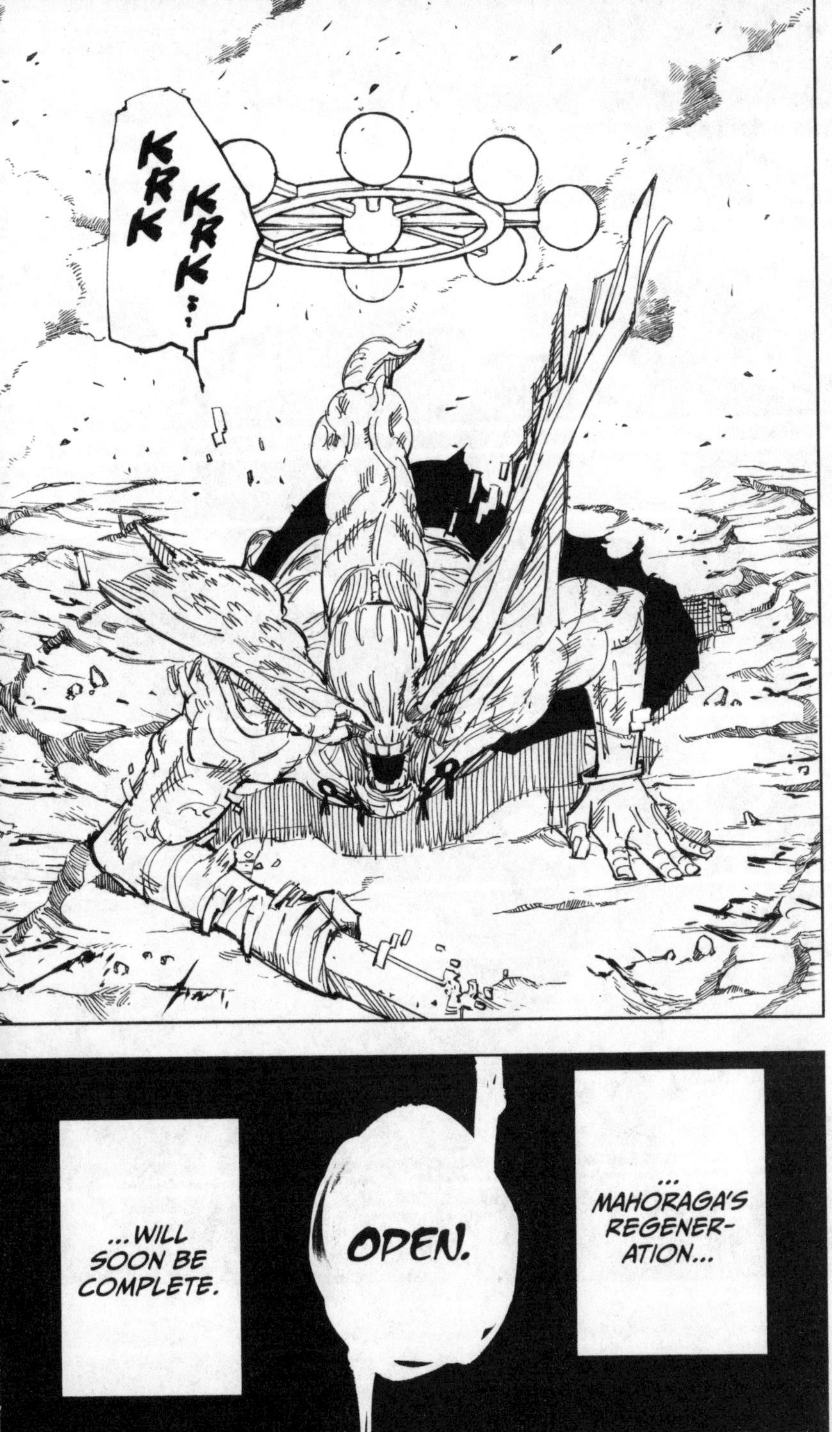
KRK KRK...
...MAHORAGA'S REGENER-ATION...
OPEN.
...WILL SOON BE COMPLETE.

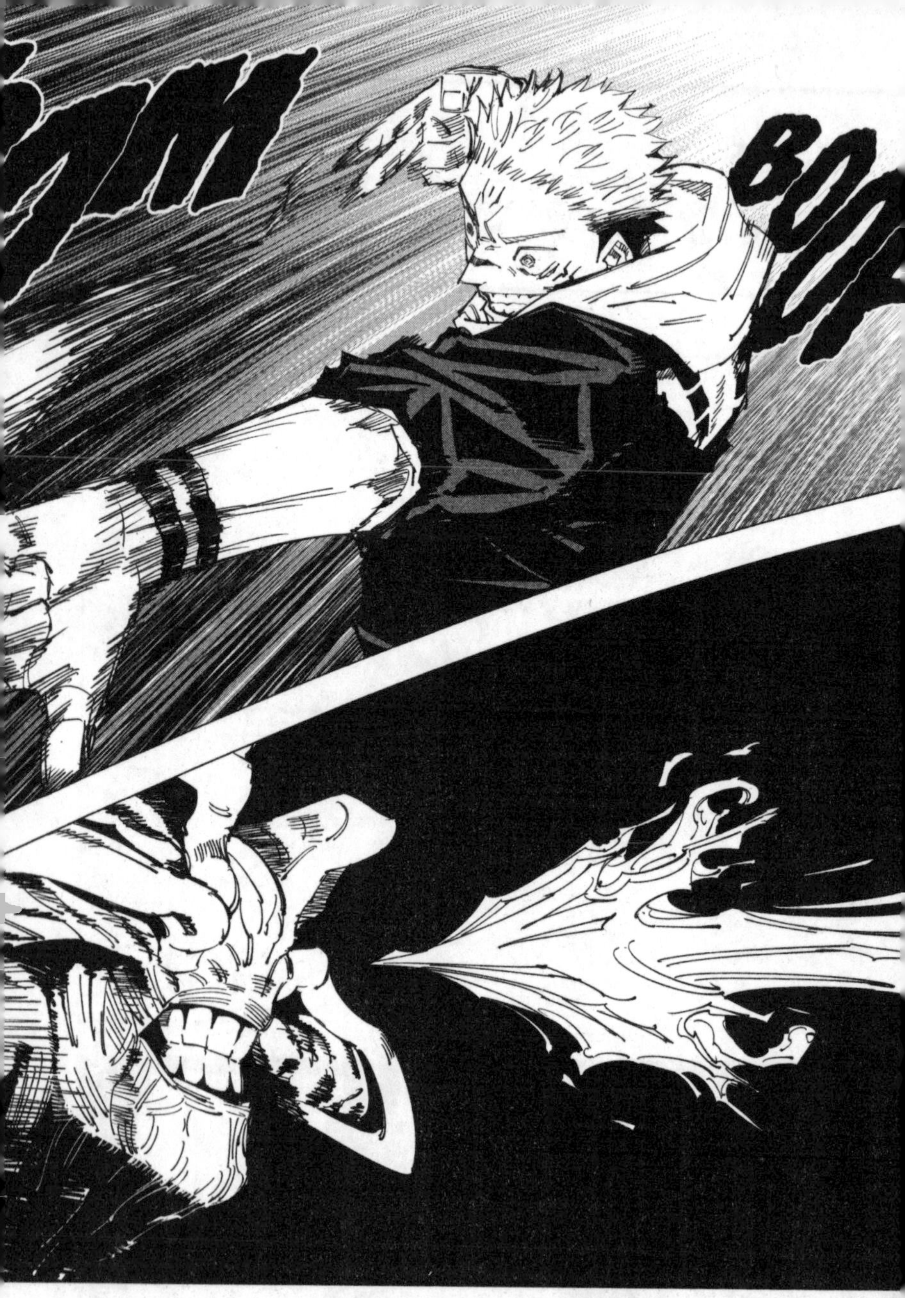
BO

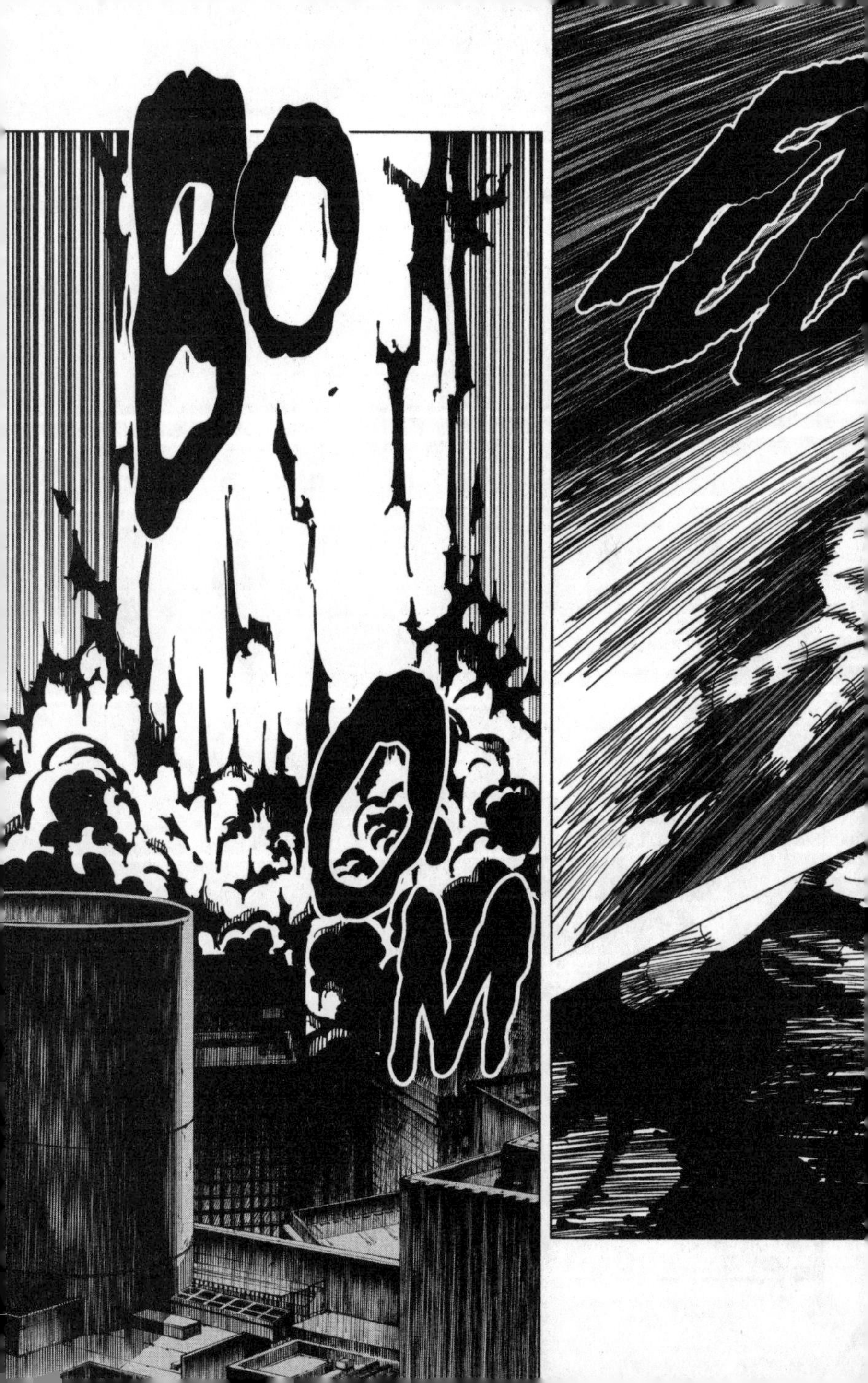
BOOM

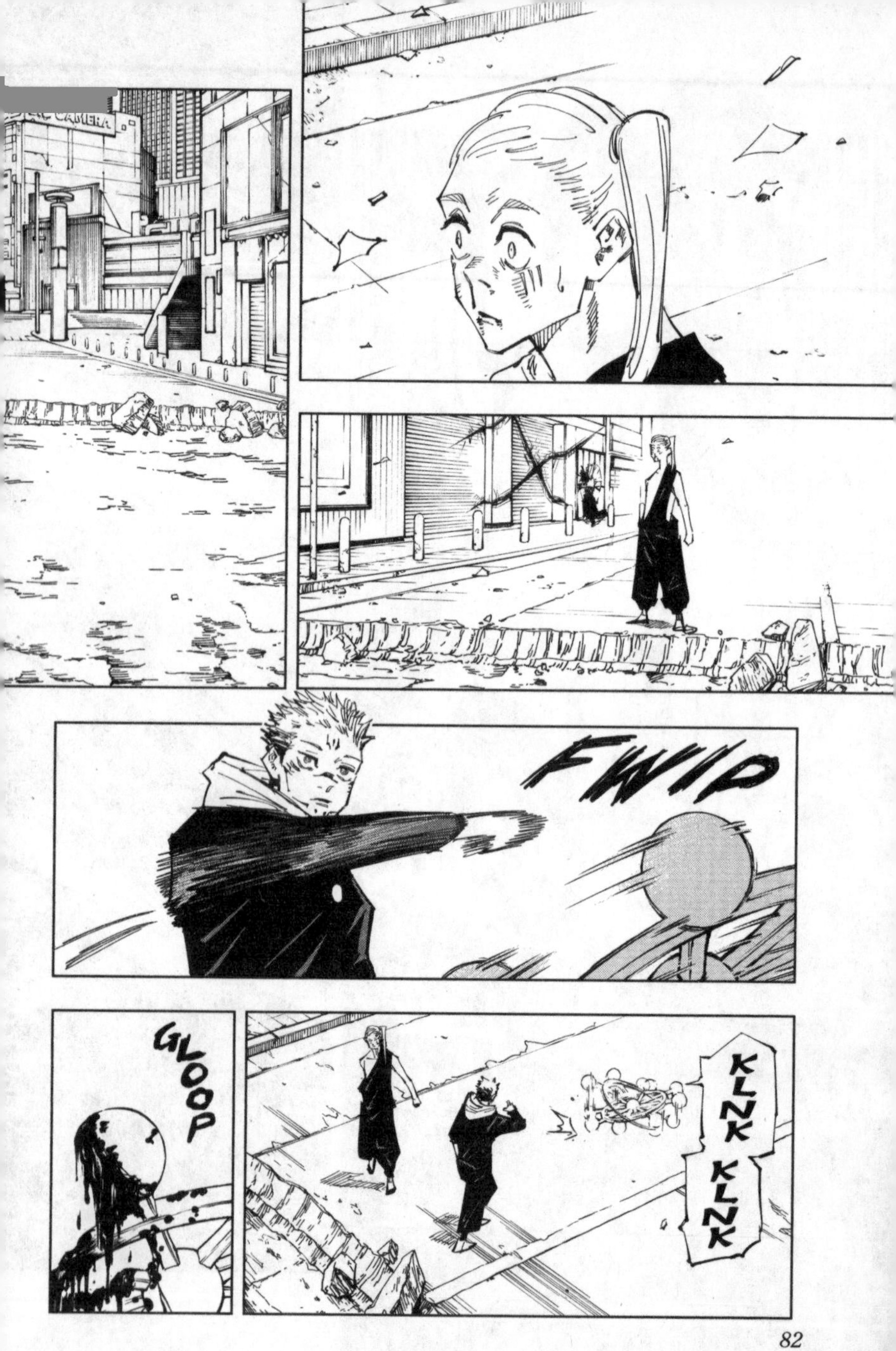
CAMERA
FWIP
KLNK
KLNK
GLOOP

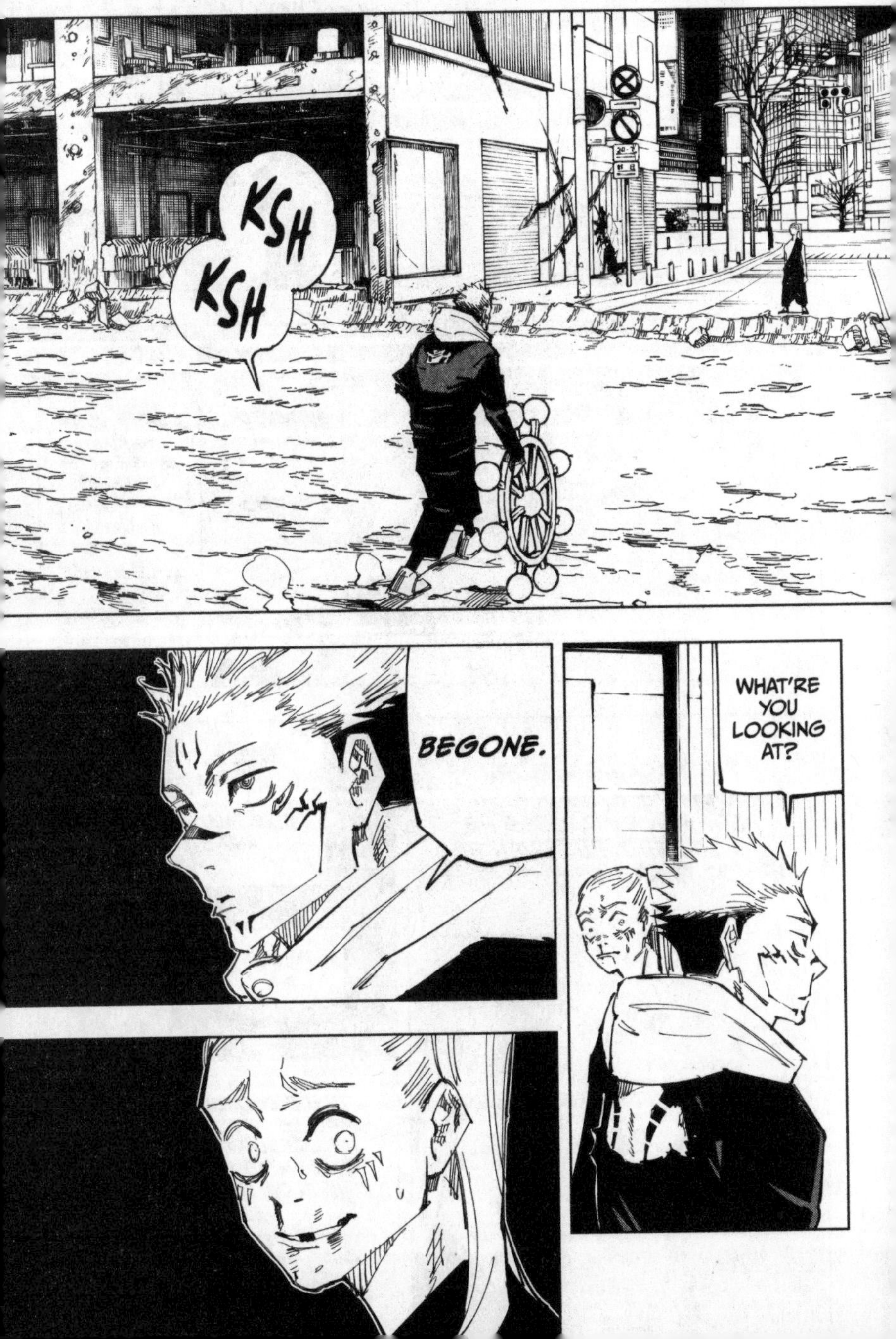
KSH KSH
WHAT'RE YOU LOOKING AT?
BEGONE.

I'M OUTTA HERE!

I...

I'LL BE ON MY WAY!

MY LUCK NEVER RUNS OUT!

...STORES MIRACLES.

I SURVIVED AGAIN!

CURSE USER HARUTA SHIGEMO'S CURSED TECHNIQUE...

THE MARKINGS UNDER SHIGEMO'S EYES INDICATE HOW MANY MIRACLES HE HAS STORED, BUT EVEN HE IS NOT AWARE OF THIS FACT.

LITTLE EVERYDAY MIRACLES ARE ERASED FROM SHIGEMO'S MEMORY AND STORED.

FOR EXAMPLE...

HEY! ALL THE SAME NUMBER!

4:44 44

ONCE AGAIN, I LIVE ...

THESE STORED MIRACLES ARE THEN RELEASED WHEN SHIGEMO'S LIFE IS IN DANGER.

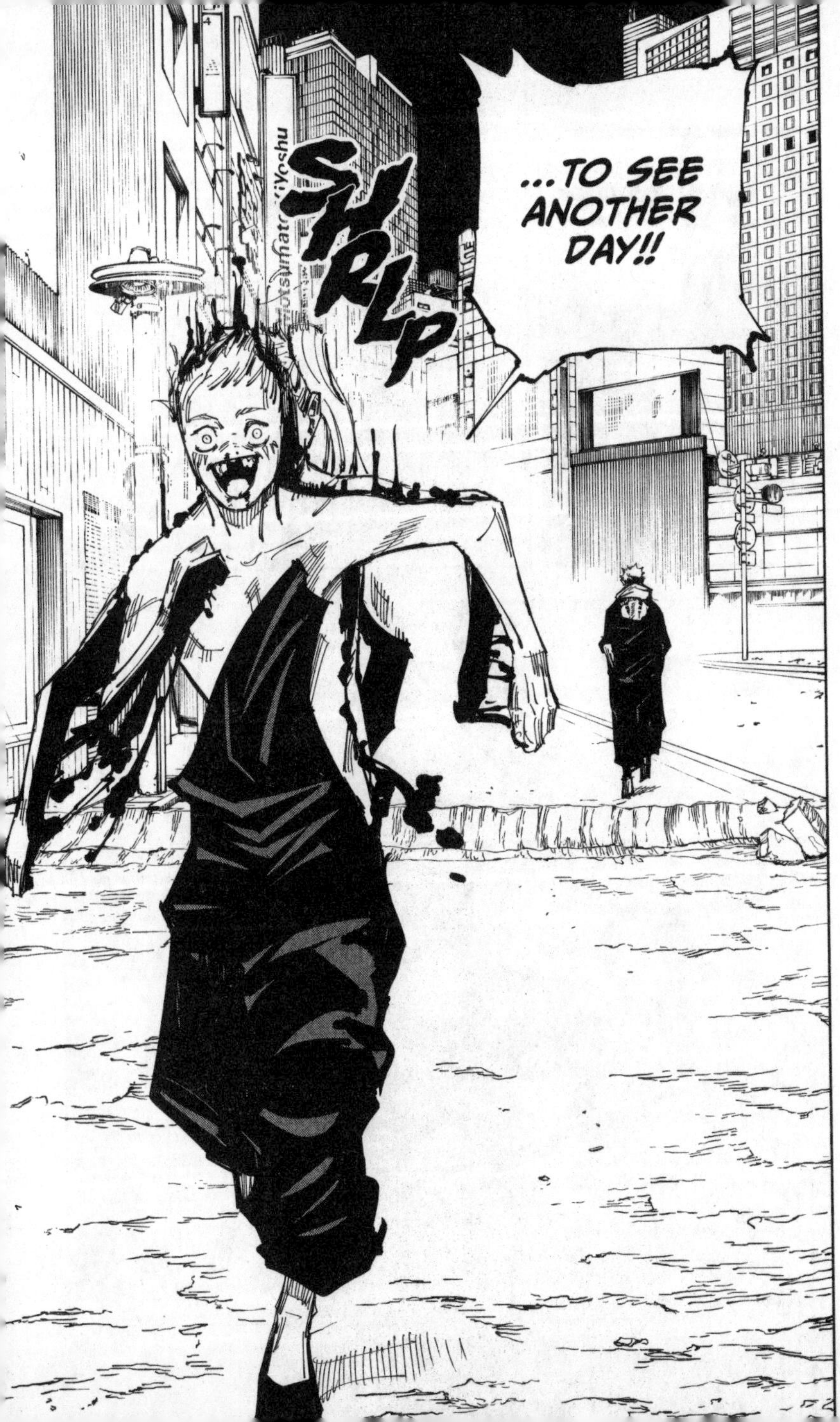
...TO SEE ANOTHER DAY!!
SHRLP

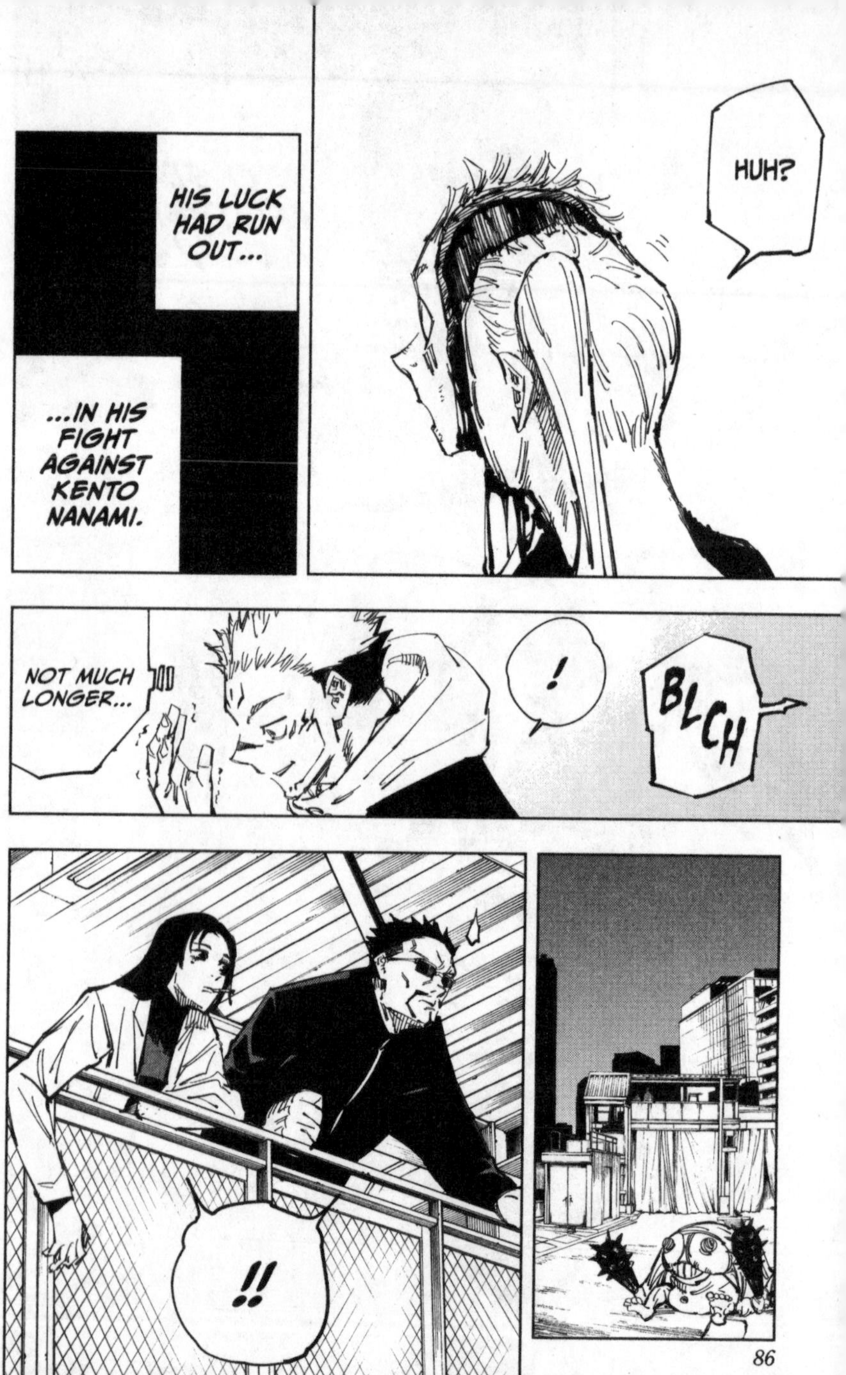
HUH?
HIS LUCK HAD RUN OUT...
...IN HIS FIGHT AGAINST KENTO NANAMI.
BLCH
!
NOT MUCH LONGER...
!!

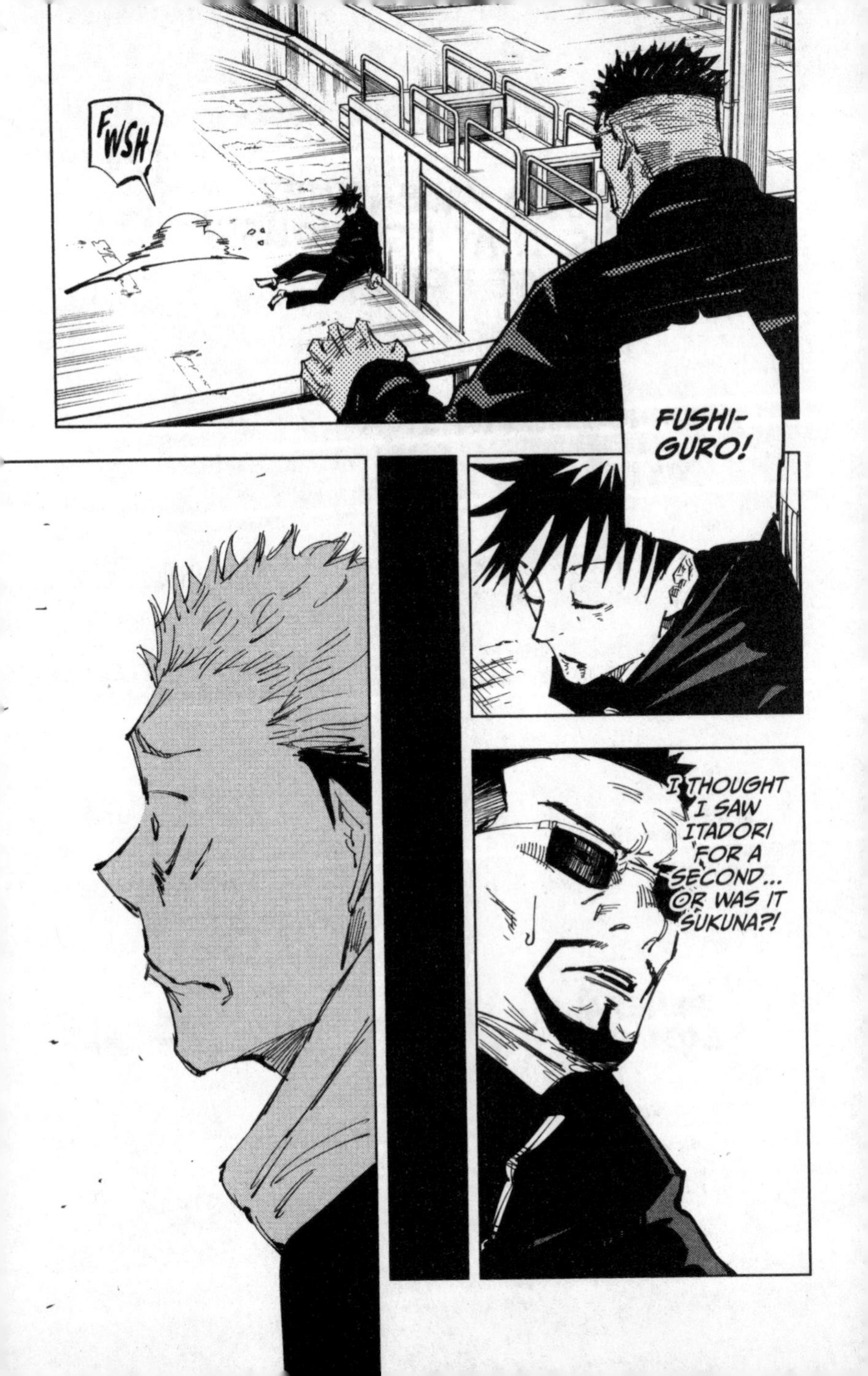
FWSH
FUSHI-GURO!
I THOUGHT I SAW ITADORI FOR A SECOND... OR WAS IT SUKUNA?!

THE 2020 VALENTINES RANKINGS THAT I SERIOUSLY ALMOST FORGOT

RANKINGS (VALENTINES RECEIVED)	CHARACTER	
17 (1)	OKKOTSU	SUKUNA
	PAPAGURO	HAIBARA
	PANDA	JUNPEI
	HANAMI	KAMO (NORITOSHI)

GENERAL COMMENT

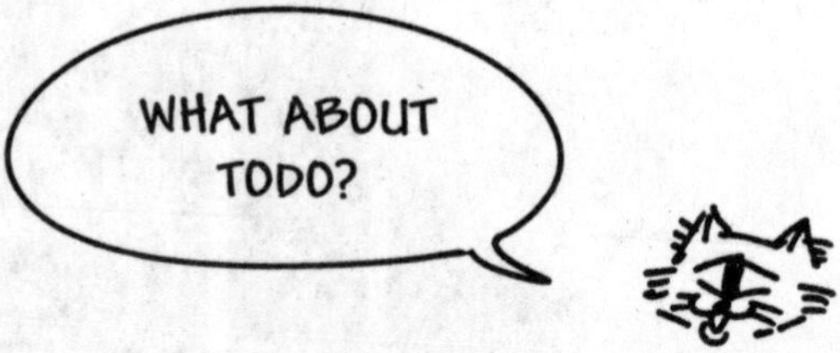
WHAT ABOUT TODO?

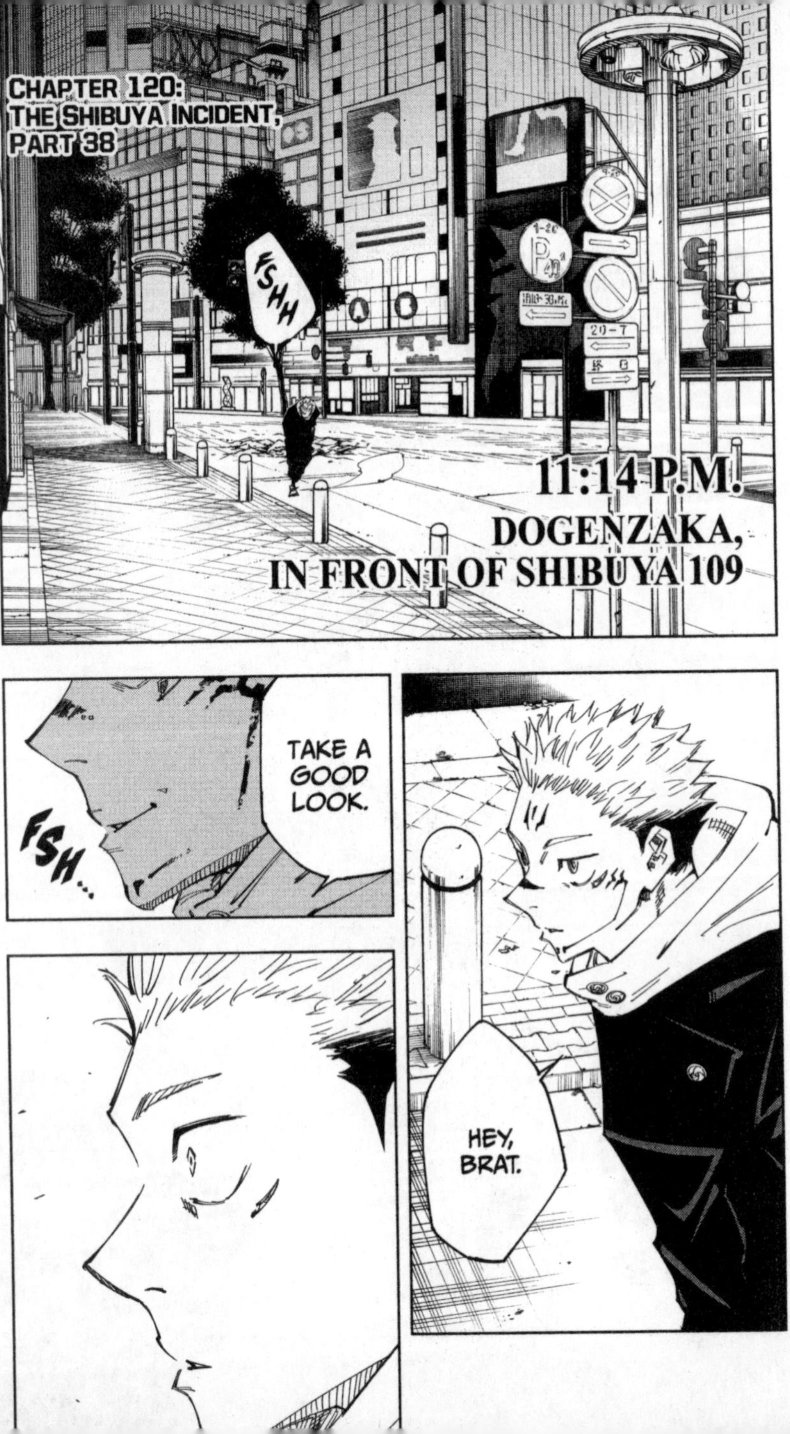
CHAPTER 120:
THE SHIBUYA INCIDENT, PART 38
FSHH
11:14 P.M.
DOGENZAKA, IN FRONT OF SHIBUYA 109
HEY, BRAT.
FSH...
TAKE A GOOD LOOK.

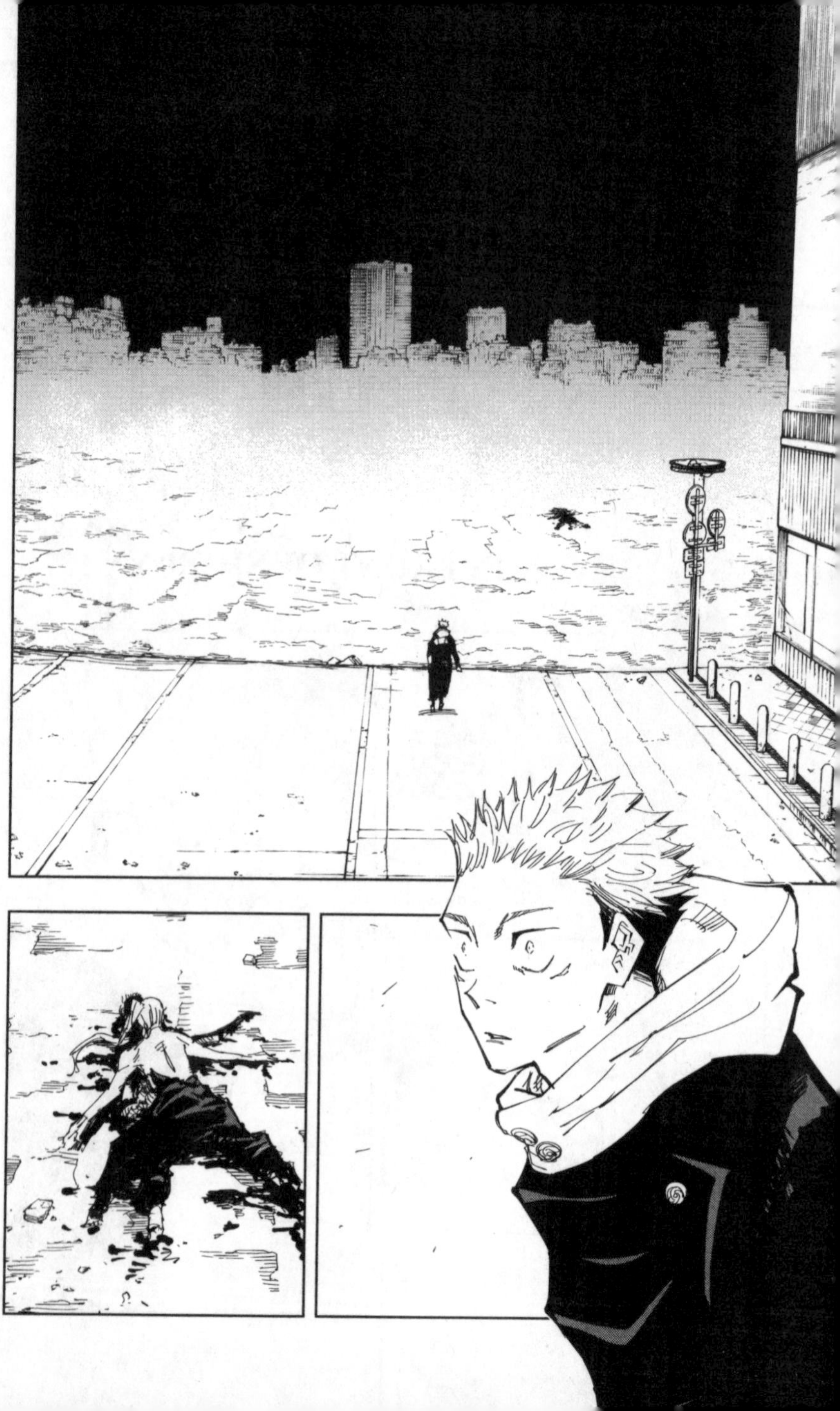

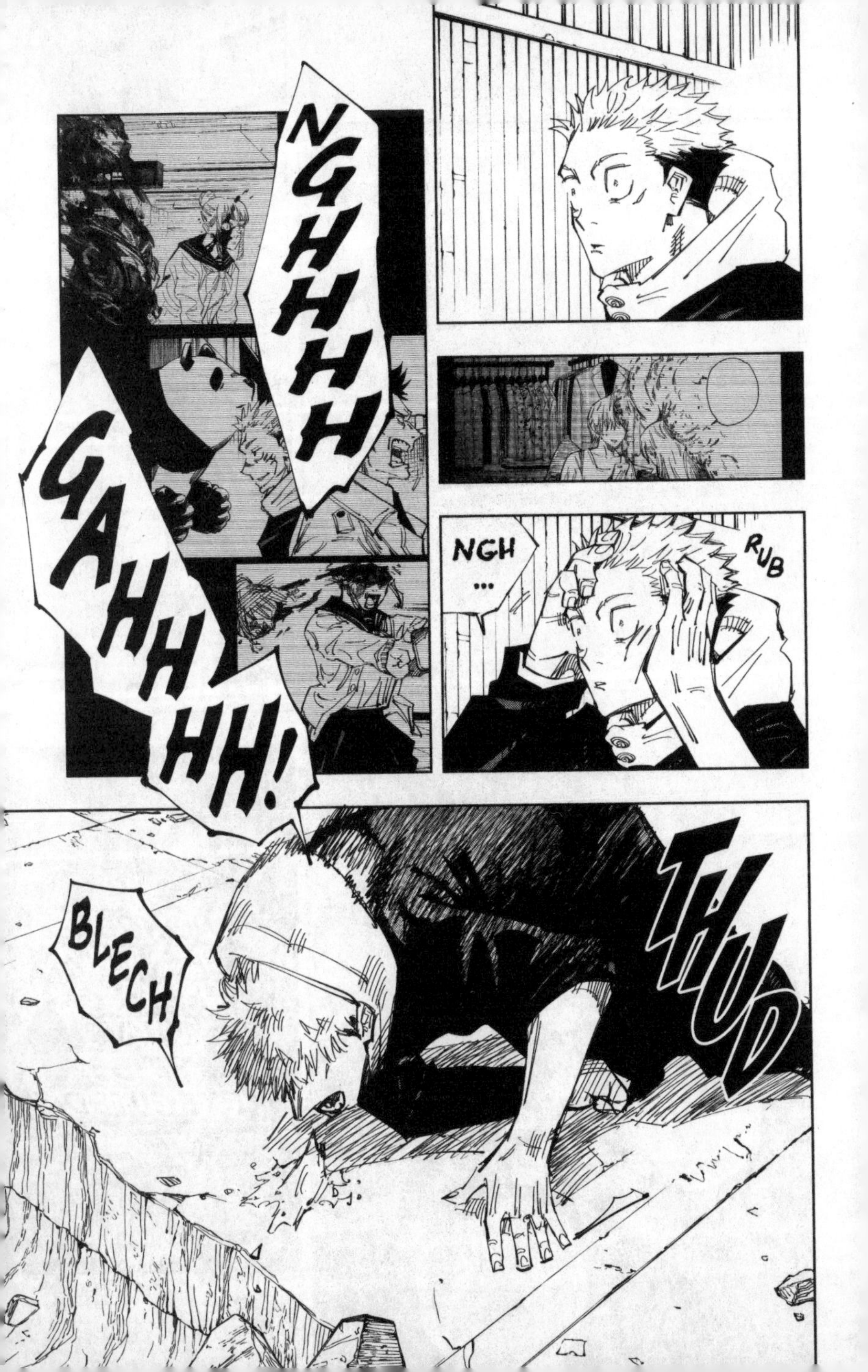
NGH ...
RUB
NGHHHHH
GAHHHHHH!
THUD
BLECH

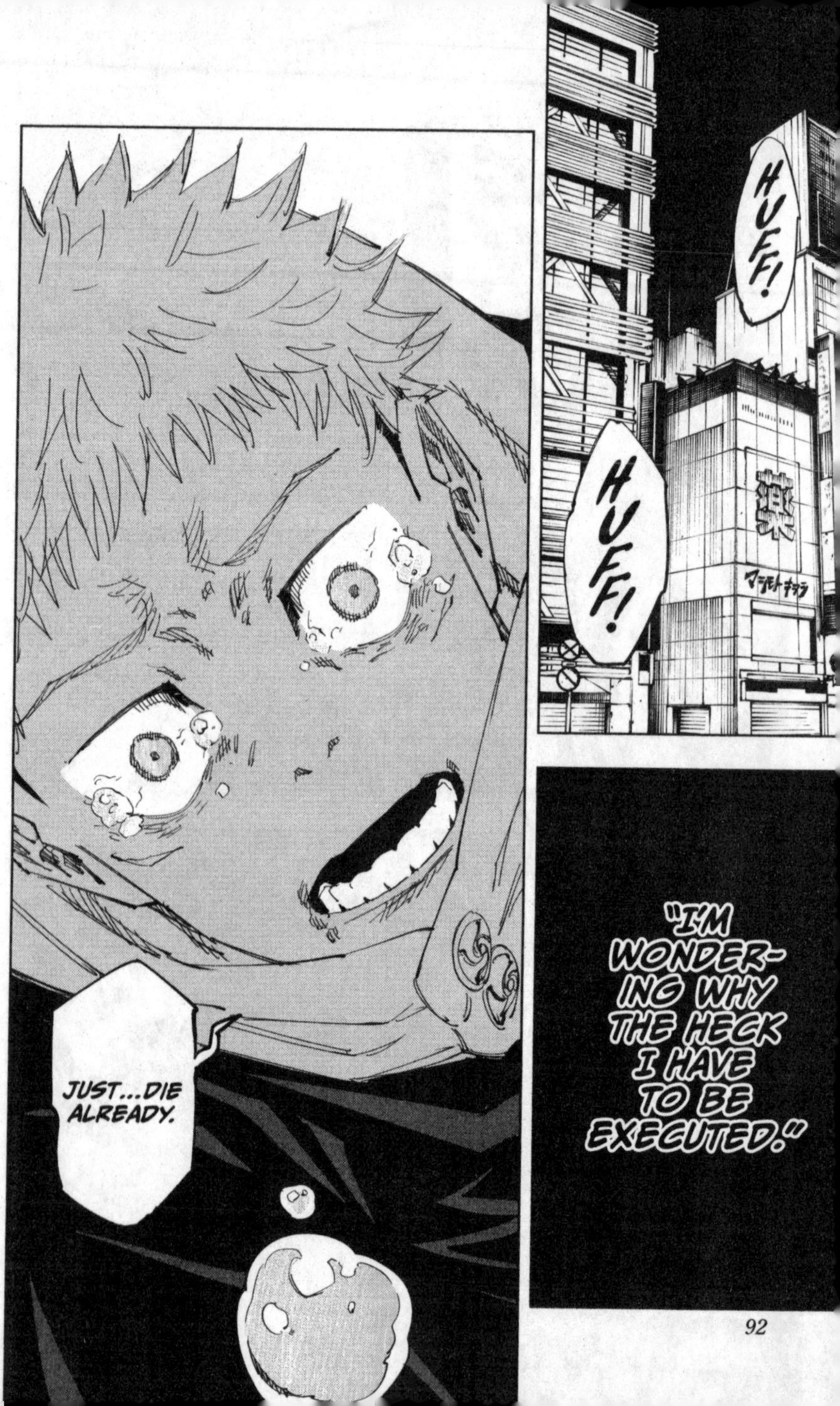
HUFF!
HUFF!
"I'M WONDERING WHY THE HECK I HAVE TO BE EXECUTED."
JUST...DIE ALREADY.

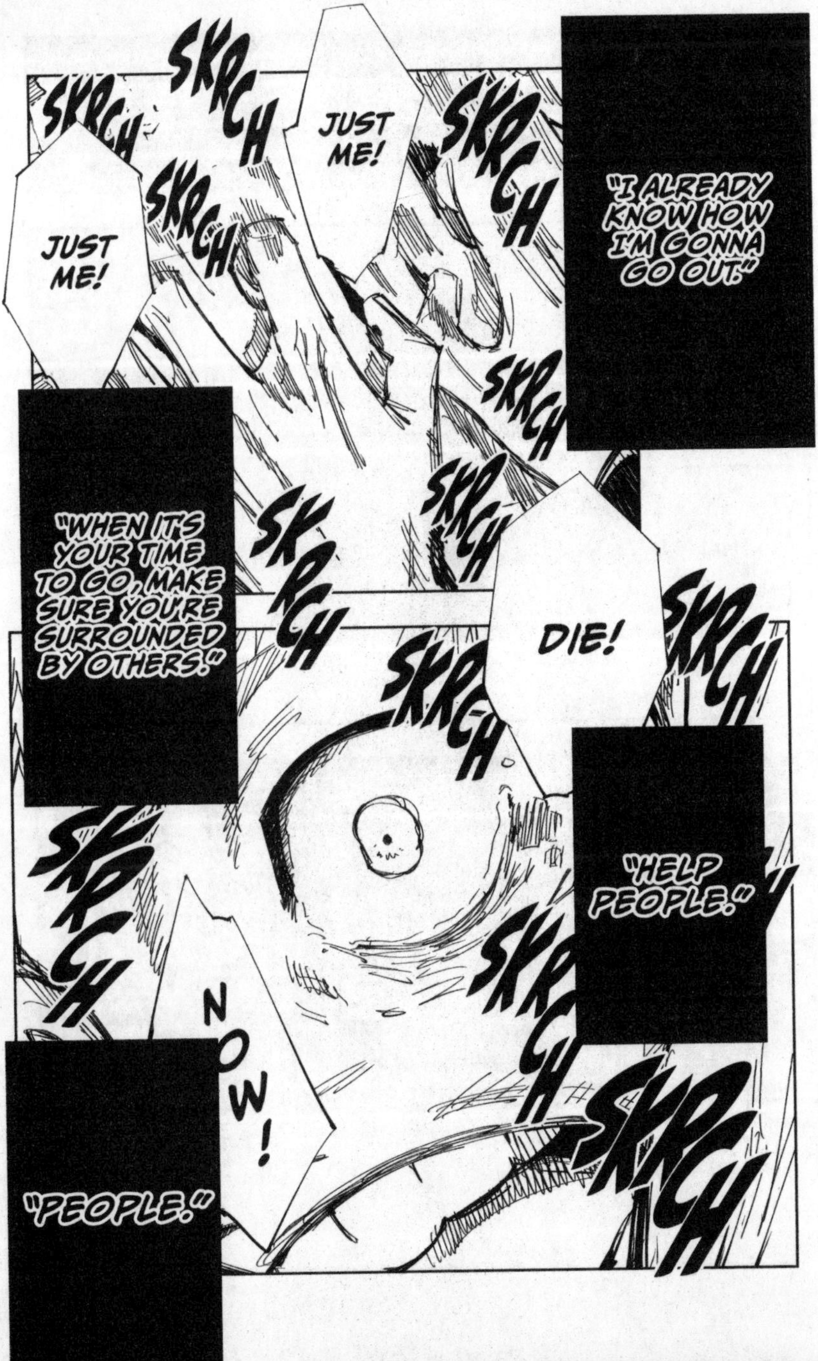
"I ALREADY KNOW HOW I'M GONNA GO OUT."
SKRCH
JUST ME!
SKRCH
SKRCH
JUST ME!
SKRCH
SKRCH
SKRCH
SKRCH
"WHEN IT'S YOUR TIME TO GO, MAKE SURE YOU'RE SURROUNDED BY OTHERS."
SKRCH
DIE!
SKRCH
"HELP PEOPLE."
SKRCH
SKRCH
SKRCH
NOW!
SKRCH
"PEOPLE."

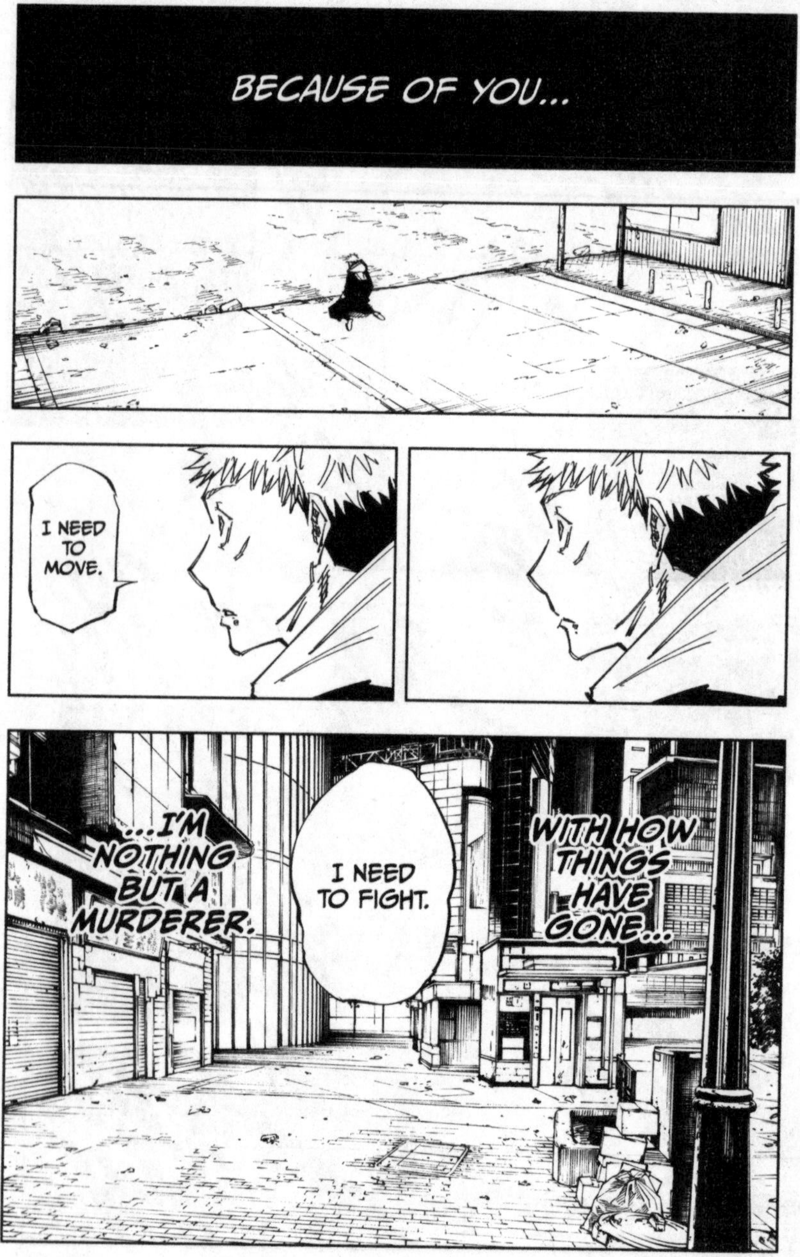
BECAUSE OF YOU...
I NEED TO MOVE.
WITH HOW THINGS HAVE GONE...
I NEED TO FIGHT.
...I'M NOTHING BUT A MURDERER.

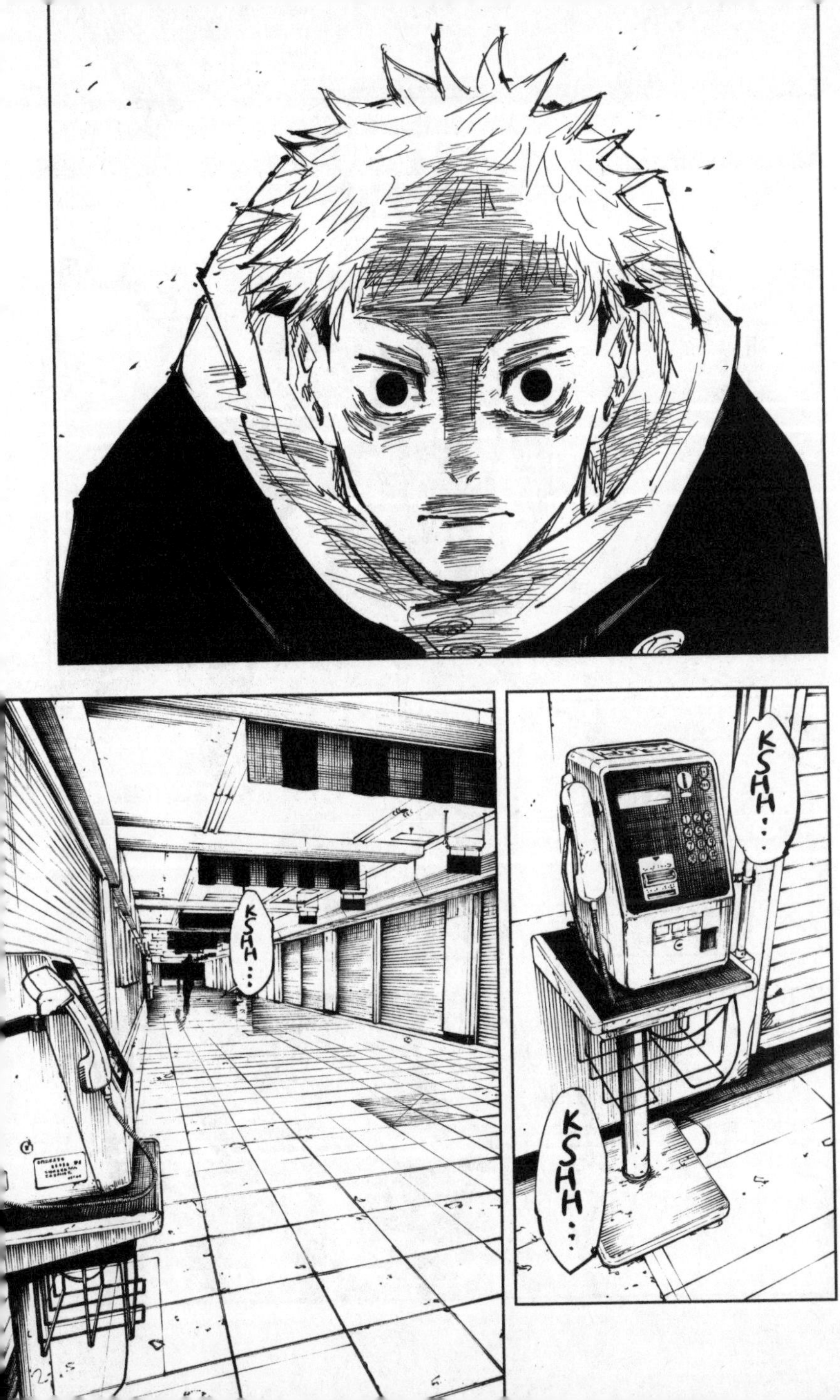
KSHH...
KSHH...
KSHH...

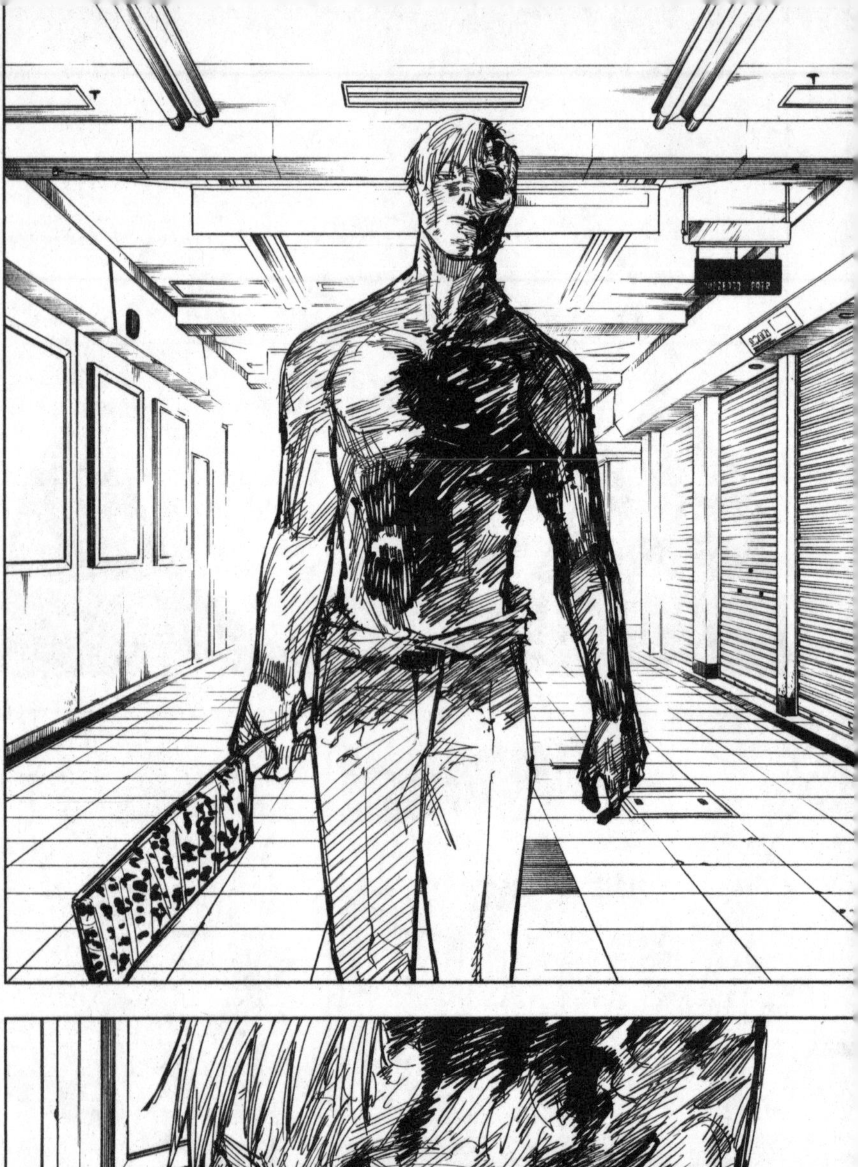

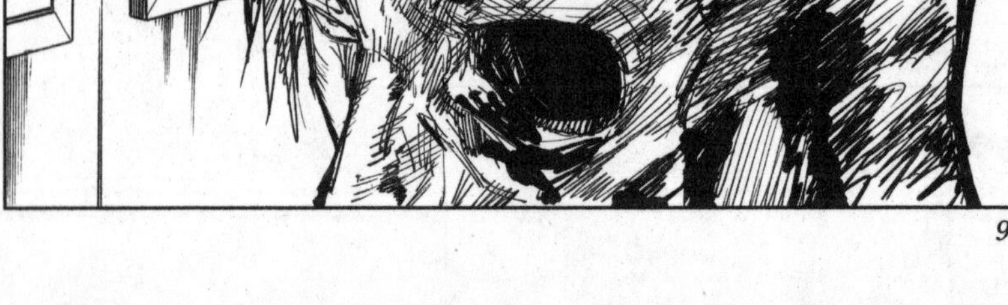

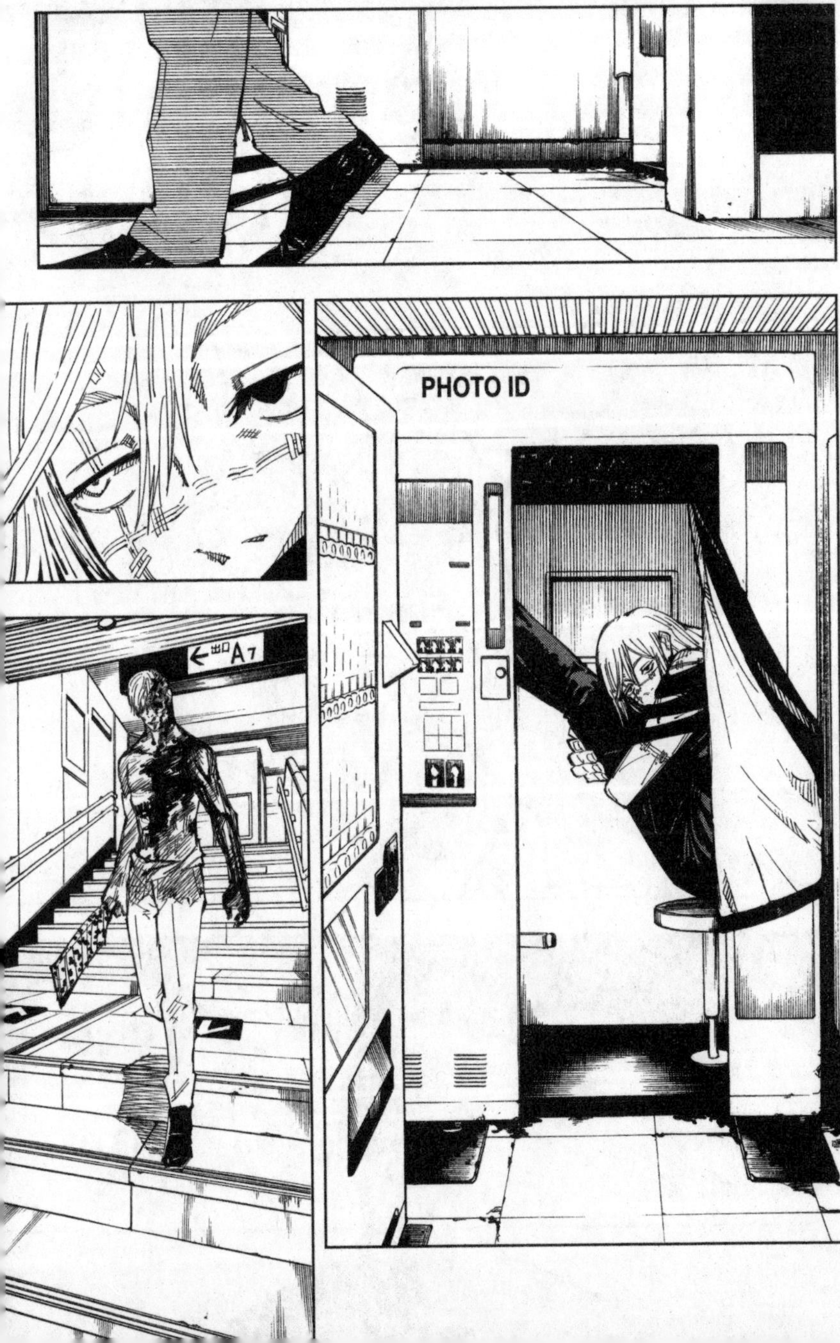
PHOTO ID
← 出口 A7

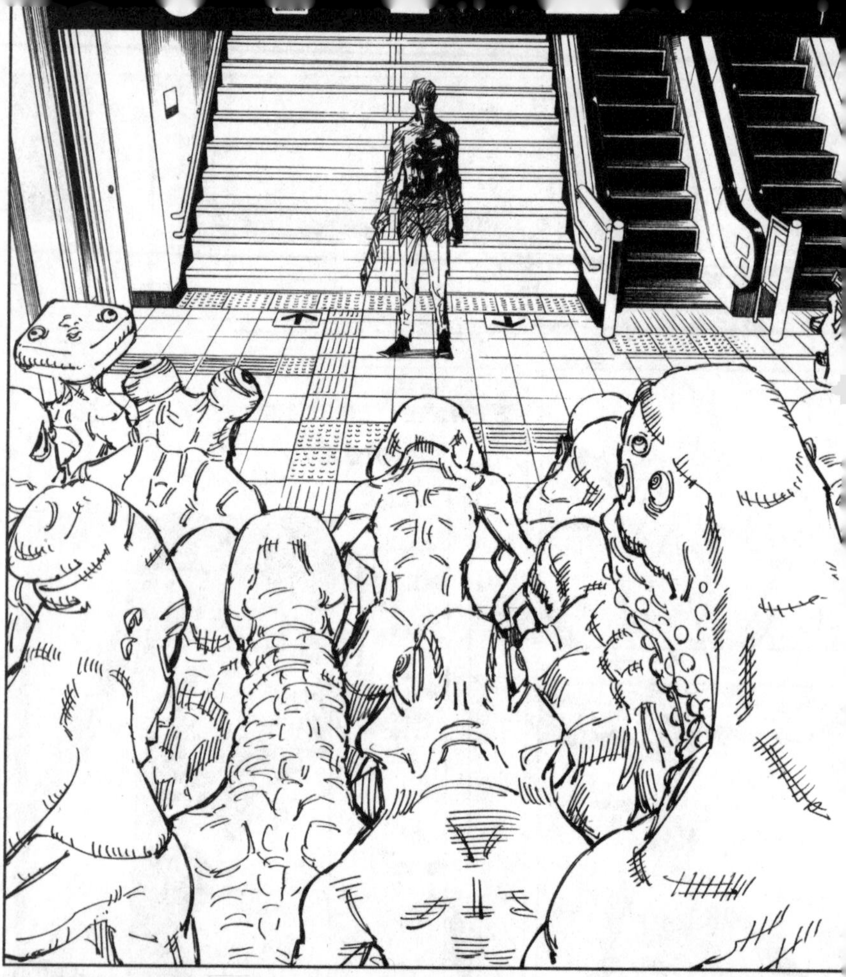

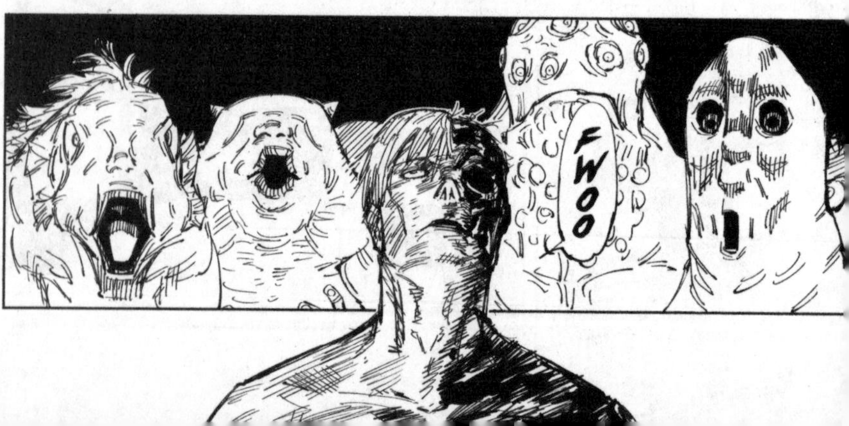
FWOO

YEAH, MALAYSIA... KUANTAN WOULD BE NICE.

MALAYSIA...

GO THROUGH THEM PAGE BY PAGE... KINDA LIKE TAKING BACK THE TIME I'VE LOST.

FINALLY GET AROUND TO THE COUNTLESS BOOKS I'VE BOUGHT BUT NEVER READ.

BUILD A HOUSE ON A SECLUDED BEACH.

WHAT HAPPENED TO THEM...?

BUT WHAT ABOUT MAKI...AND NAOBITO?

YOU'RE HEADING OVER TO SAVE FUSHIGURO...

NO, RIGHT NOW YOU'RE...

I'VE DONE ENOUGH, HAVEN'T I?

YEAH, I'M JUST TIRED.

TIRED... SO TIRED.

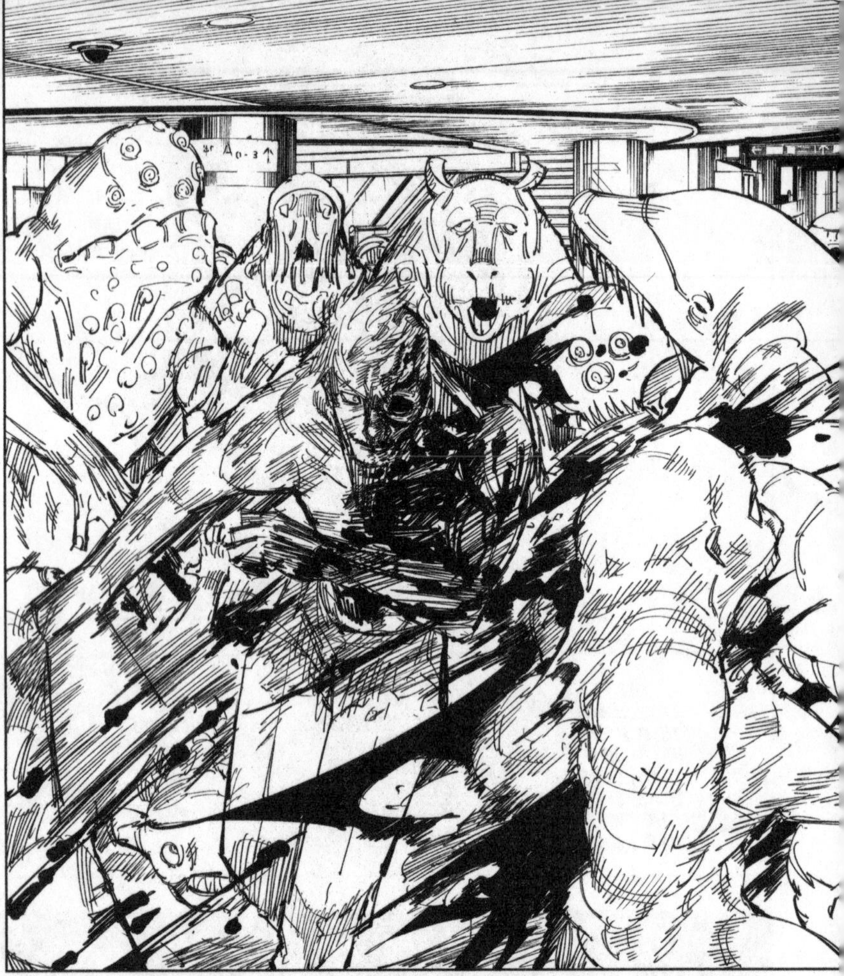
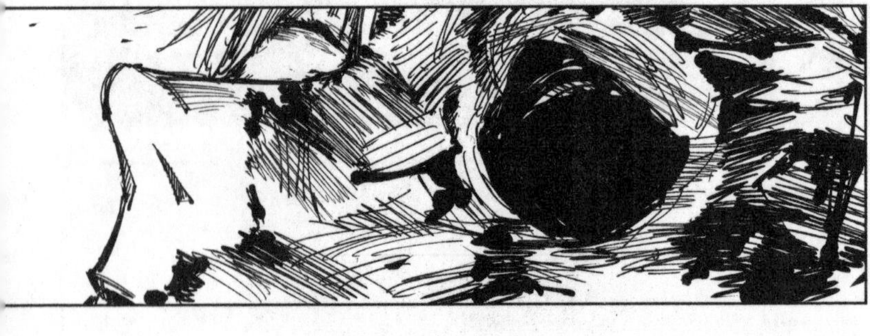

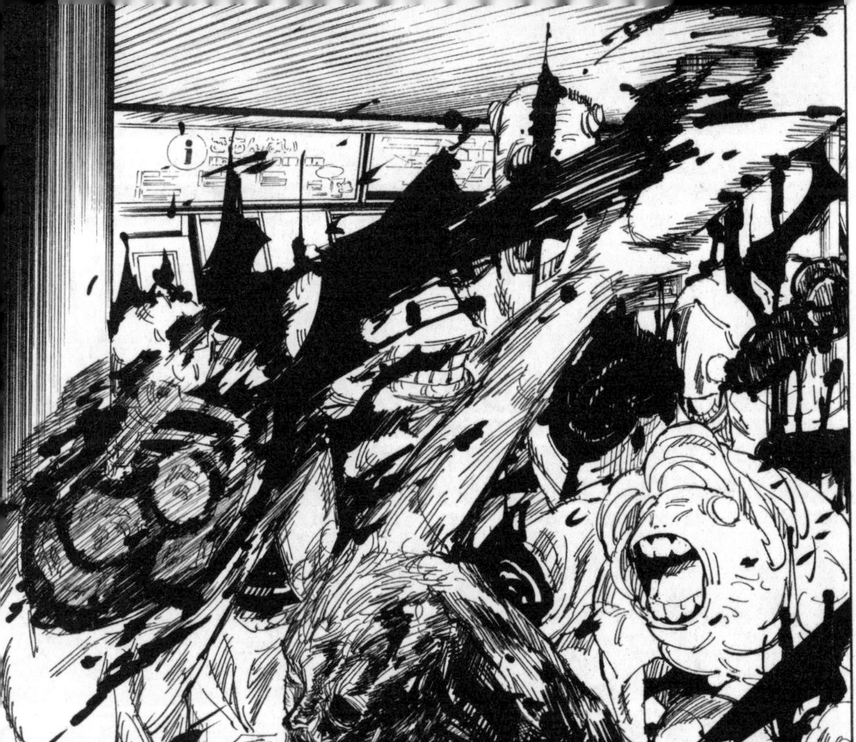
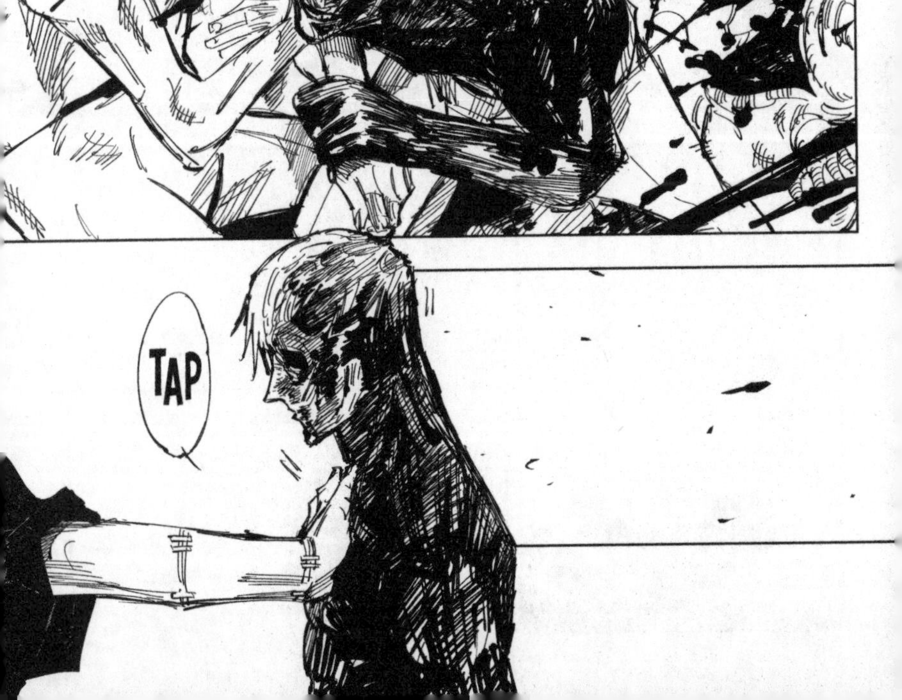
TAP

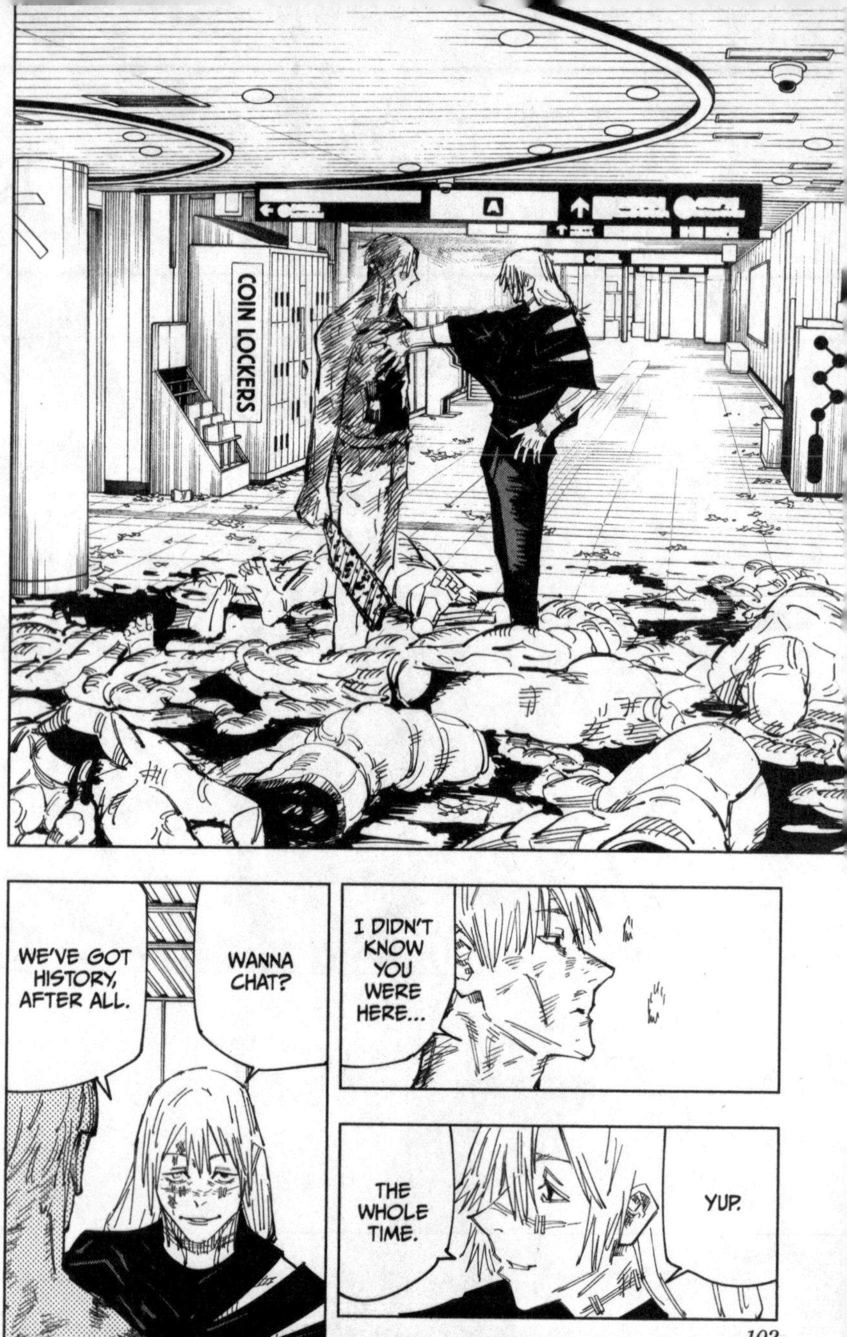
COIN LOCKERS
I DIDN'T KNOW YOU WERE HERE...
YUP.
THE WHOLE TIME.
WANNA CHAT?
WE'VE GOT HISTORY, AFTER ALL.

I RAN. EVEN THOUGH I RAN AWAY, I CAME BACK WITH THE VAGUE REASON OF FINDING THE WORK WORTHWHILE.

WHAT WAS I TRYING TO DO ANYWAY?

HAIBARA...

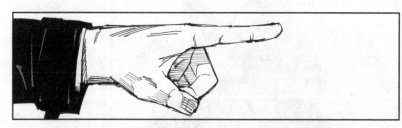

104

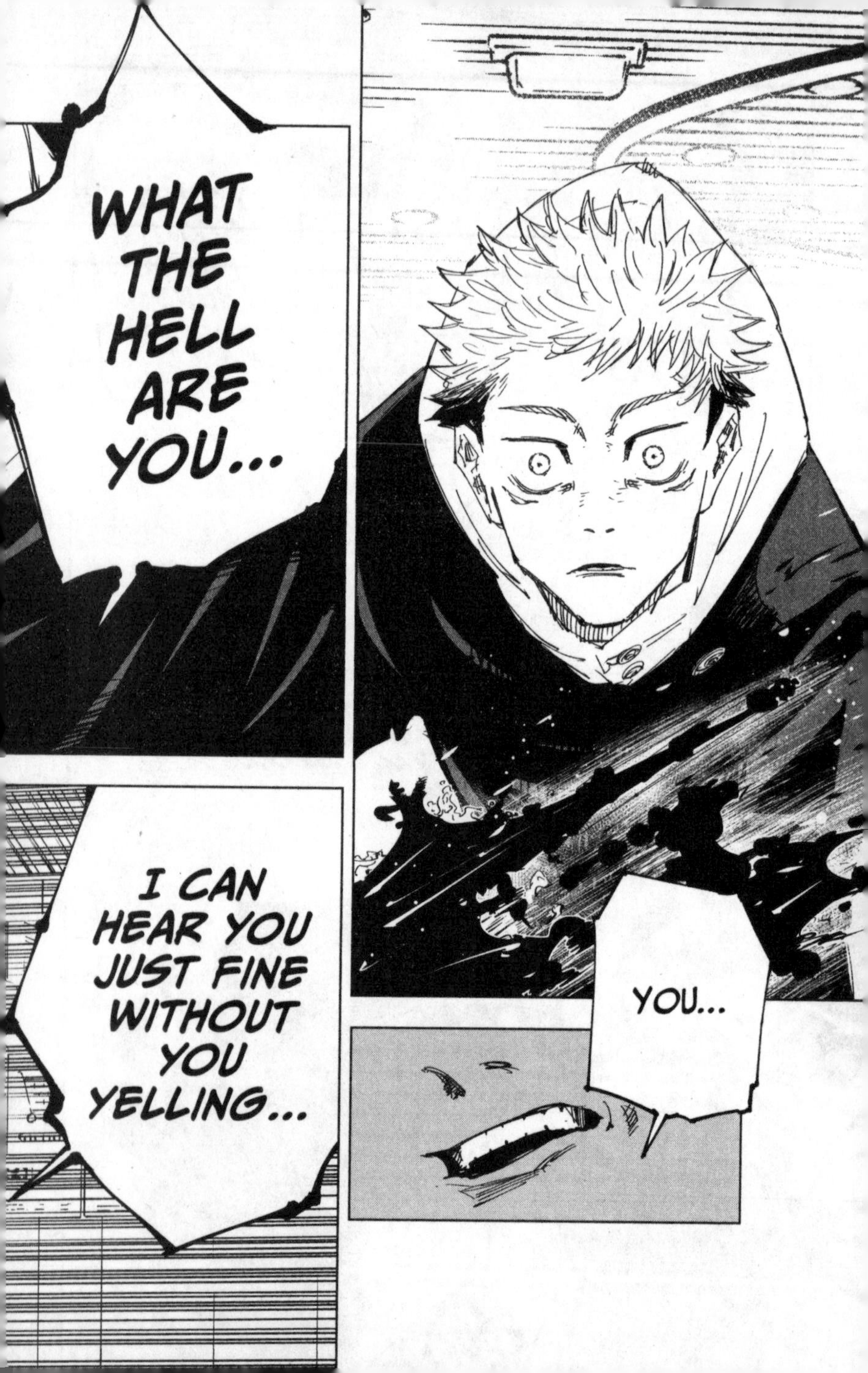
WHAT THE HELL ARE YOU...
YOU...
I CAN HEAR YOU JUST FINE WITHOUT YOU YELLING...

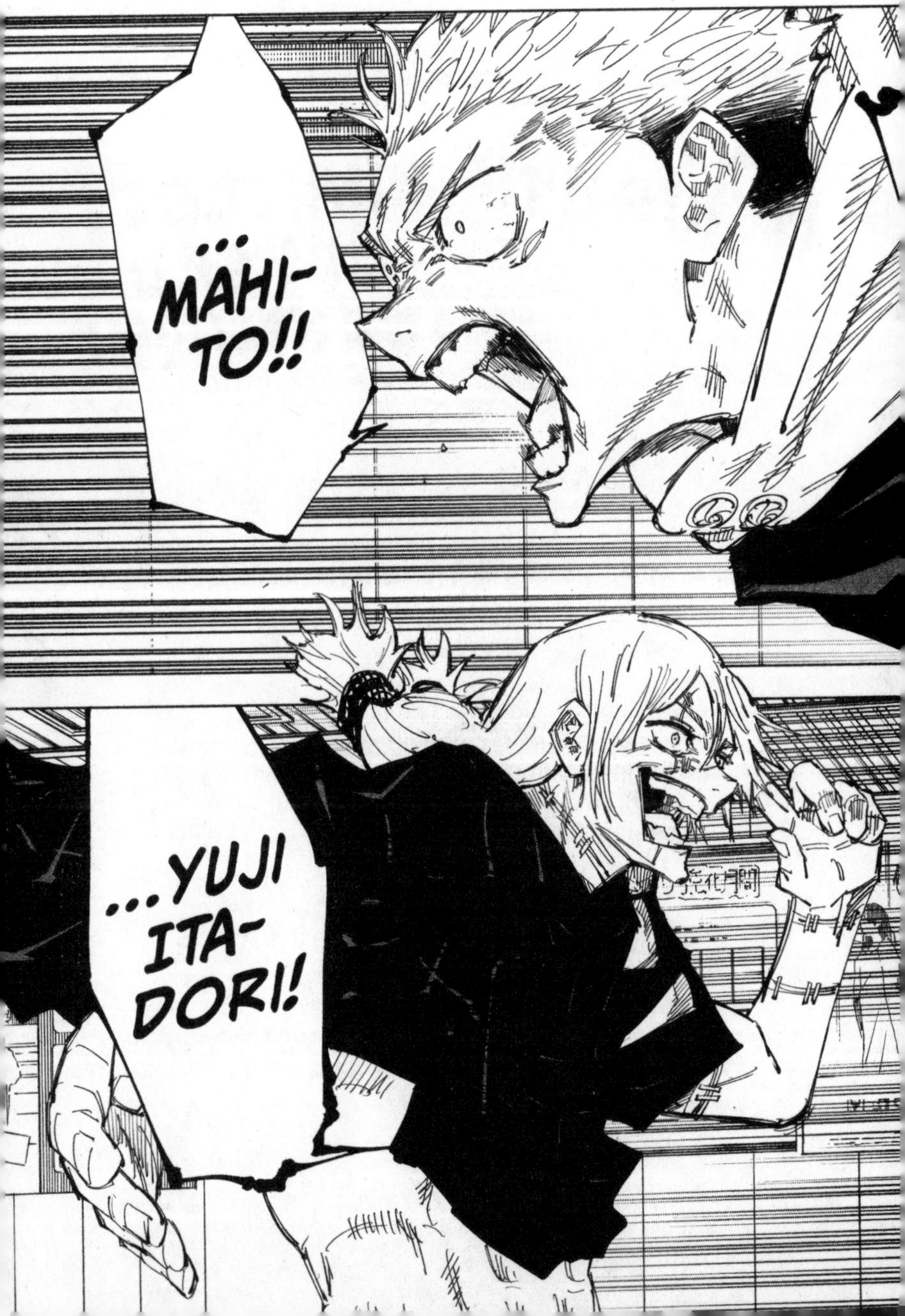
...MAHI-
TO!!
...YUJI
ITA-
DORI!

GETTING IT RIGHT!! LIMITLESS CURSED TECHNIQUE

• Now that the anime has begun, more people in Japan and overseas will check out *Jujutsu Kaisen*. Because of that, I can't keep bluffing my way through stuff. Yes, I'm talking about Gojo's cursed technique.

• So I asked my editor to find someone knowledgeable about mathematics for their input, and the inquiry in the *Jump* editorial staff turned up T-san, who has a master's degree in engineering (information geometry)!!

• I hope to share what I've learned in this volume and the next.

• I should've done this from the start!!

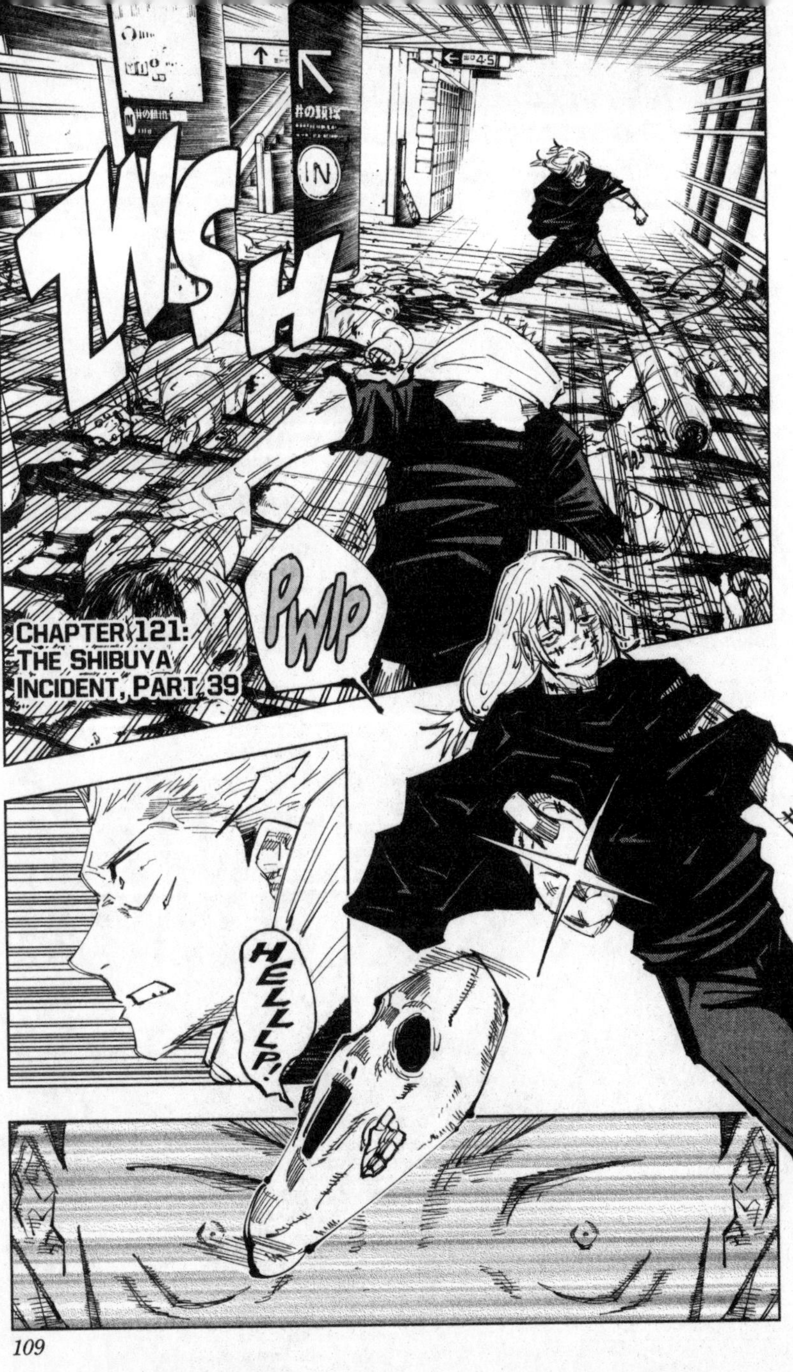
ZWSH
PWIP
CHAPTER 121:
THE SHIBUYA INCIDENT, PART 39
IN
HELLLP!

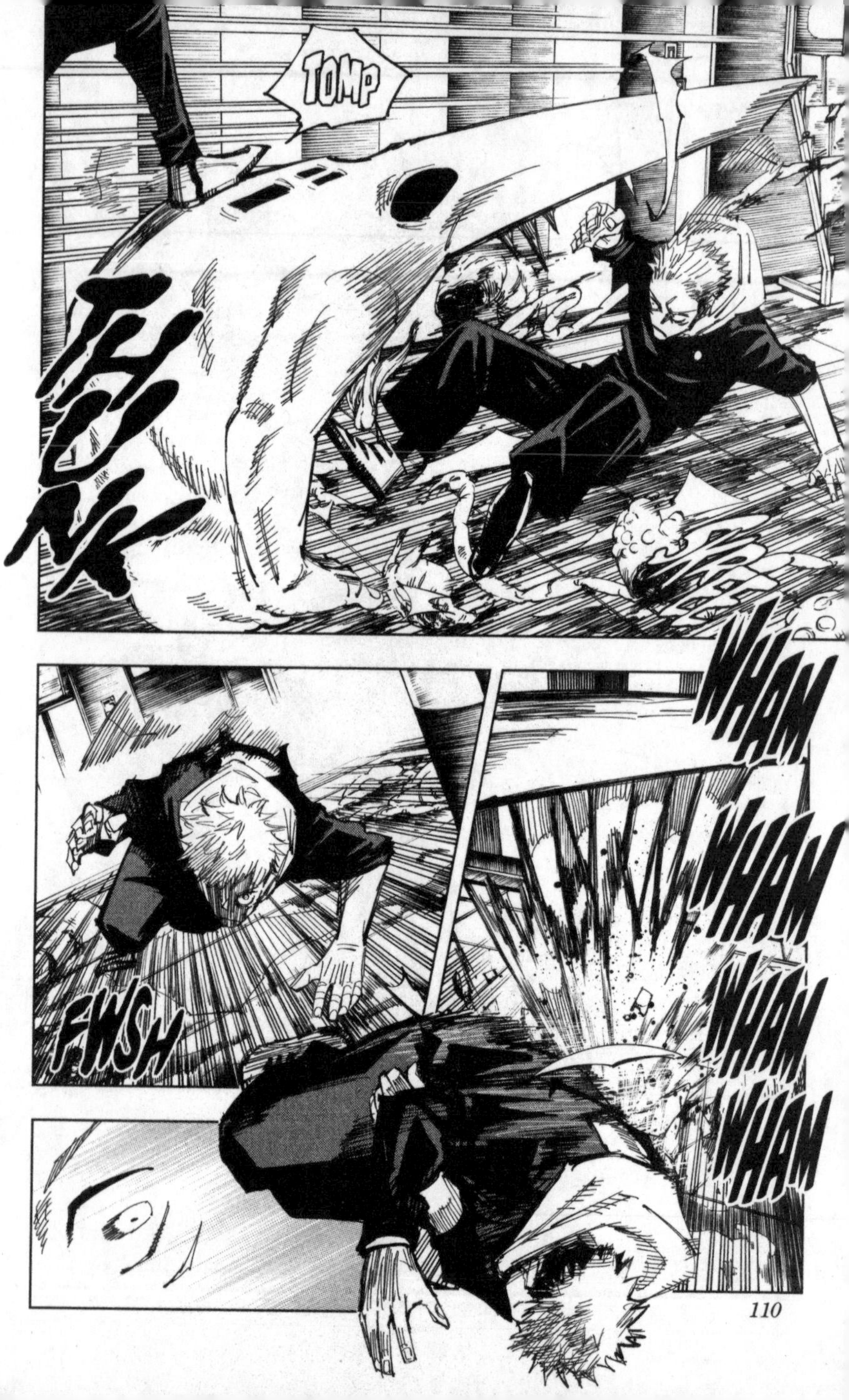
TOMP
THUNK
WHAM
WHAM
WHAM
WHAM
FWSH

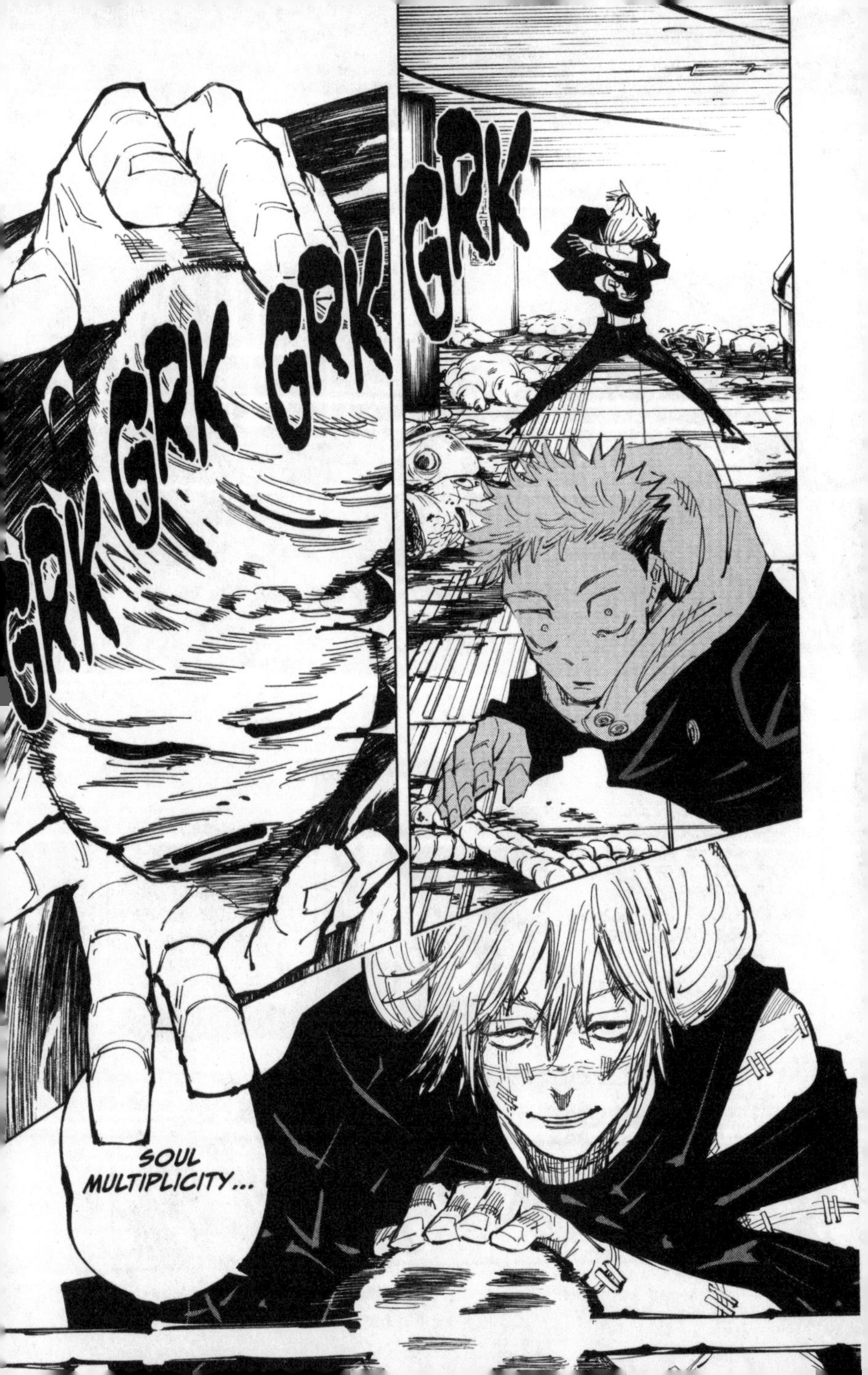
GRK
GRK GRK GRK GRK
SOUL MULTIPLICITY...

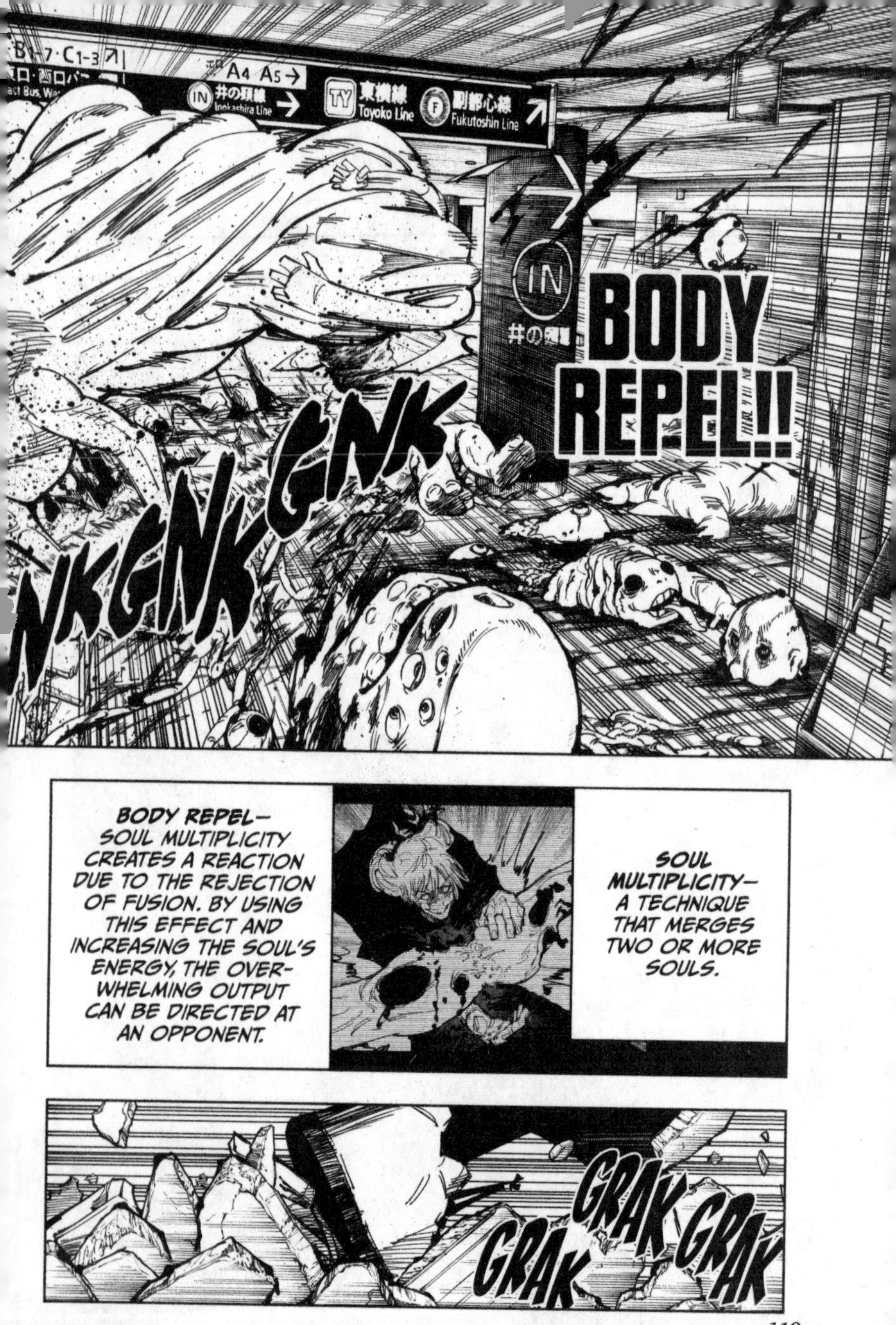
B1-7·C1-3
A4 A5
IN 井の頭線 Inokashira Line
TY 東横線 Toyoko Line
F 副都心線 Fukutoshin Line
NKGNKGNK GNK
BODY REPEL!!
SOUL MULTIPLICITY— A TECHNIQUE THAT MERGES TWO OR MORE SOULS.
BODY REPEL— SOUL MULTIPLICITY CREATES A REACTION DUE TO THE REJECTION OF FUSION. BY USING THIS EFFECT AND INCREASING THE SOUL'S ENERGY, THE OVER-WHELMING OUTPUT CAN BE DIRECTED AT AN OPPONENT.
GRAK GRAK GRAK GRAK

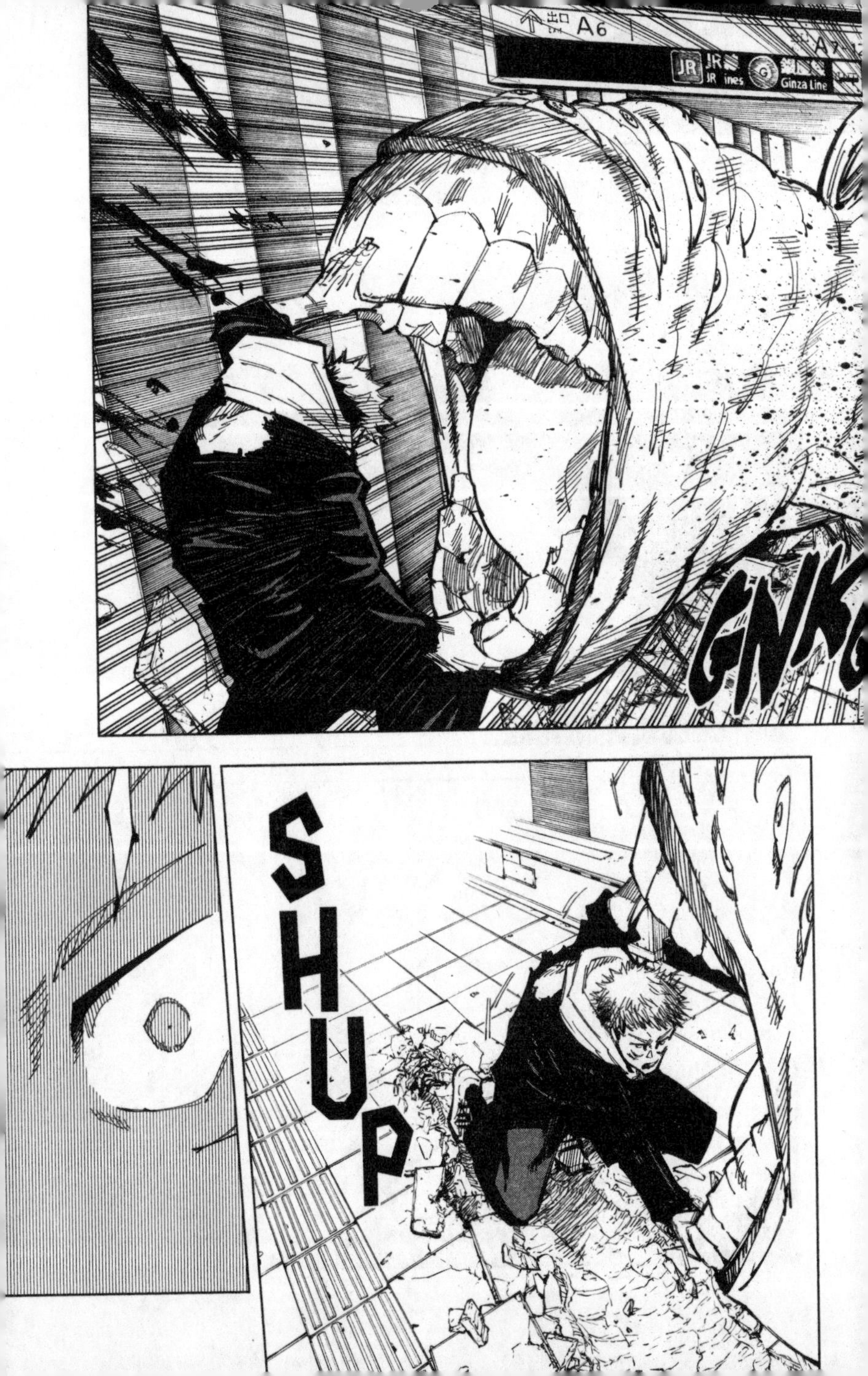
出口 A6
JR
Ginza Line
GNK
SHUP

BOO!

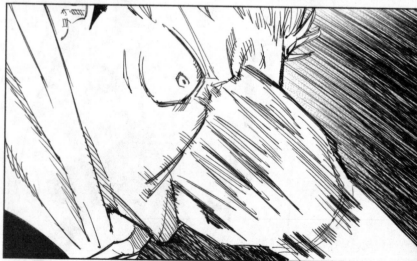

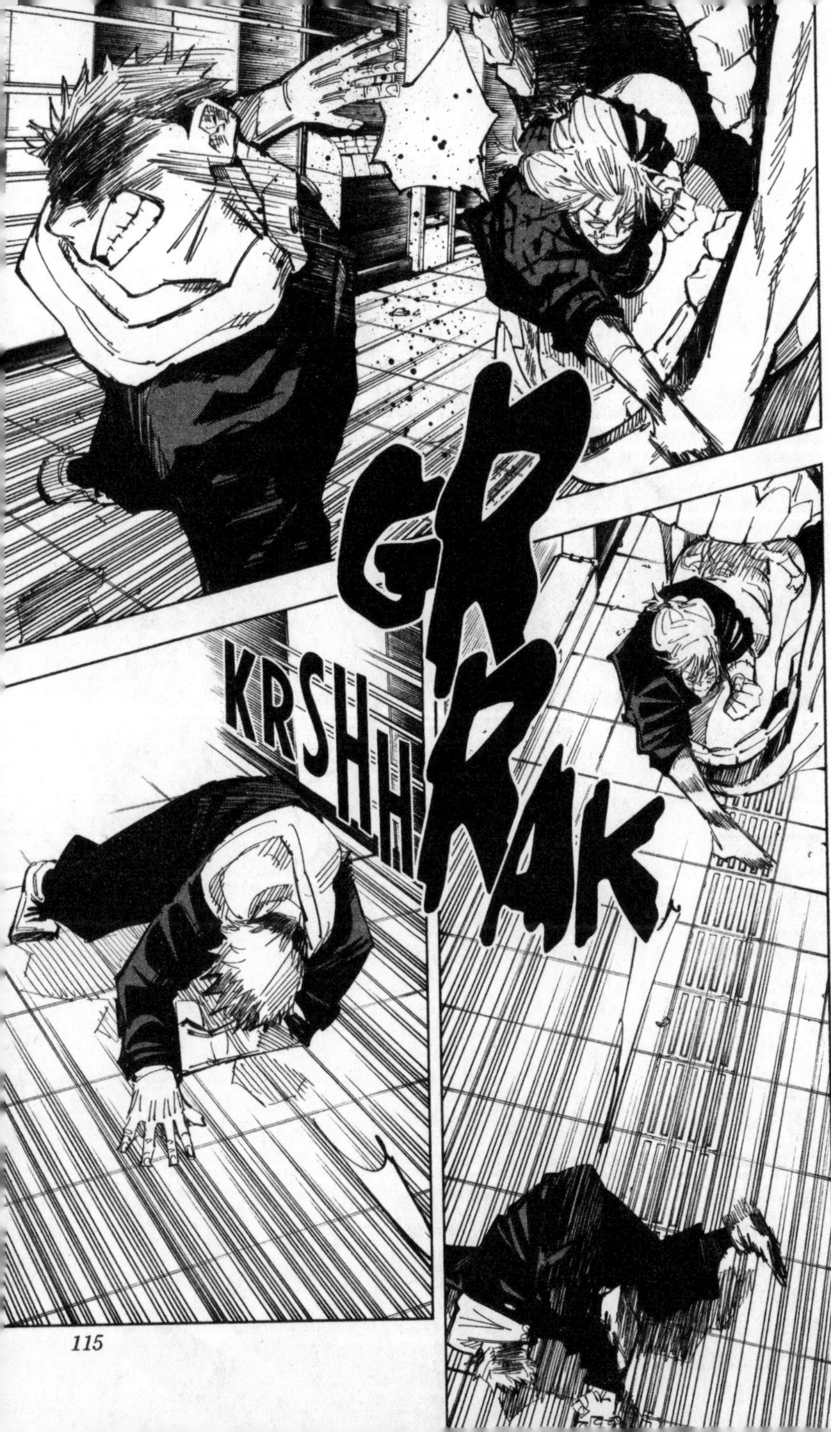
GRRAK
KRSHH

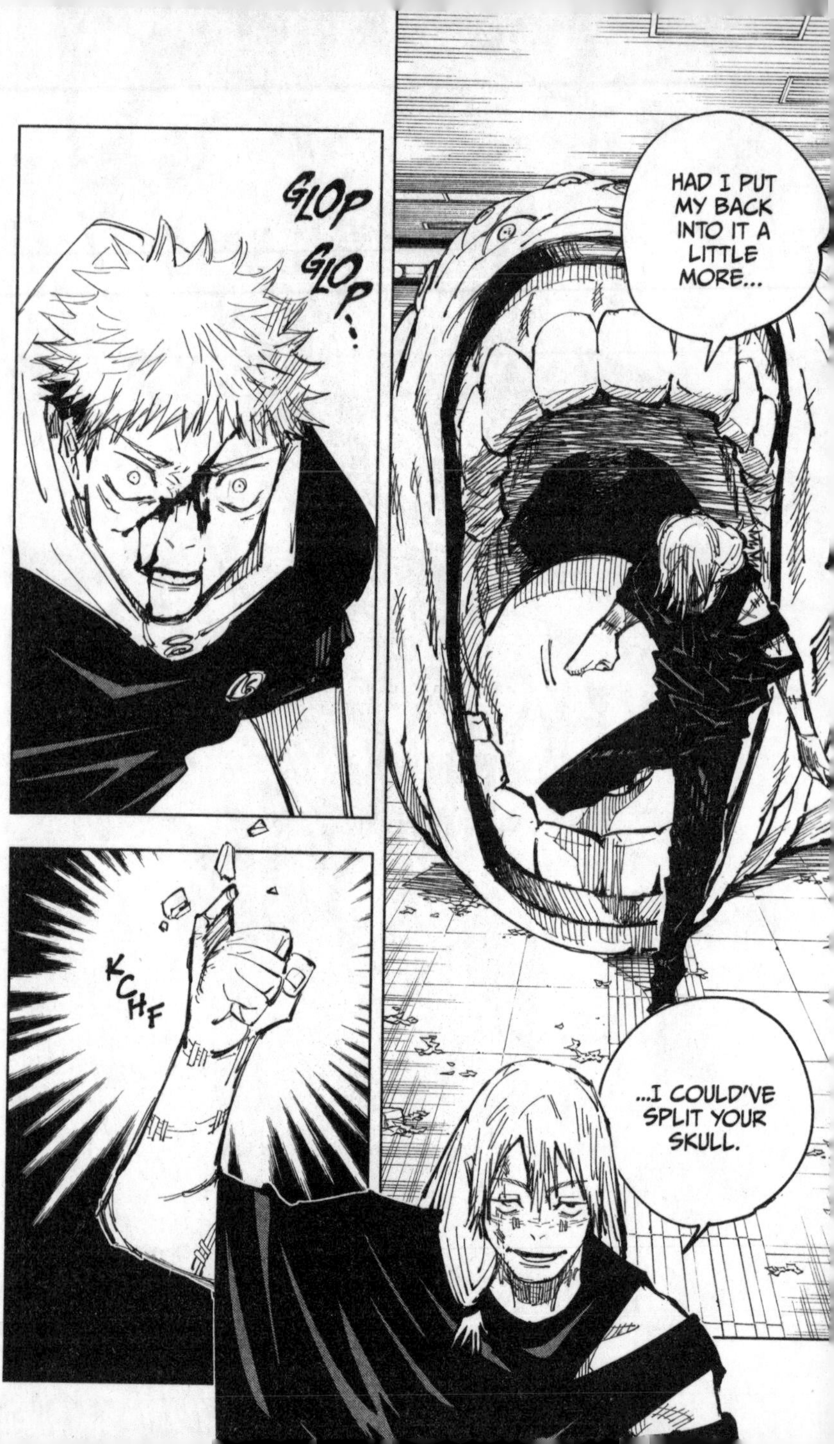
HAD I PUT MY BACK INTO IT A LITTLE MORE...
...I COULD'VE SPLIT YOUR SKULL.
GLOP
GLOP...
KCHF

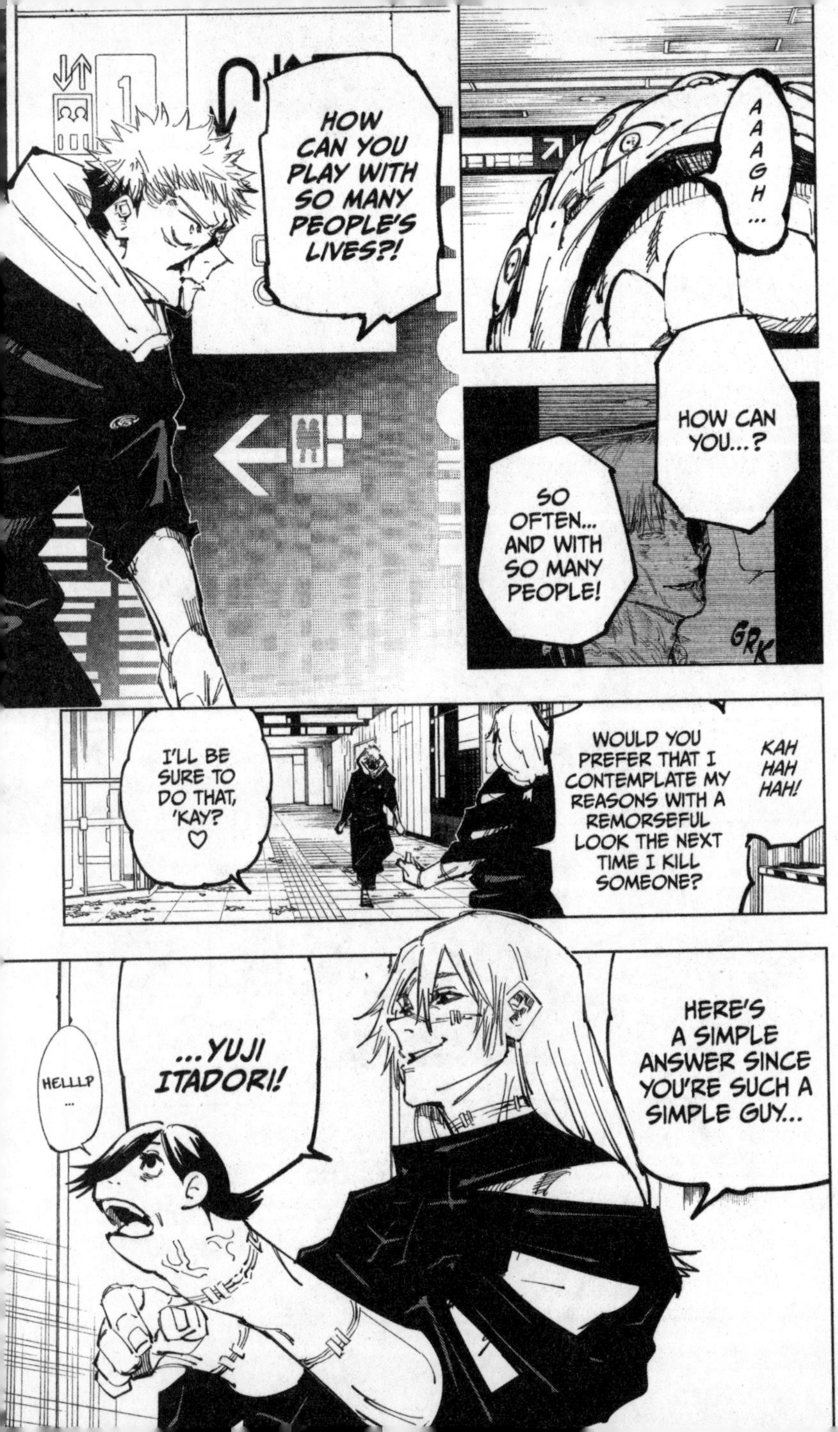
AAAGH...
HOW CAN YOU...?
SO OFTEN... AND WITH SO MANY PEOPLE!
GRK
HOW CAN YOU PLAY WITH SO MANY PEOPLE'S LIVES?!
KAH HAH HAH!
WOULD YOU PREFER THAT I CONTEMPLATE MY REASONS WITH A REMORSEFUL LOOK THE NEXT TIME I KILL SOMEONE?
I'LL BE SURE TO DO THAT, 'KAY? ♡
HERE'S A SIMPLE ANSWER SINCE YOU'RE SUCH A SIMPLE GUY...
...YUJI ITADORI!
HELLLP...

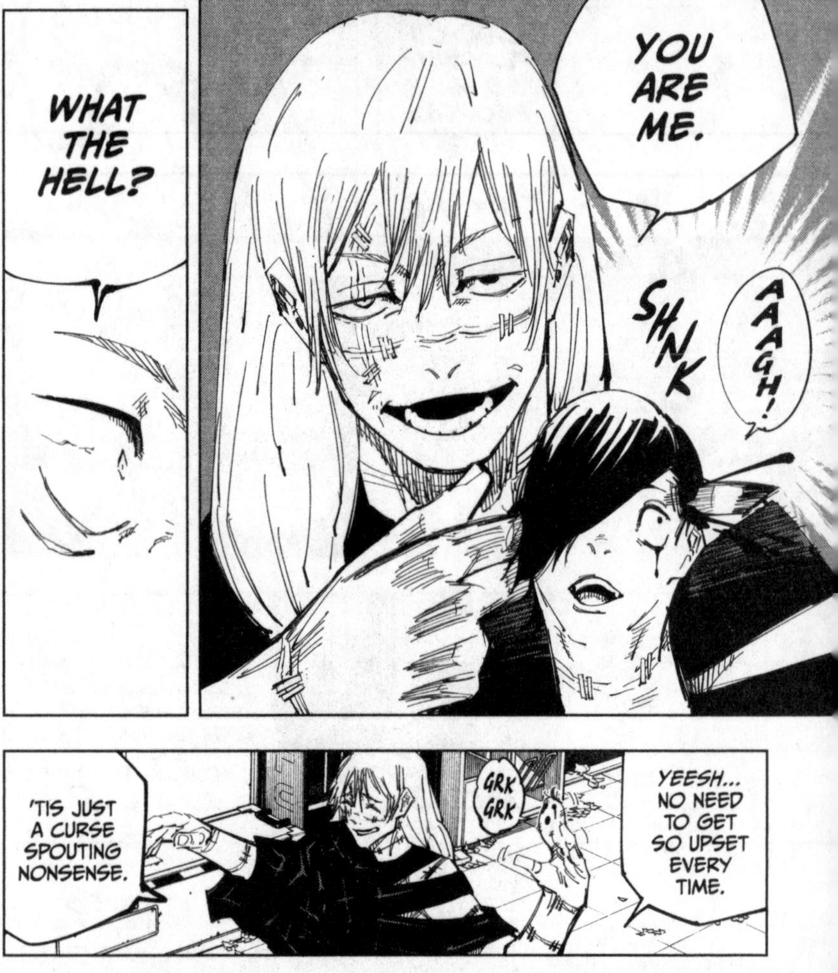
YOU ARE ME.
SHNK
AAAGH!
WHAT THE HELL?
YEESH... NO NEED TO GET SO UPSET EVERY TIME.
GRK GRK
'TIS JUST A CURSE SPOUTING NONSENSE.
BUT YOU KNOW WHAT?

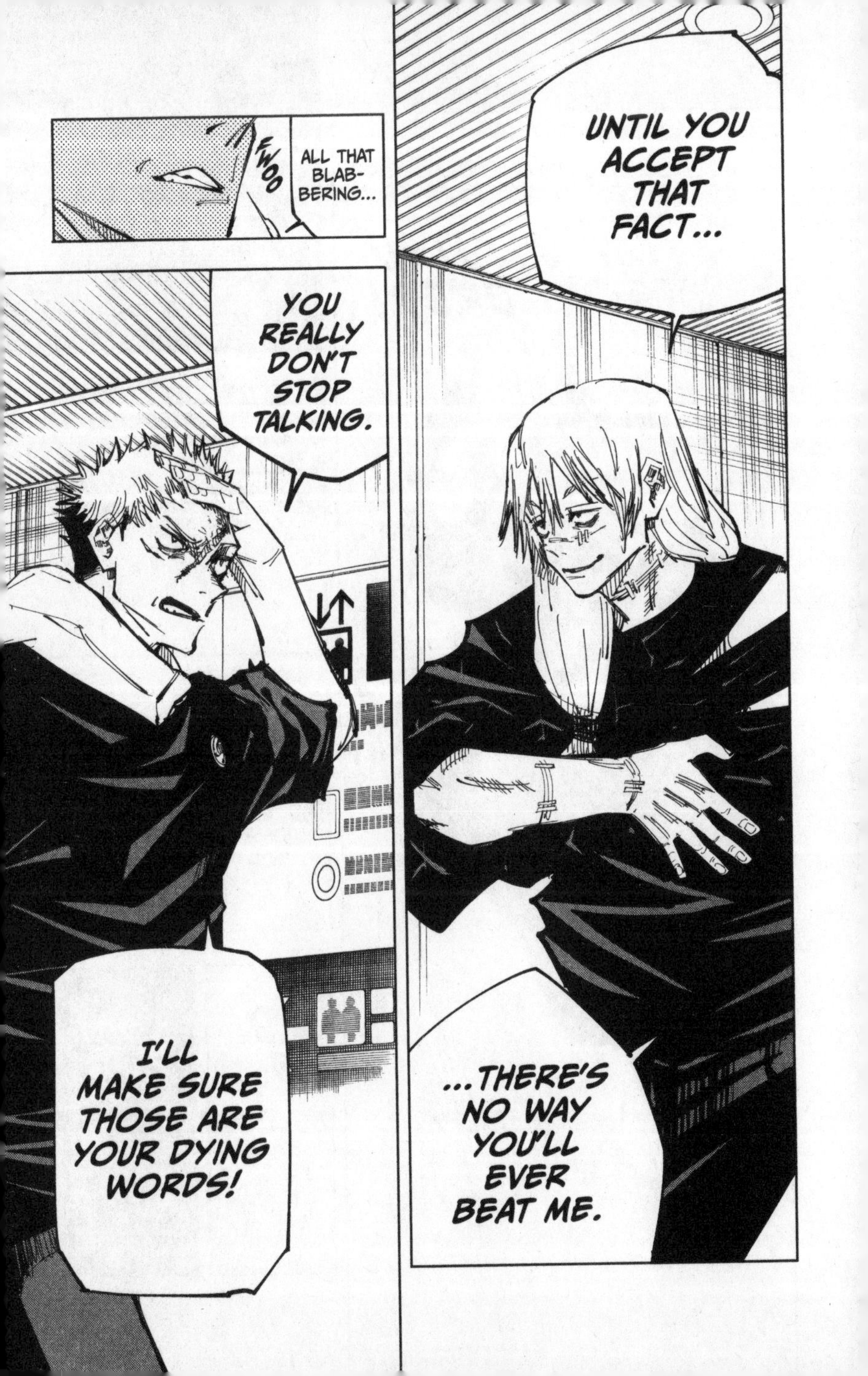
UNTIL YOU ACCEPT THAT FACT...
...THERE'S NO WAY YOU'LL EVER BEAT ME.
FWOO
ALL THAT BLAB-BERING...
YOU REALLY DON'T STOP TALKING.
I'LL MAKE SURE THOSE ARE YOUR DYING WORDS!

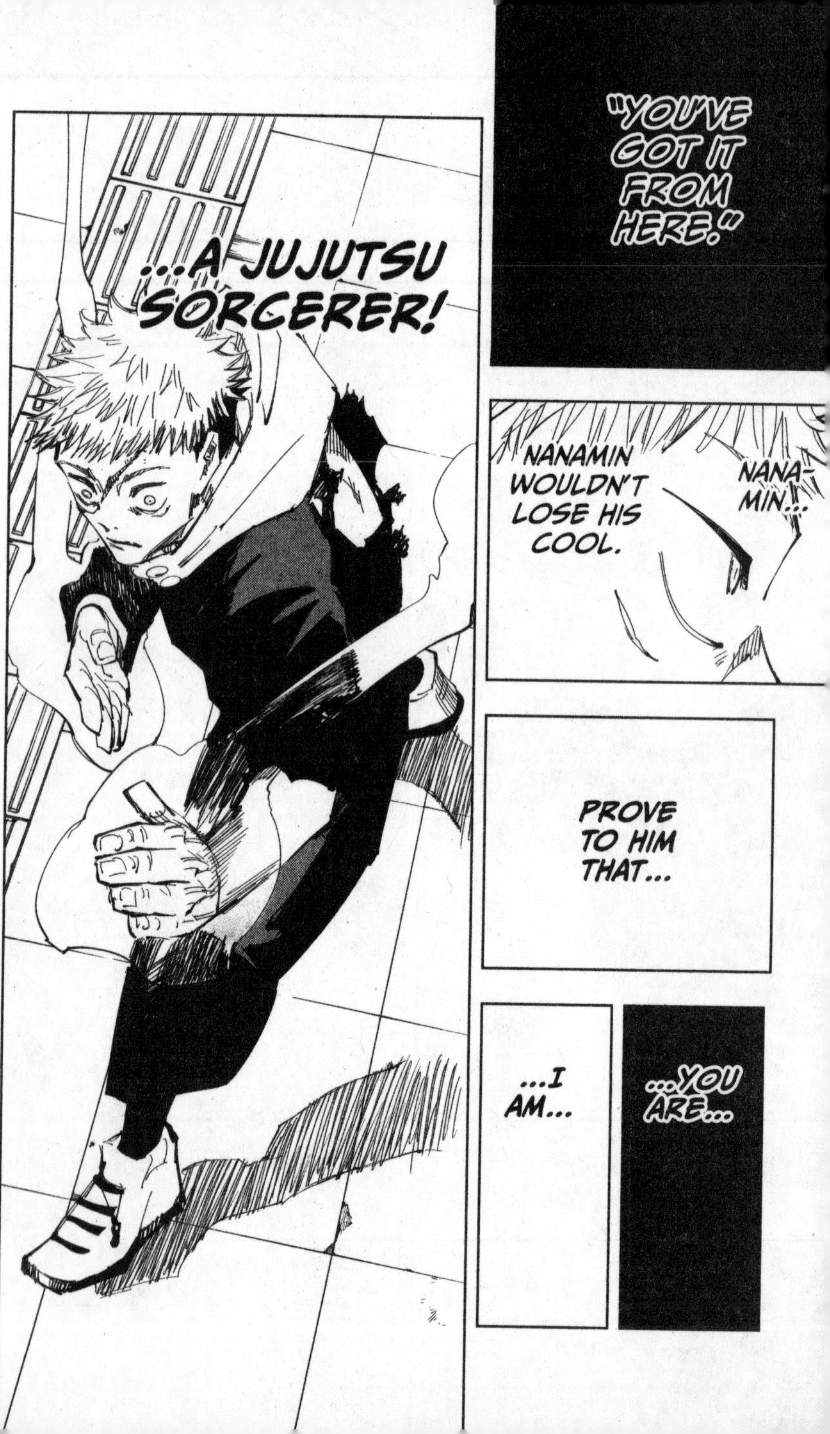
"YOU'VE GOT IT FROM HERE."
NANA-MIN...
NANAMIN WOULDN'T LOSE HIS COOL.
PROVE TO HIM THAT...
...YOU ARE...
...I AM...
...A JUJUTSU SORCERER!

GWOOOO

I'LL STICK WITH MANIPULATING LIMBS, WHICH SHOULDN'T BE A PROBLEM TO SACRIFICE JUST LIKE A MOMENT AGO.

"I NEED TO FOCUS ON CONCENTRATING MY BODY'S FORM TO MAINTAIN TOUGHNESS"...

IDLE TRANSFIGURATION DOESN'T WORK ON ITADORI.

INCREASING MY SIZE BY MANIPULATING MY SOUL WOULD JUST MAKE ME A BIGGER TARGET. THAT MIGHT AS WELL BE SUICIDE.

KRA KK

WHILE MAHITO'S FIST PIERCES THROUGH AIR...

...ITADORI DISAPPEARS FROM HIS SIGHT.

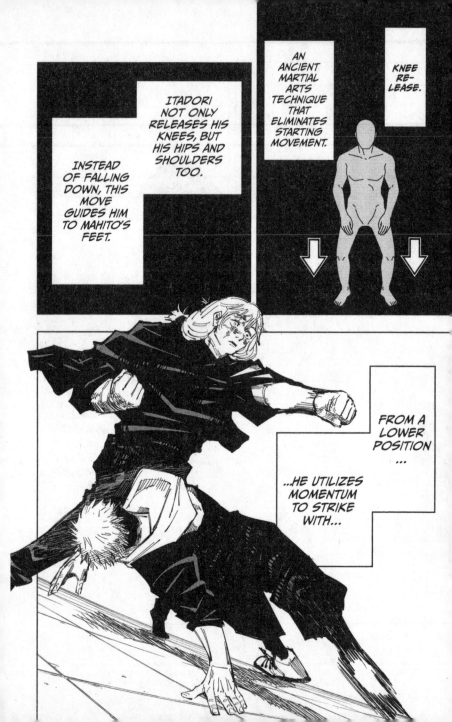

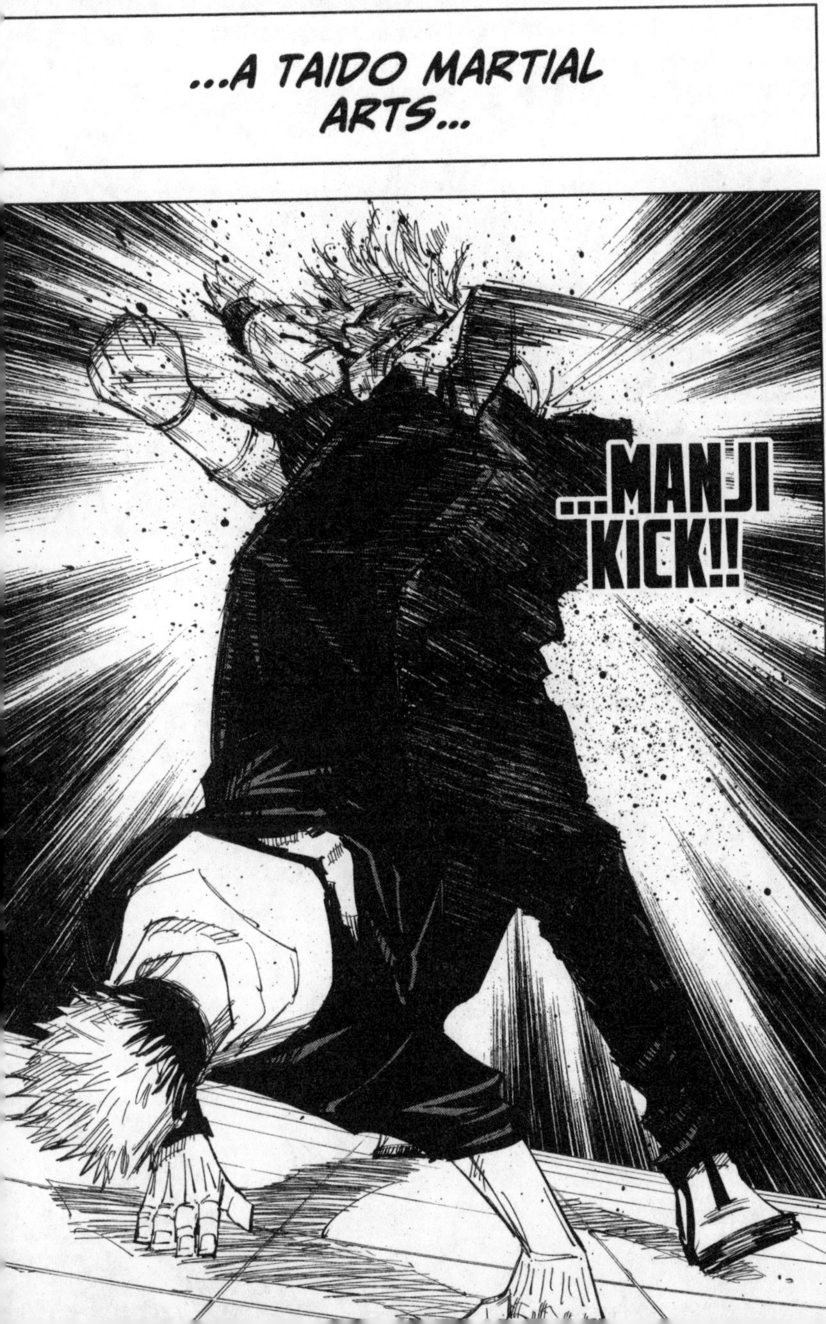
...A TAIDO MARTIAL ARTS...
...MANJI KICK!!

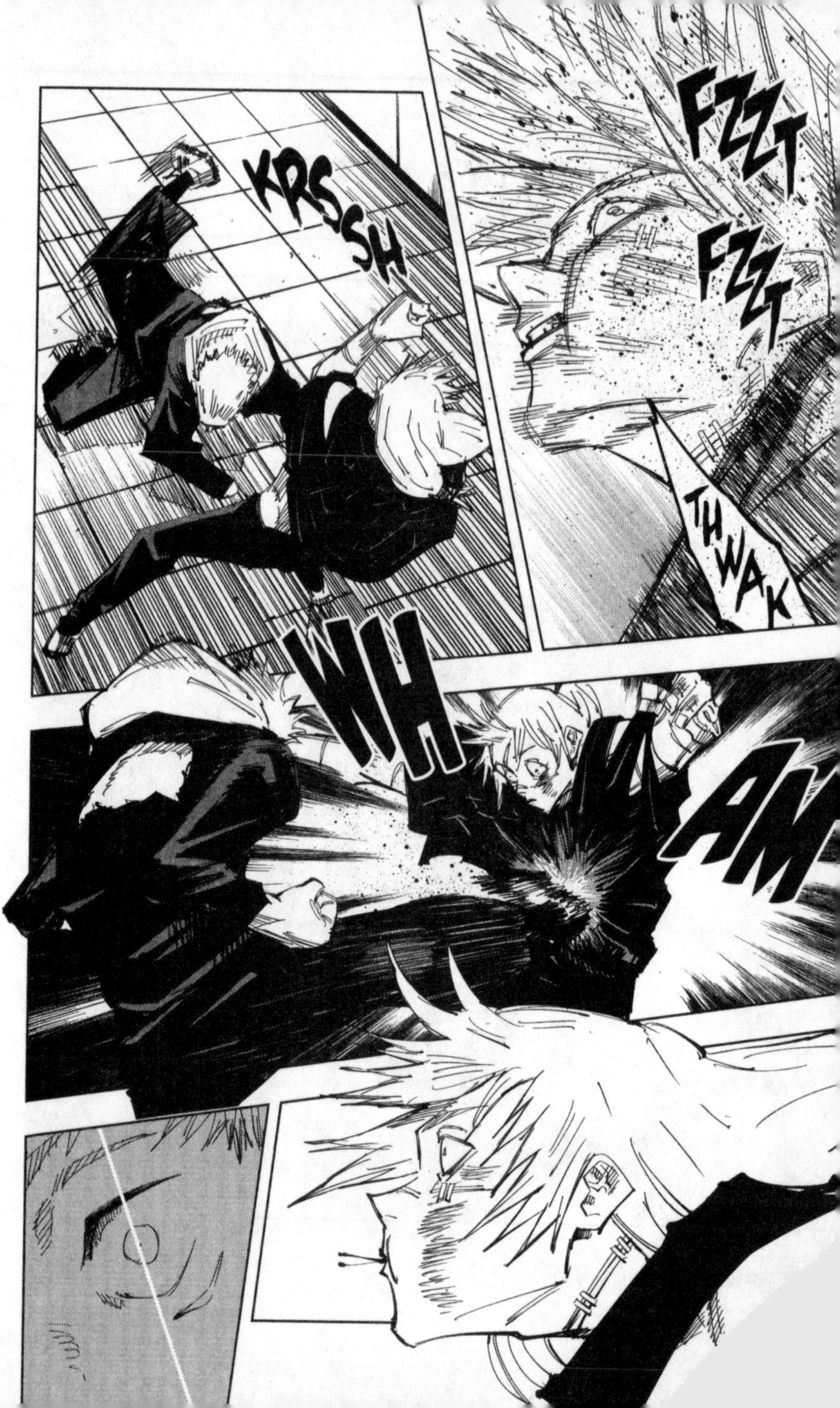
FZZZT
FZZZT
THWAK
KRSSH
WH
AM

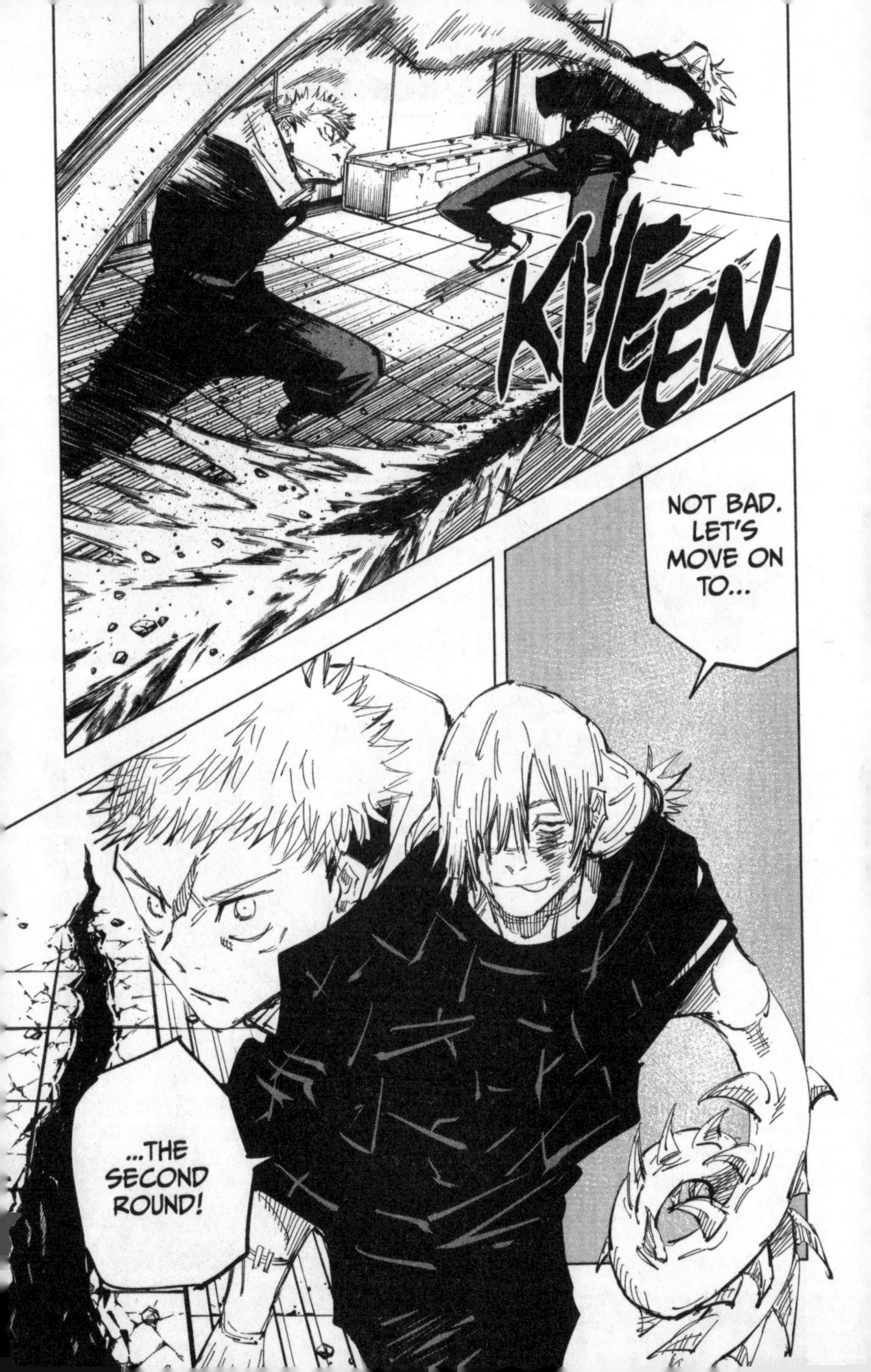
KVEEN
NOT BAD. LET'S MOVE ON TO...
...THE SECOND ROUND!

GETTING IT RIGHT!!
LIMITLESS CURSED TECHNIQUE ~INTRODUCTION~

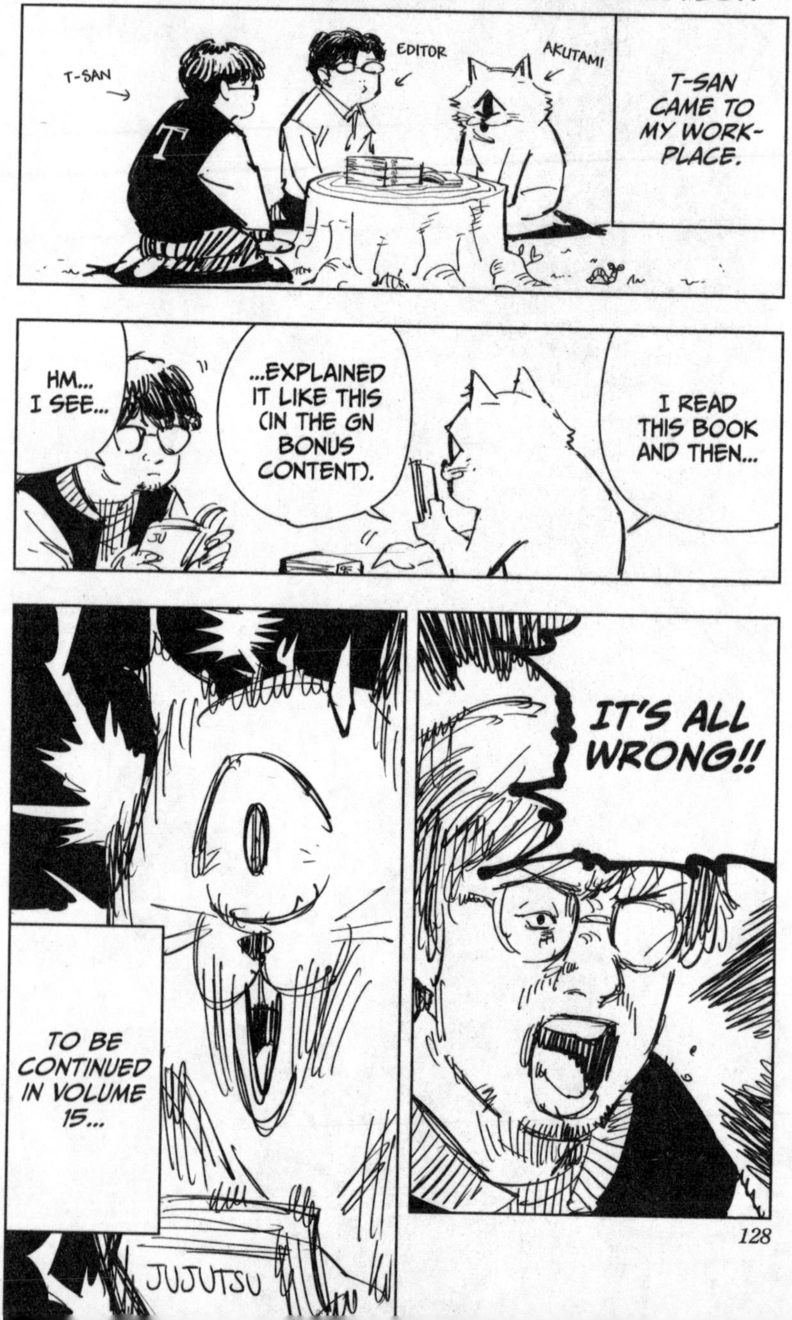
T-SAN CAME TO MY WORKPLACE.
T-SAN
EDITOR
AKUTAMI
I READ THIS BOOK AND THEN...
...EXPLAINED IT LIKE THIS (IN THE GN BONUS CONTENT).
HM... I SEE...
JU
IT'S ALL WRONG!!
TO BE CONTINUED IN VOLUME 15...
JUJUTSU

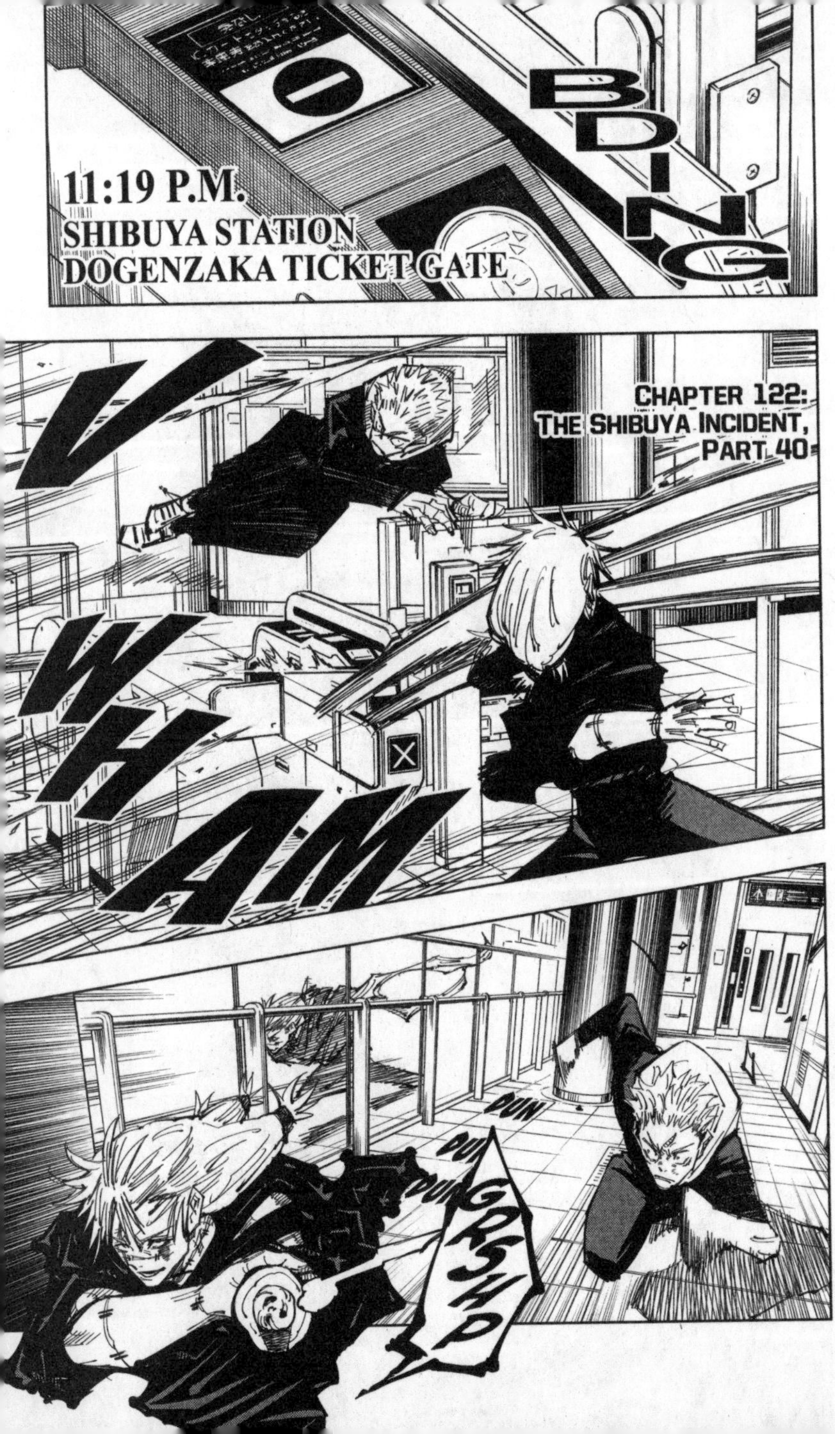
11:19 P.M.
SHIBUYA STATION
DOGENZAKA TICKET GATE
BDING
Chapter 122: The Shibuya Incident, Part 40
WHAM
DUN
DUN
DUN
GRSHP

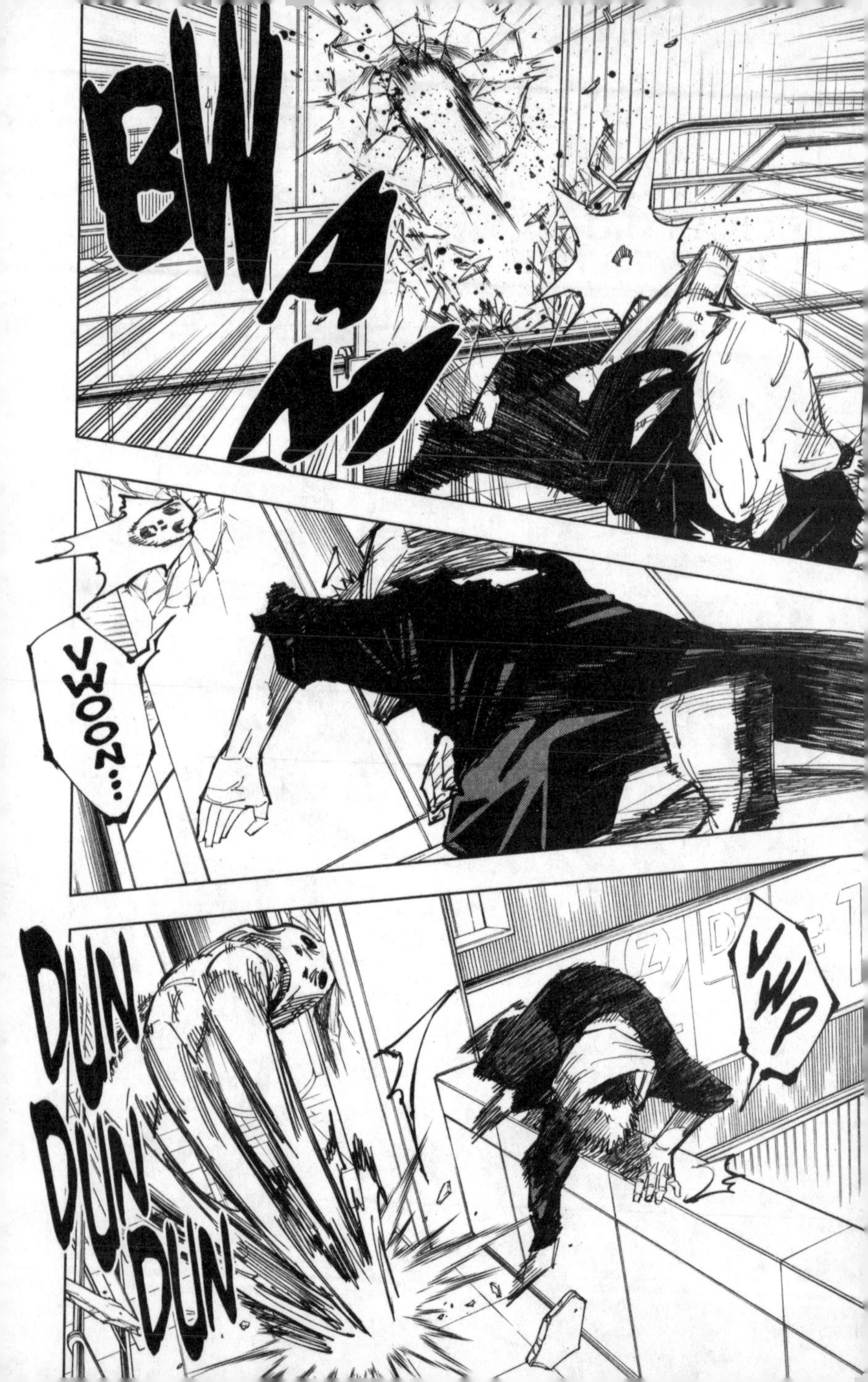
BWAM
VWOON...
VWP
DUN DUN DUN

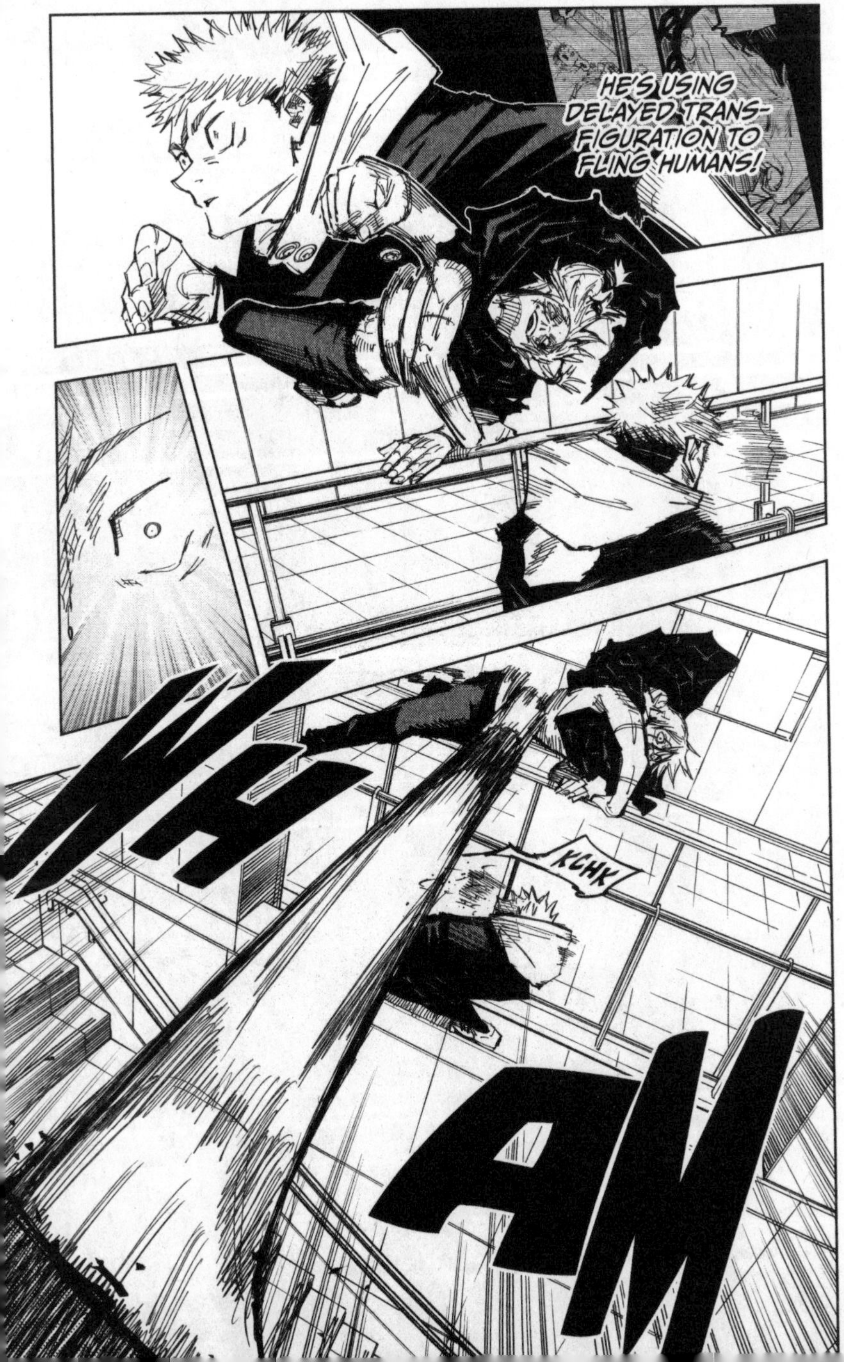
HE'S USING DELAYED TRANS-FIGURATION TO FLING HUMANS!
KCHK
WHAM

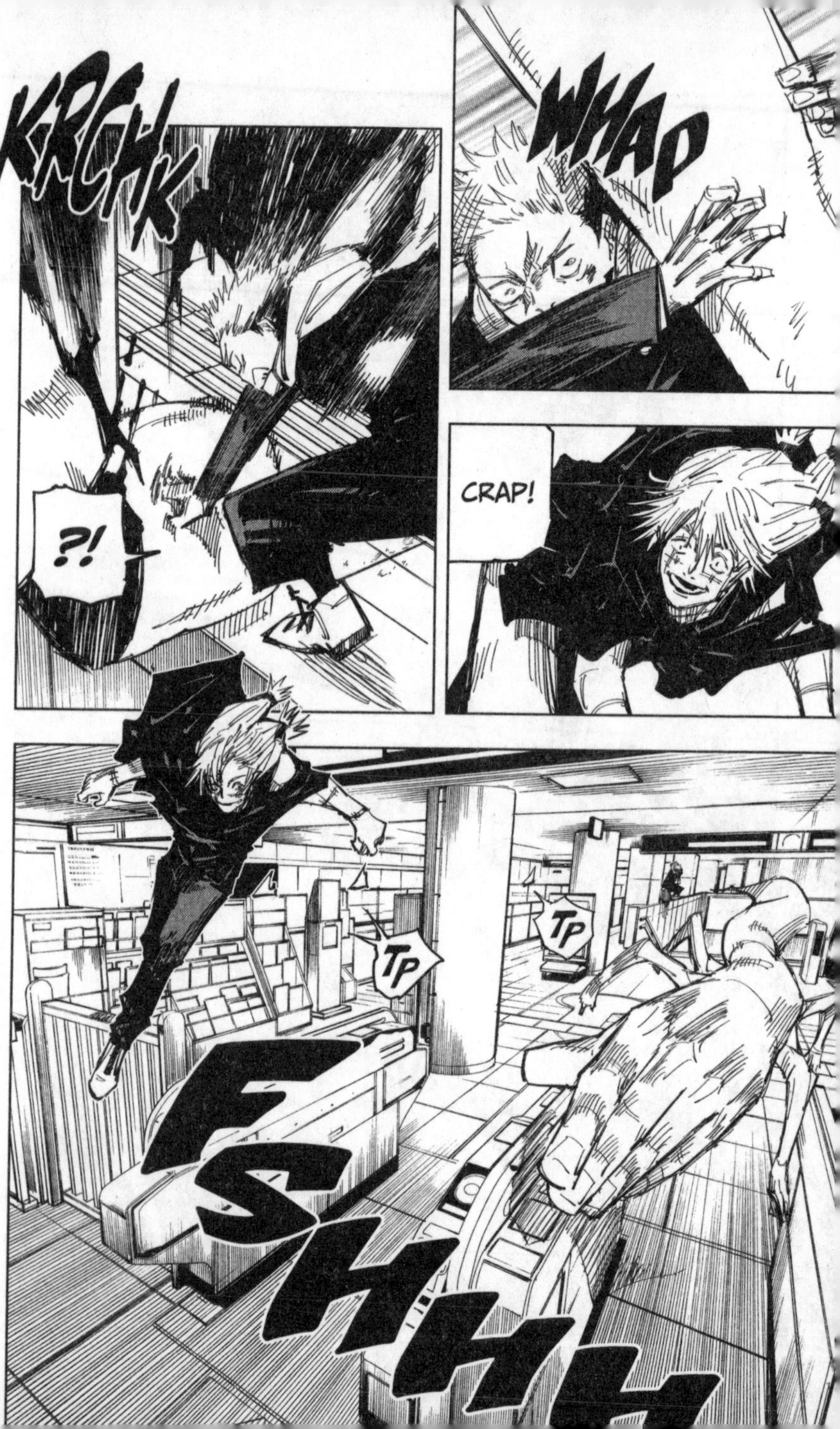
WHAD
CRAP!
KRCHK
?!
TP
TP
FSHHH

OHH... THAT WAS SCARY!

IF I TAKE A RISK AND MESS UP THE TIMING, I COULD END UP DEAD. I'LL STICK TO USING TRANSFIGURED HUMANS FOR NOW.

MWP
MWP
MWP

REDUCING RISK ISN'T THE ONLY REASON I'M USING TRANS-FIGURED HUMANS.

HE HAS MORE MOVES NOW.

DELAYED TRANS-FIGURATION, BODY DISMEMBER-MENT, AND MERGING...

!

DUN

IT'S DANGEROUS OVER THERE WITH ALL THOSE MONSTERS!

HEY, COME THIS WAY!

A STUDENT?!

TRY TO STAY SOMEW—

SORRY, BUT NOWHERE'S SAFE IN SHIBUYA.

WHERE'S MAHITO...?

UPSTAIRS!

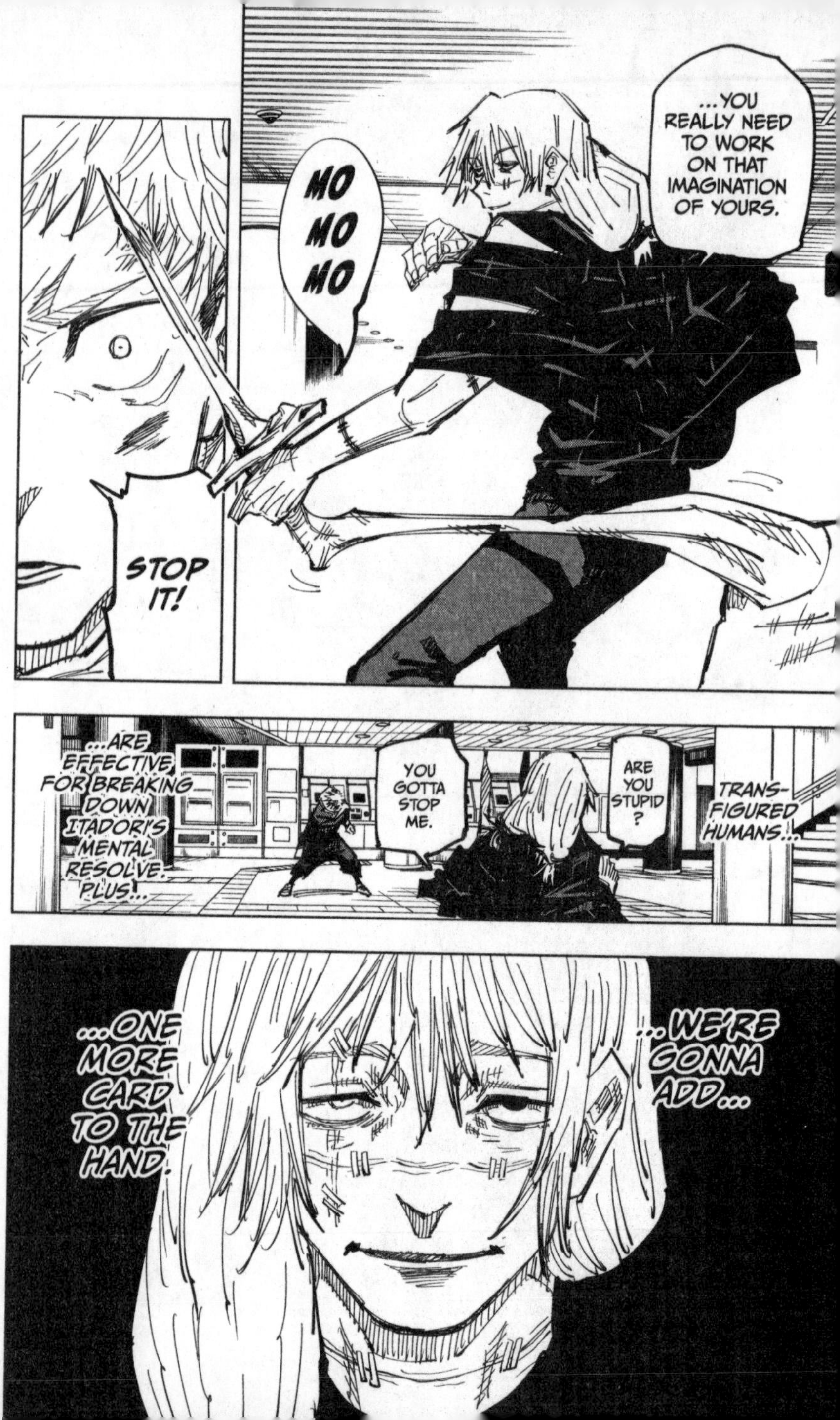
...YOU REALLY NEED TO WORK ON THAT IMAGINATION OF YOURS.
MO MO MO
STOP IT!
TRANS-FIGURED HUMANS...
ARE YOU STUPID?
YOU GOTTA STOP ME.
...ARE EFFECTIVE FOR BREAKING DOWN ITADORI'S MENTAL RESOLVE. PLUS...
...WE'RE GONNA ADD...
...ONE MORE CARD TO THE HAND.

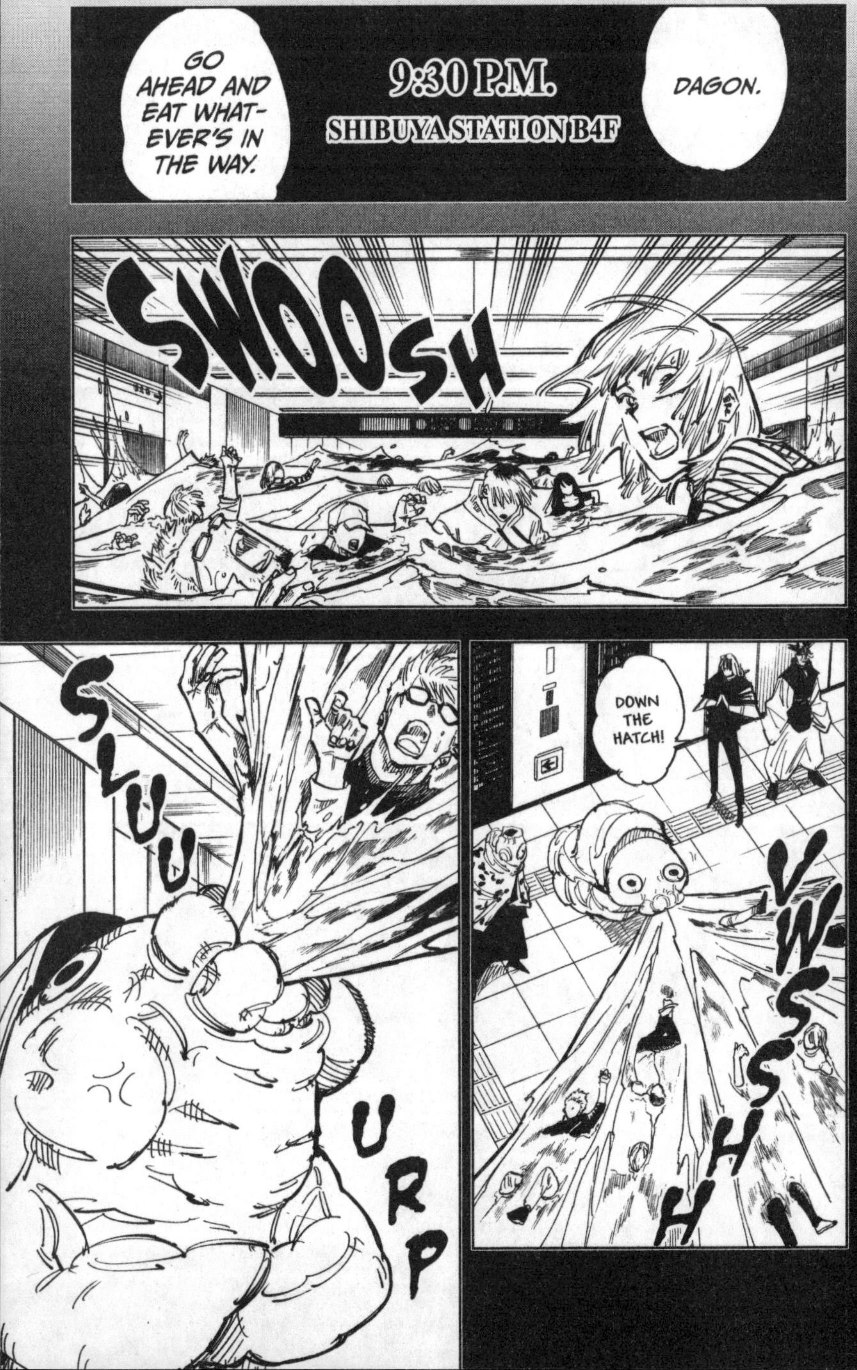
DAGON.
9:30 P.M.
SHIBUYA STATION B4F
GO AHEAD AND EAT WHATEVER'S IN THE WAY.
SWOOSH
DOWN THE HATCH!
VWSSHHH
SLUU
URP

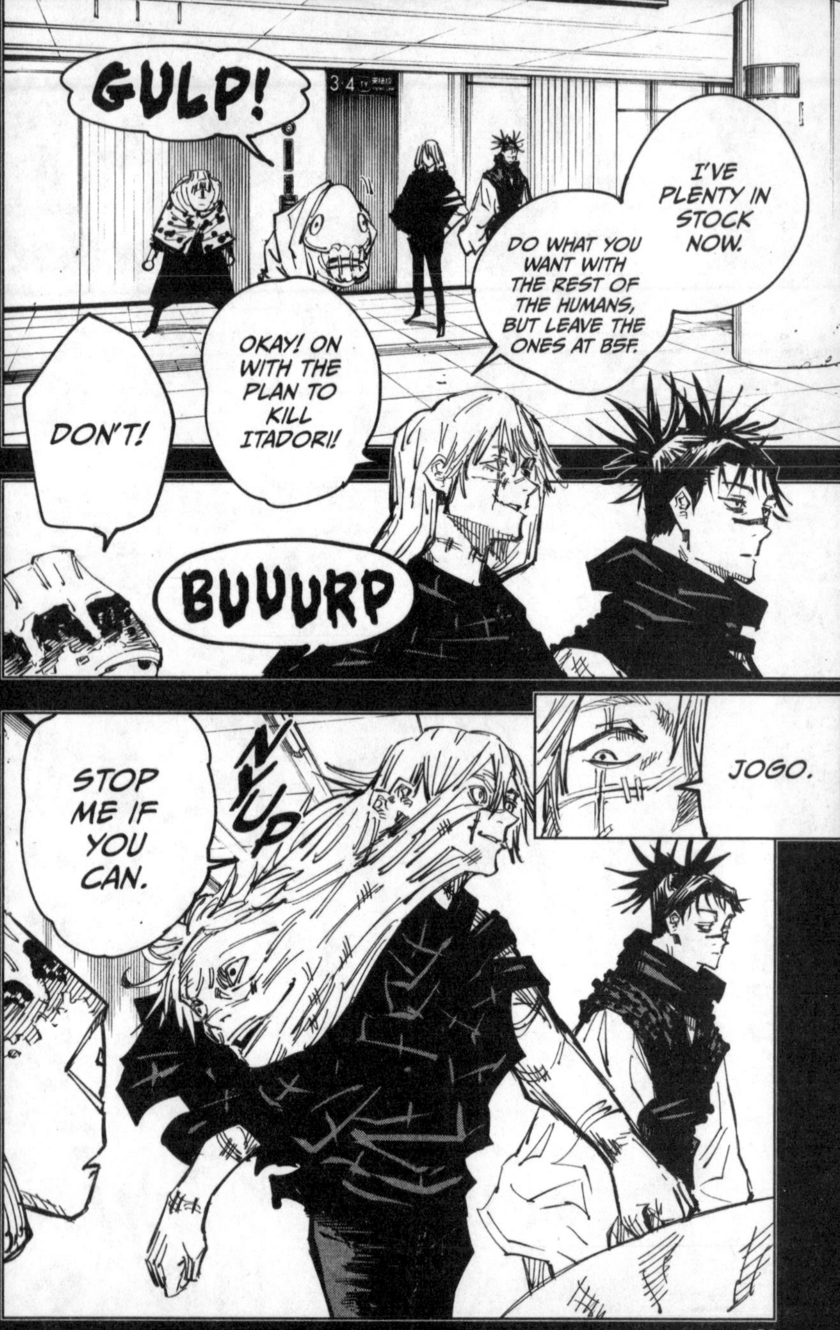
I'VE PLENTY IN STOCK NOW.
DO WHAT YOU WANT WITH THE REST OF THE HUMANS, BUT LEAVE THE ONES AT B5F.
GULP!
OKAY! ON WITH THE PLAN TO KILL ITADORI!
DON'T!
BUUURP
JOGO.
NYUP
STOP ME IF YOU CAN.

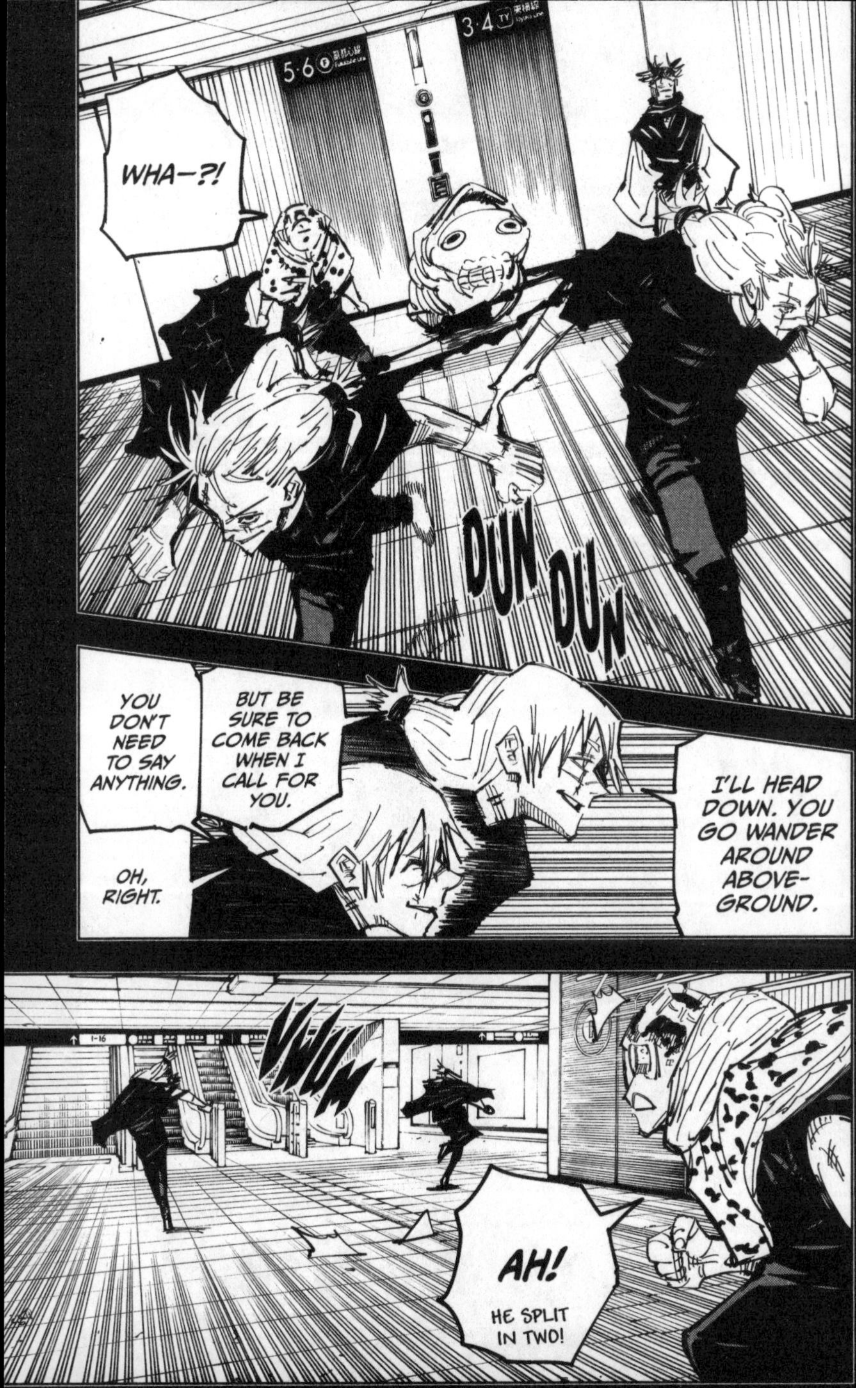
WHA—?!
DUN DUN
I'LL HEAD DOWN. YOU GO WANDER AROUND ABOVE-GROUND.
BUT BE SURE TO COME BACK WHEN I CALL FOR YOU.
YOU DON'T NEED TO SAY ANYTHING.
OH, RIGHT.
AH! HE SPLIT IN TWO!

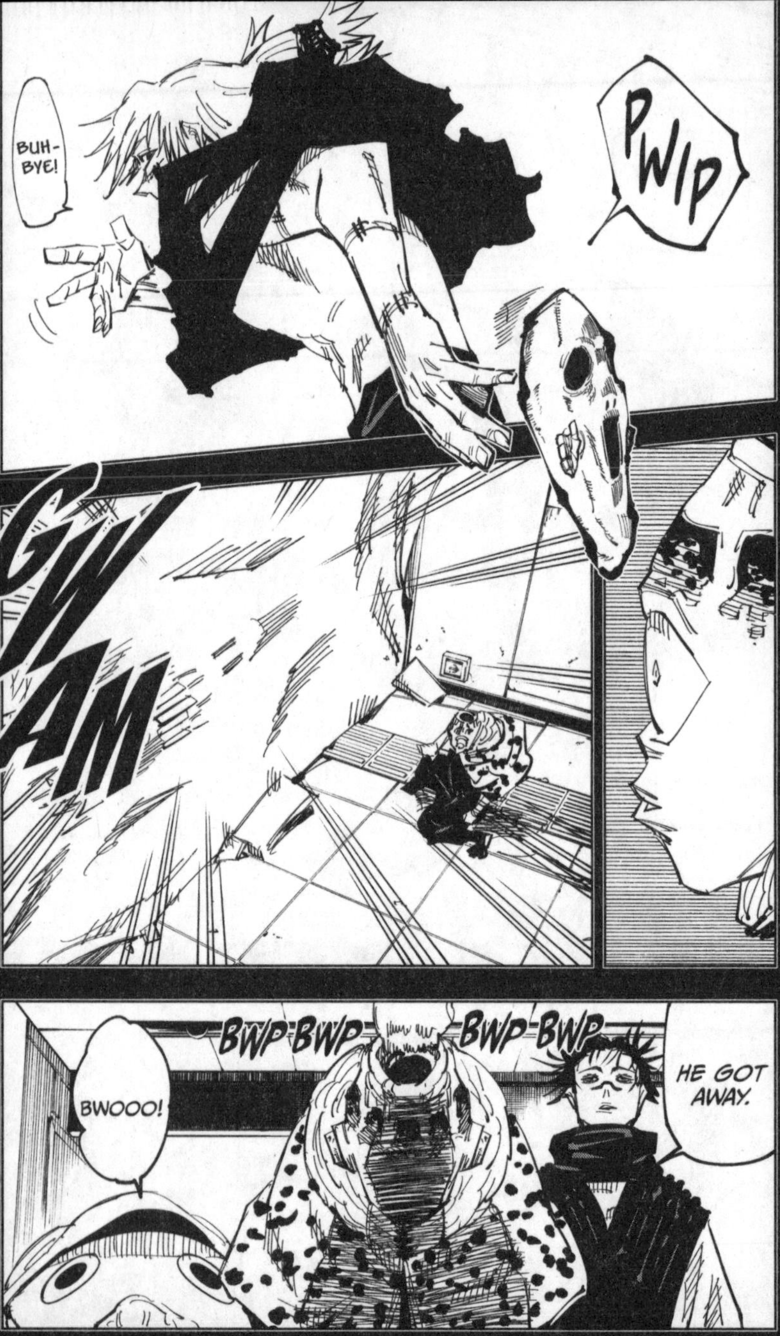
PWIP
BUH-BYE!
GWAM
BWP BWP
BWP BWP
HE GOT AWAY.
BWOOO!

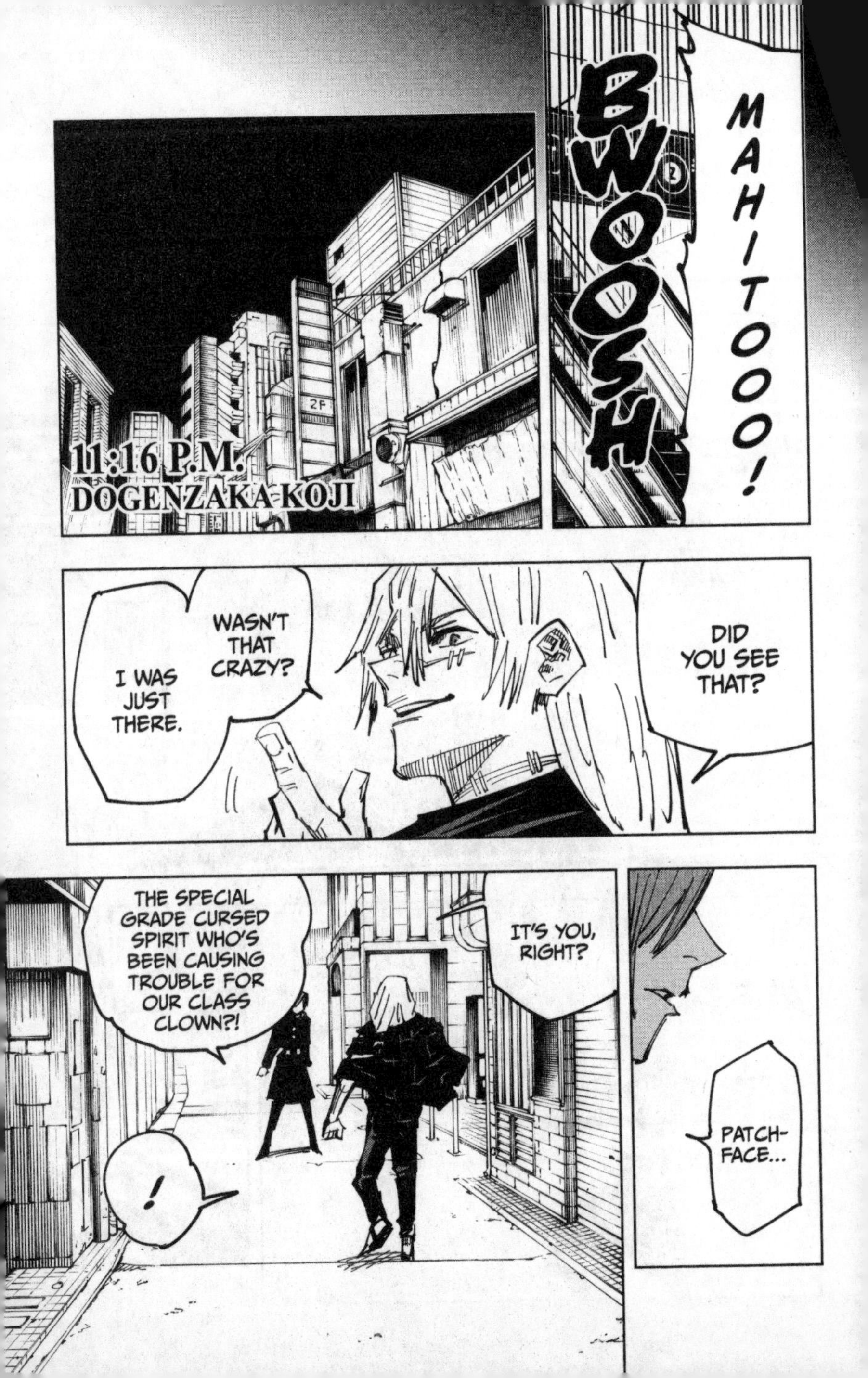
MAHITOOO!
BWOOSH
11:16 P.M.
DOGENZAKA KOJI
DID YOU SEE THAT?
WASN'T THAT CRAZY?
I WAS JUST THERE.
PATCH-FACE...
IT'S YOU, RIGHT?
THE SPECIAL GRADE CURSED SPIRIT WHO'S BEEN CAUSING TROUBLE FOR OUR CLASS CLOWN?!
!

...NOT TO LET HIM TOUCH ME WITH HIS HANDS.

THEY TOLD ME...

...SO YOU'LL HAVE TO AT LEAST LET ME SQUASH A FLEEING BUG LIKE YOU.

I THINK HIS CURSED TECHNIQUE HAS SOMETHING TO DO WITH THE SOUL!!!

I DON'T HAVE MUCH TO SHOW FOR TODAY...

SHK

...FROM BACK THEN.

REMEMBER THE FEELING...

...CURSED ENERGY!

FEEL THE CORE OF...

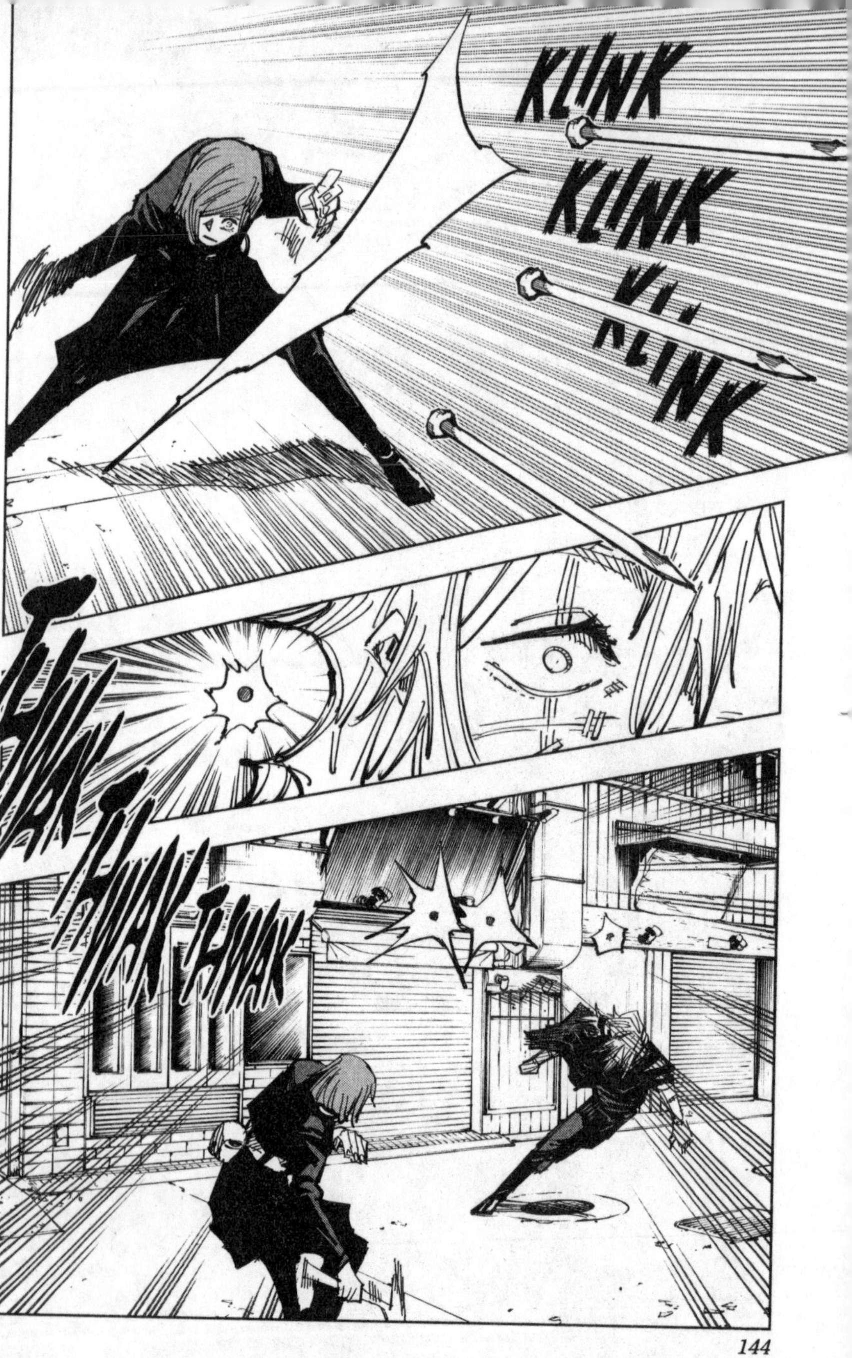
KLINK
KLINK
KLINK
THWAK
THWAK
THWAK
THWAK

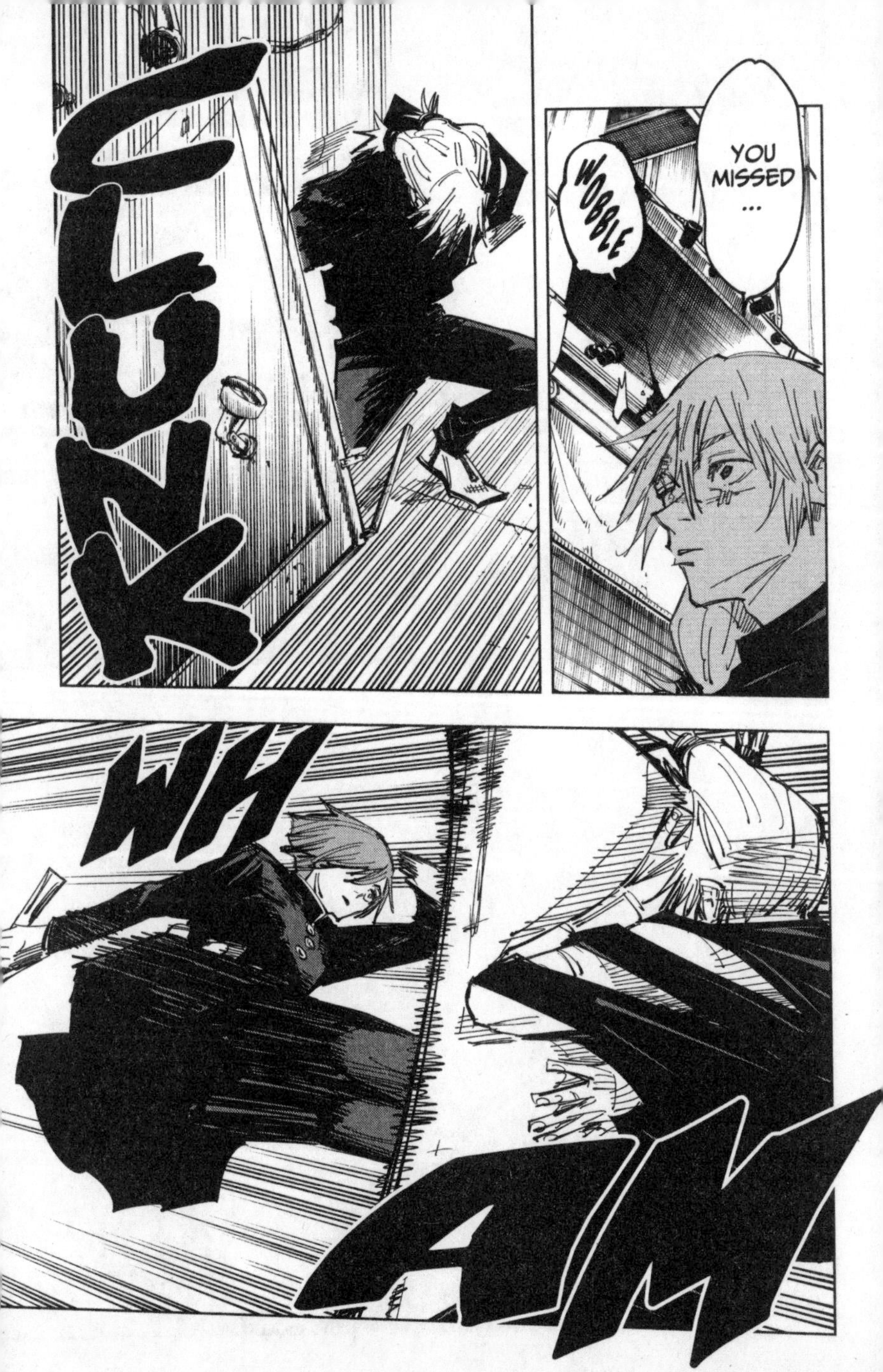
YOU MISSED ...
WOBBLE
WHAM

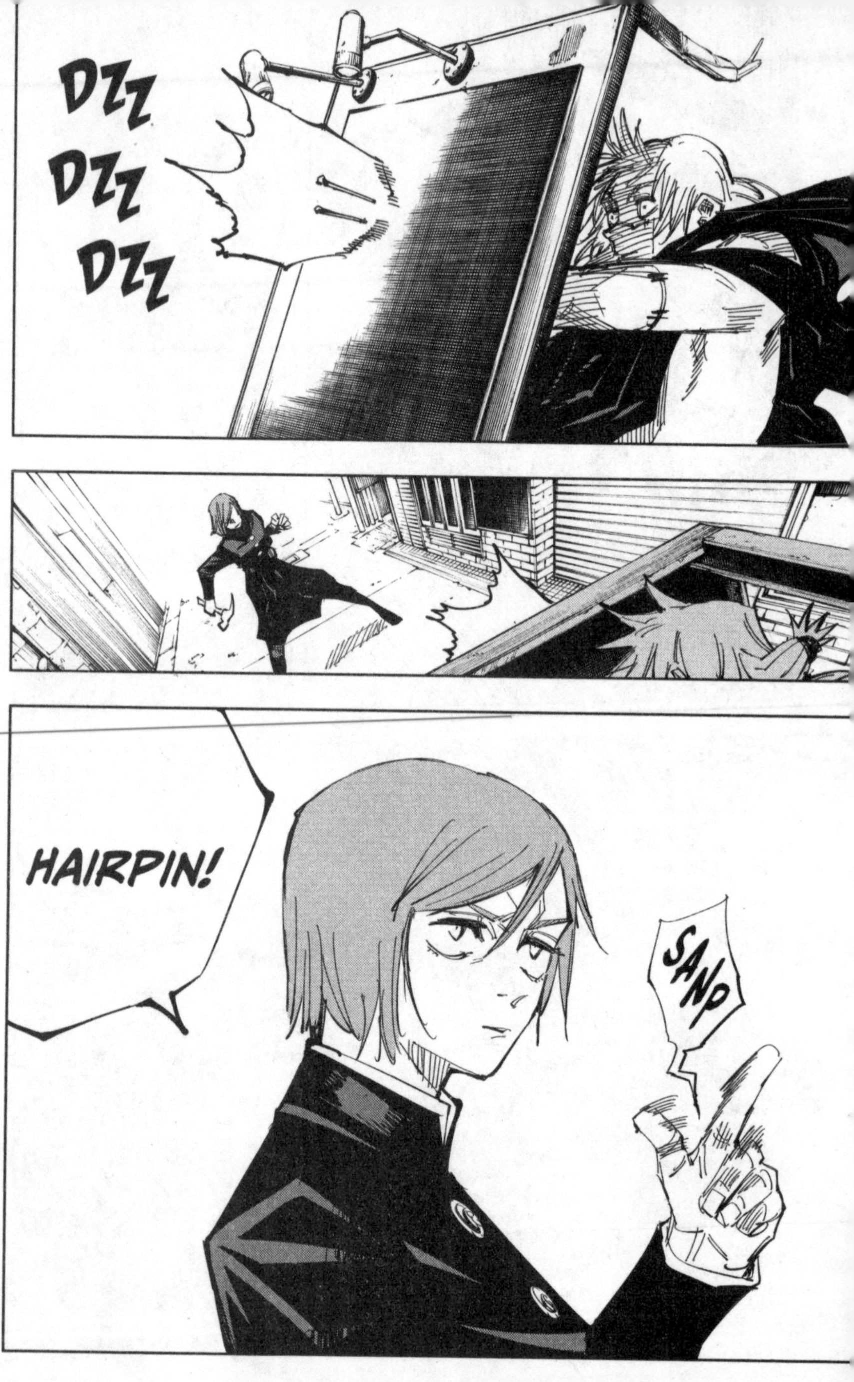
DZZ
DZZ
DZZ
SNAP
HAIRPIN!

WHAK
WHAK

NOT BAD. BUT...

HA HA HA!

I'LL BRING HER DEAD BODY TO YUJI ITA-DORI...

...AND DESTROY HIS SOUL!

...THAT WON'T WORK ON ME.

JUDGING BY THE WAY SHE TALKS...

...I'D SAY SHE'S A FRIEND OF HIS.

Extra Info

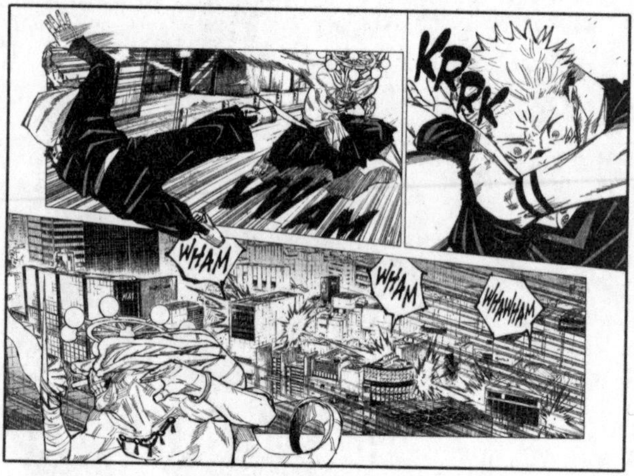
KRRK
VWAM
WHAM
WHAM
WHAWHAM

• Sukuna actually flew all the way outside the curtain in this scene.
• Since there was no particular effect on either Sukuna or Mahoraga and visually it had no particular bearing on the fight, I left it out.

DON'T DO IT, KUGI-SAKI!!

NANAMI SAID SO TOO!

AND...WE DIDN'T TELL YOU SHOKO WAS HERE BECAUSE—

11:14 P.M.
SHOTO BUNKAMURA STREET
(OUTSIDE THE CURTAIN)

THE PARAMEDIC TEAM WAS PROBABLY LATE FOR THE SAME REASON.

BECAUSE YOU DIDN'T WANT ME DOING SOMETHING RECKLESS, RIGHT?

...WHILE THEY'RE STILL FIGHTING.

...I CAN'T JUST LEAVE...

EVEN SO...

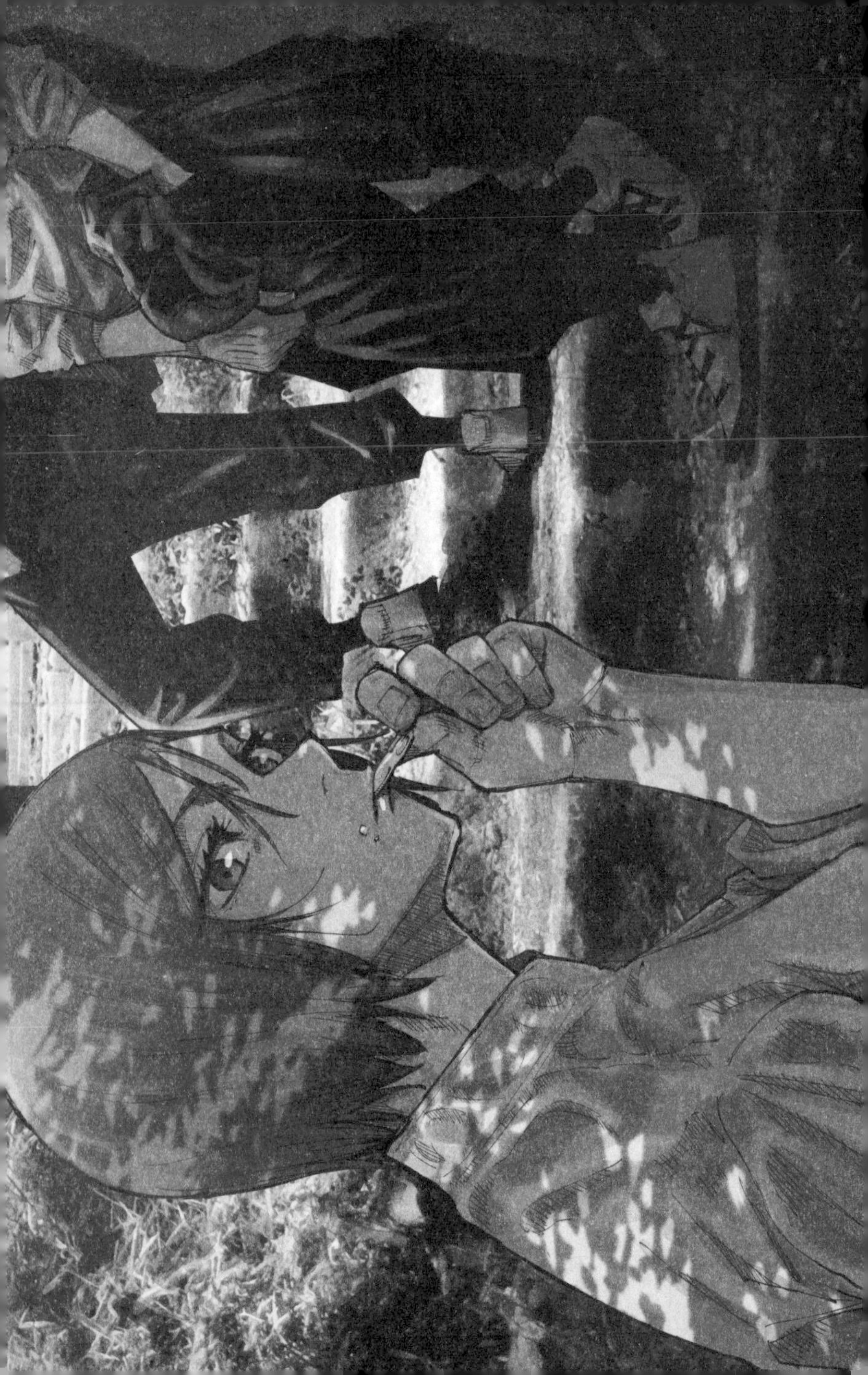

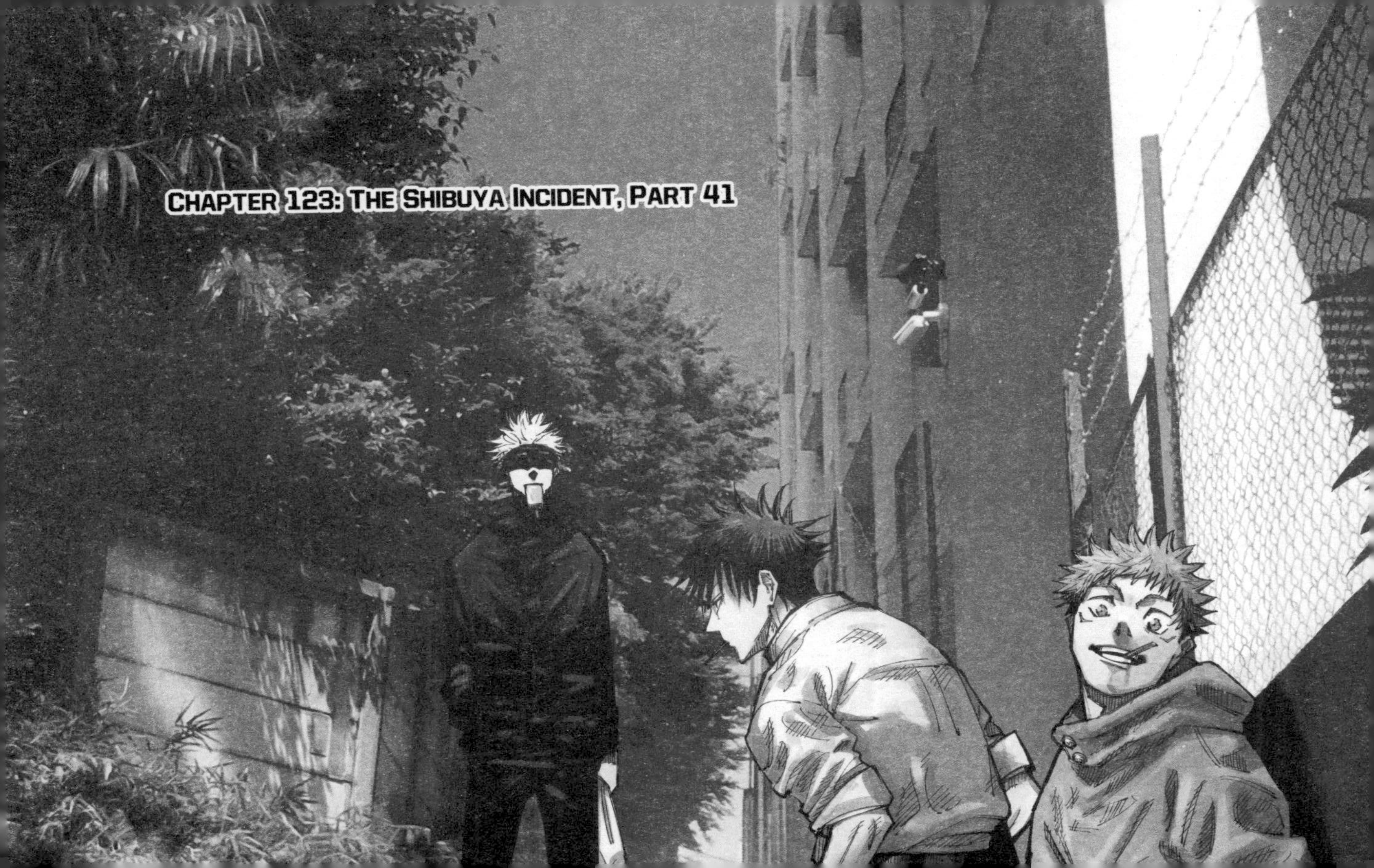
CHAPTER 123: THE SHIBUYA INCIDENT, PART 41

JUJUTSU KAISEN

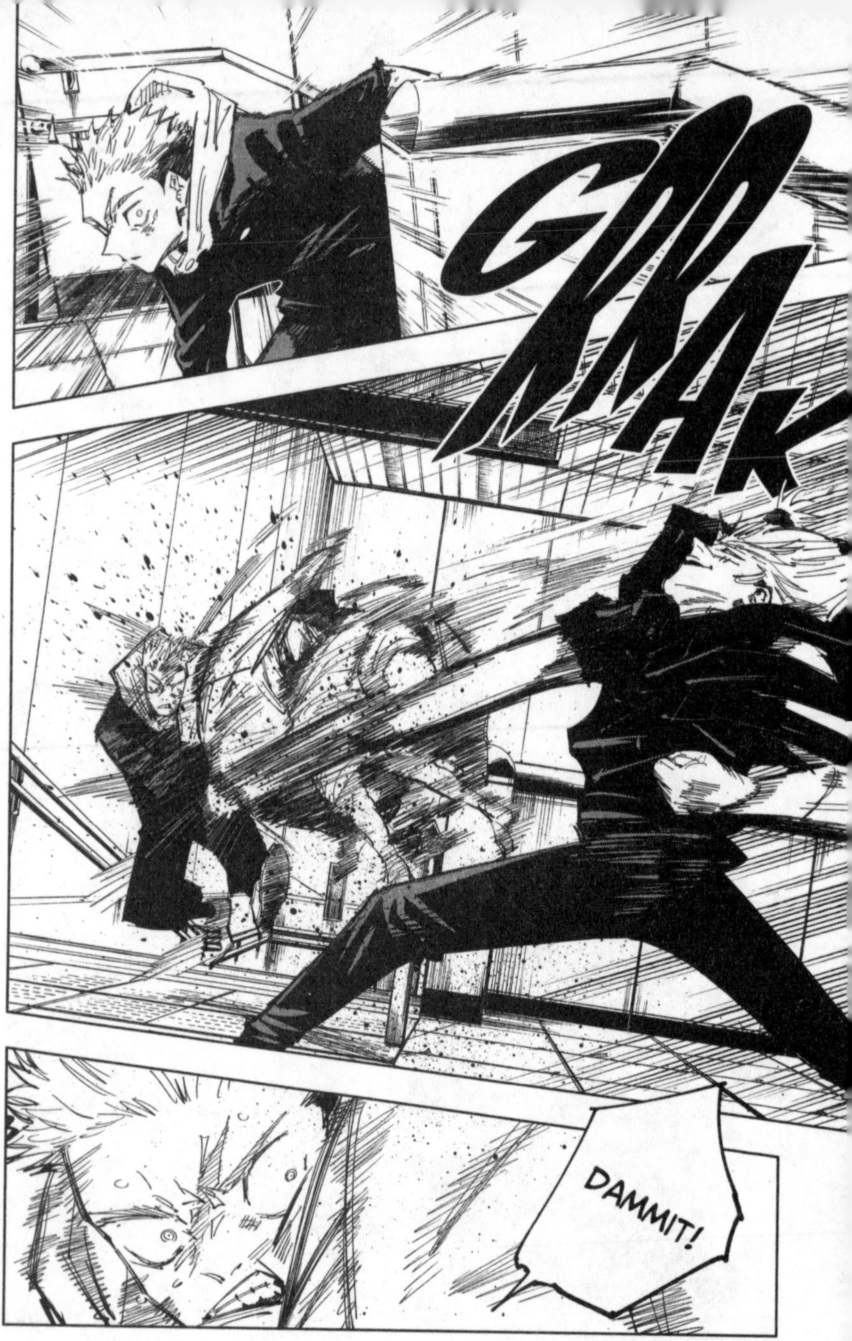
GONK
DAMMIT!

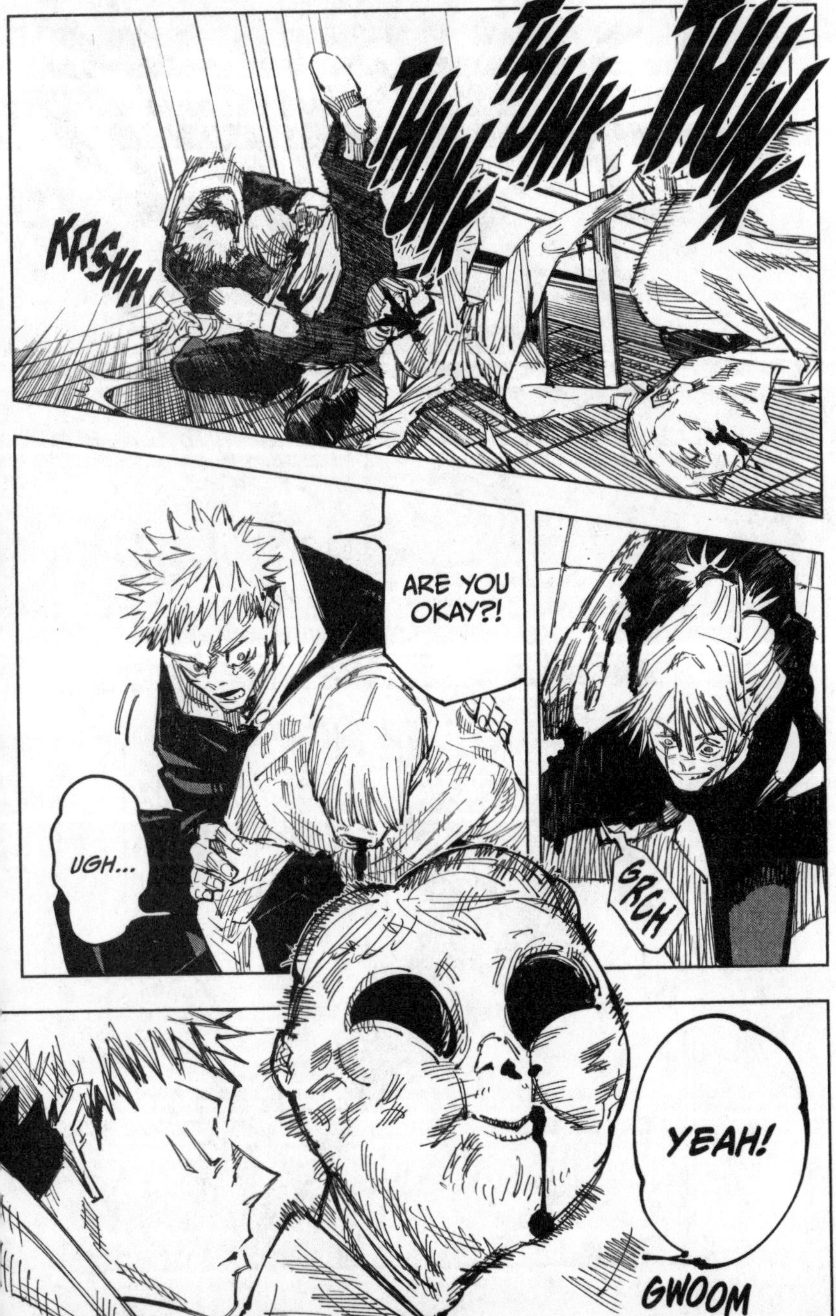
THUNK
THUNK
THUNK
KRSHH
GRCH
ARE YOU OKAY?!
UGH...
YEAH!
GWOOM

POP

SPLAT
SPLAT

CRAP, I—

KLINK
KLINK

KLINK

KLINK

KLINK

VWUM

KRSH

I'M JUST A DOUBLE THOUGH.

HOW BORING.

SHE'S AVOIDING MY HANDS... THE 7:3 HAIRSTYLE SORCERER MUST HAVE WARNED HER.

I CAN CHANGE MY FORM LIKE THE ORIGINAL, BUT...

...I CAN'T MANIPULATE TRANSFIGURED HUMANS OR OTHER SOULS.

BWOOM

...BUT THANKS FOR WEARING YOUR-SELF DOWN...

...FOR ME!

I'M NOT FIGHTING ITADORI. I CAN MANIPULATE MY FORM AS MUCH AS I WANT WITHOUT INCURRING RISKS.

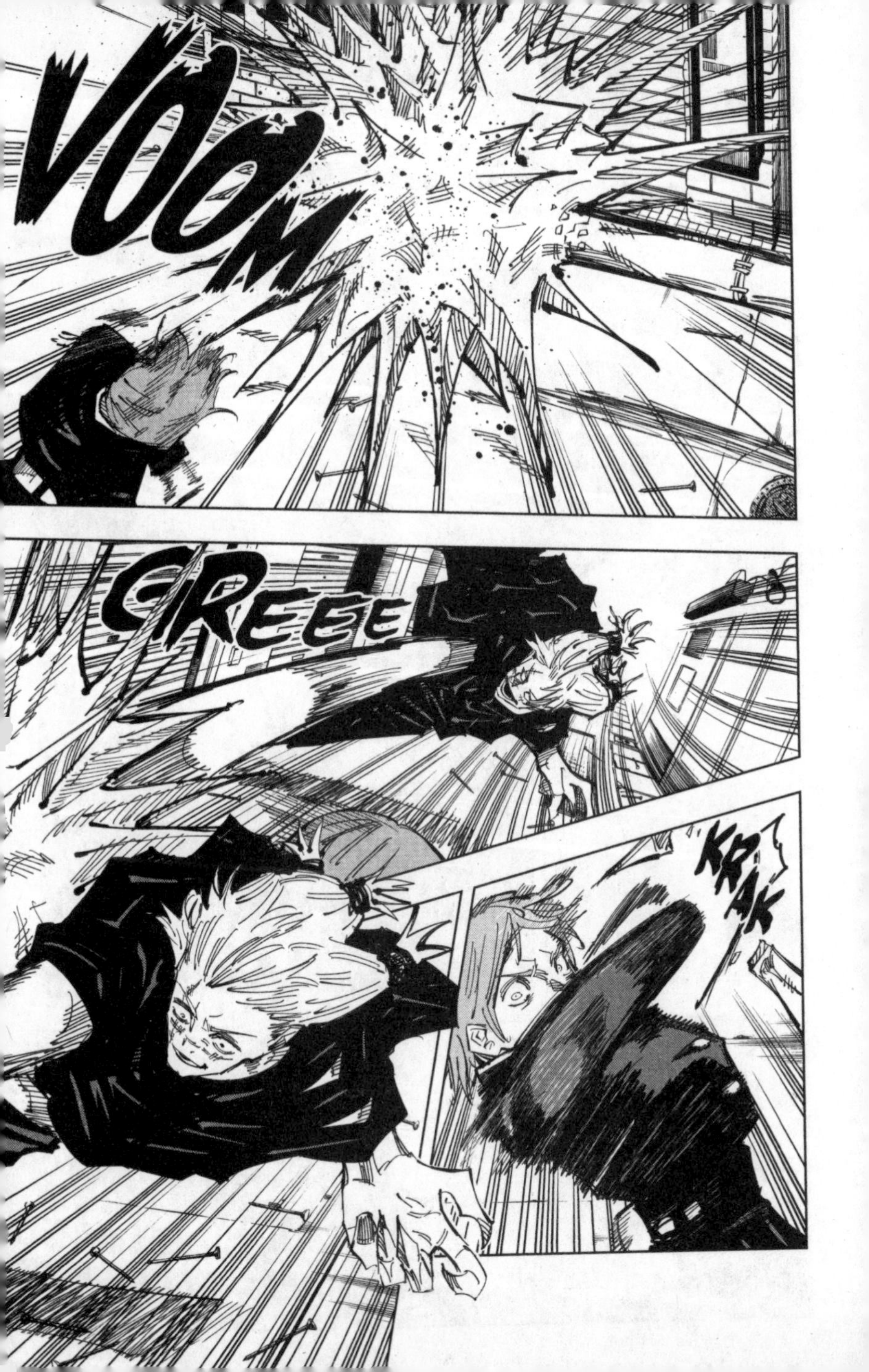
VOOM
GREEEE
KRAK

SOOO LAME!

... SOMETIMES YOU JUST GOTTA TRY!

I KNOW THAT, BUT...

KLINK

KLINK

SWP

2F

!

TP TP

VVP

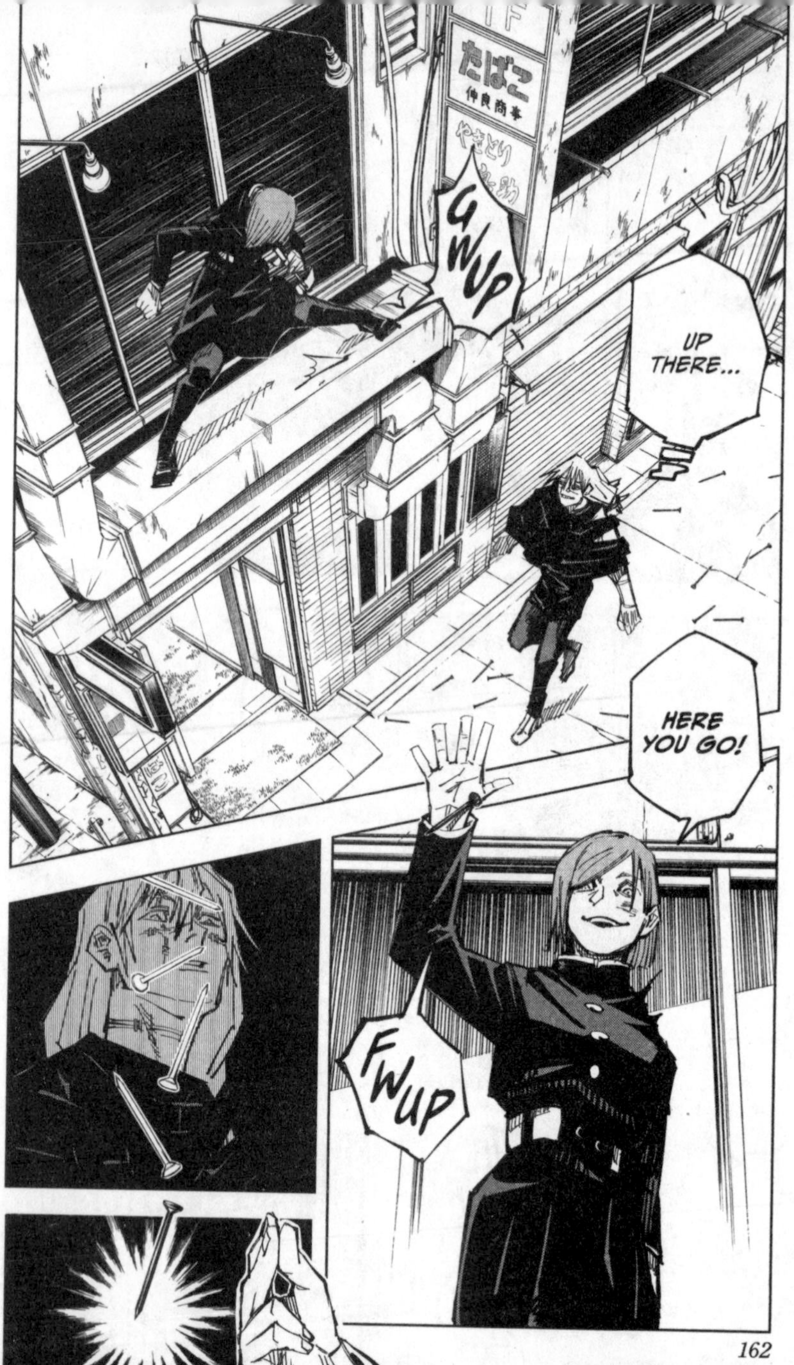
たばこ
仲良商事
やきとり
GWUP
UP THERE...
HERE YOU GO!
FWUP

THOK
THOK

!!

THOK
THOK

HAIR-PIN!!

THE FIRST ONE RATTLED THE NAILS TO MAKE THEM POINT UPRIGHT!

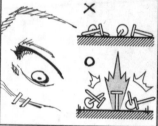

THUNK

...

I'VE BEEN
THINKING
ABOUT IT.

BUT WHAT
DOES THAT
MATTER?

...THIS...

EVER SINCE
I WAS TOLD
ABOUT YOUR
CURSED
TECHNIQUE,
I'VE
THOUGHT...

!!

...WOULD
BE
EFFECTIVE
AGAINST
YOU.

SHE WAS
BLUFFING
TO MAKE
IT SEEM
LIKE SHE
DIDN'T
HAVE A
PLAN!

BEFORE...

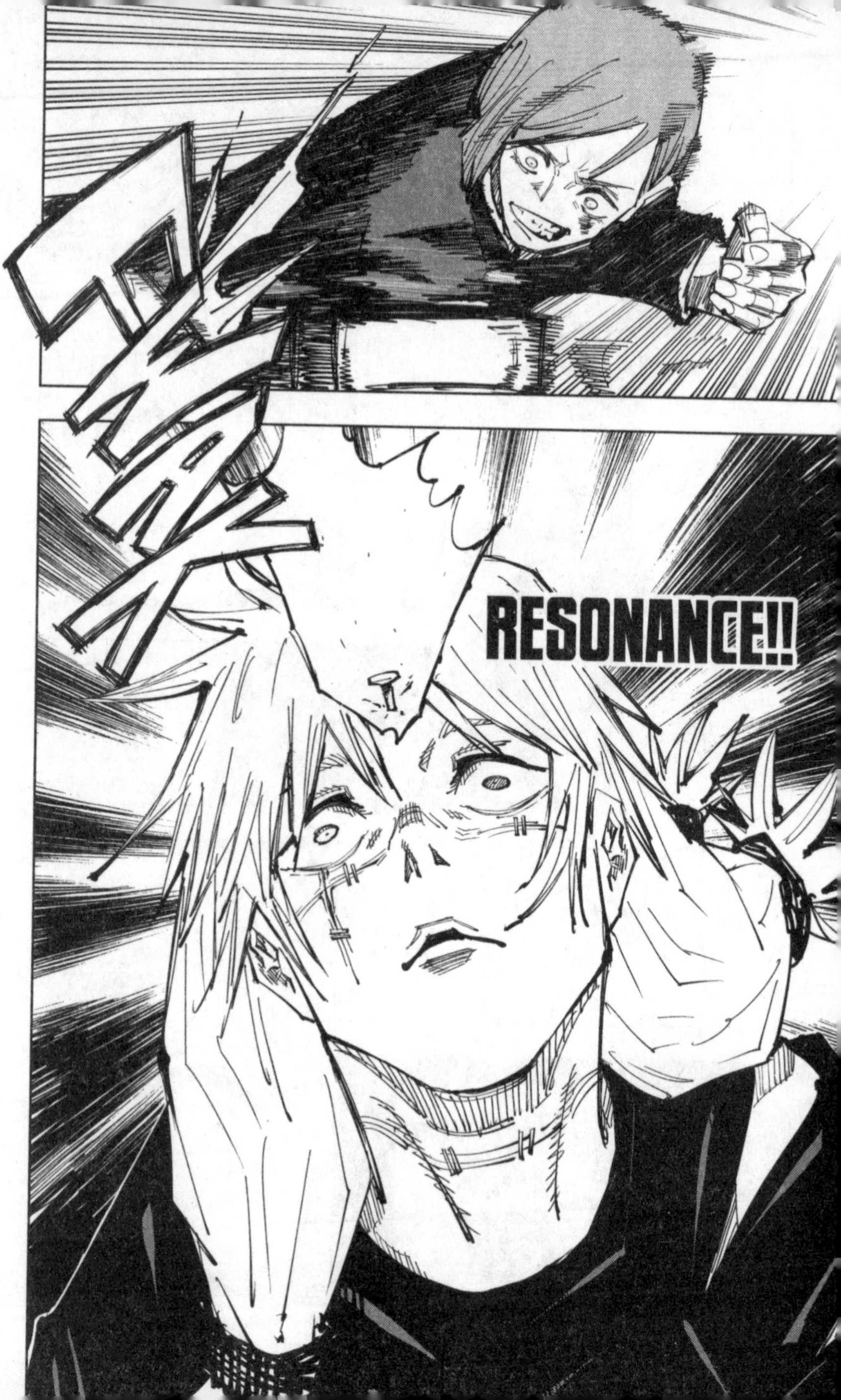
RESONANCE!!

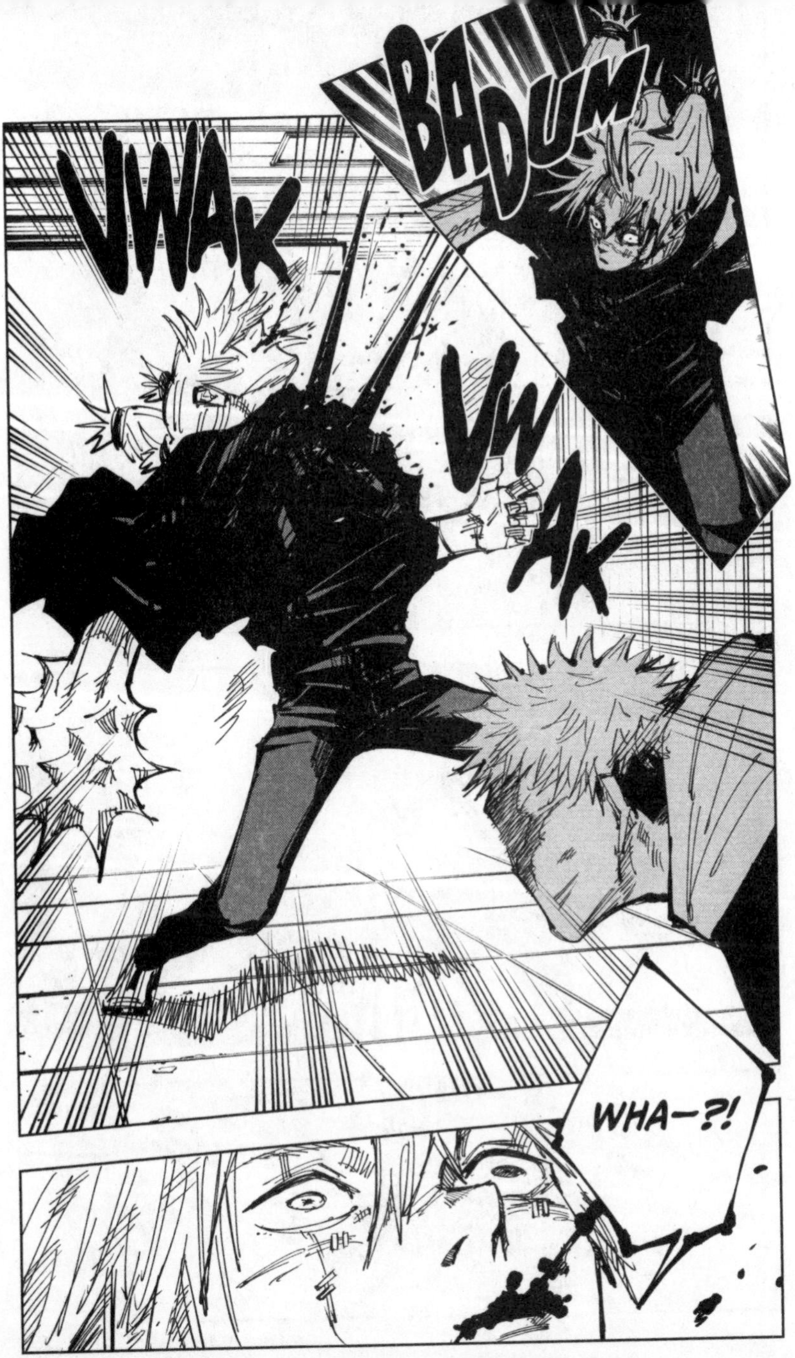
BADUM
VWAK
VWAK
WHA-?!

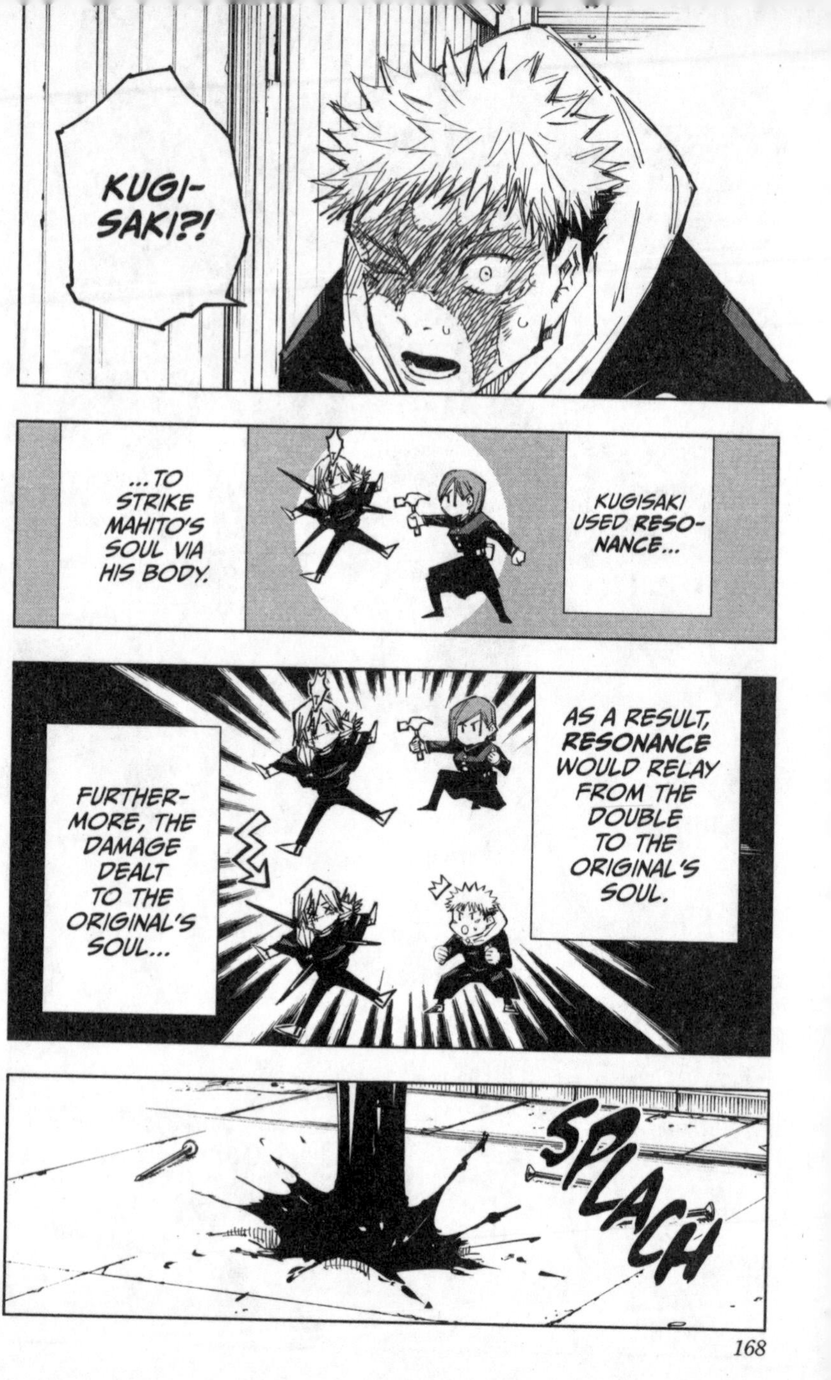
KUGI-SAKI?!
KUGISAKI USED RESO-NANCE...
...TO STRIKE MAHITO'S SOUL VIA HIS BODY.
AS A RESULT, RESONANCE WOULD RELAY FROM THE DOUBLE TO THE ORIGINAL'S SOUL.
FURTHER-MORE, THE DAMAGE DEALT TO THE ORIGINAL'S SOUL...
SPLACH

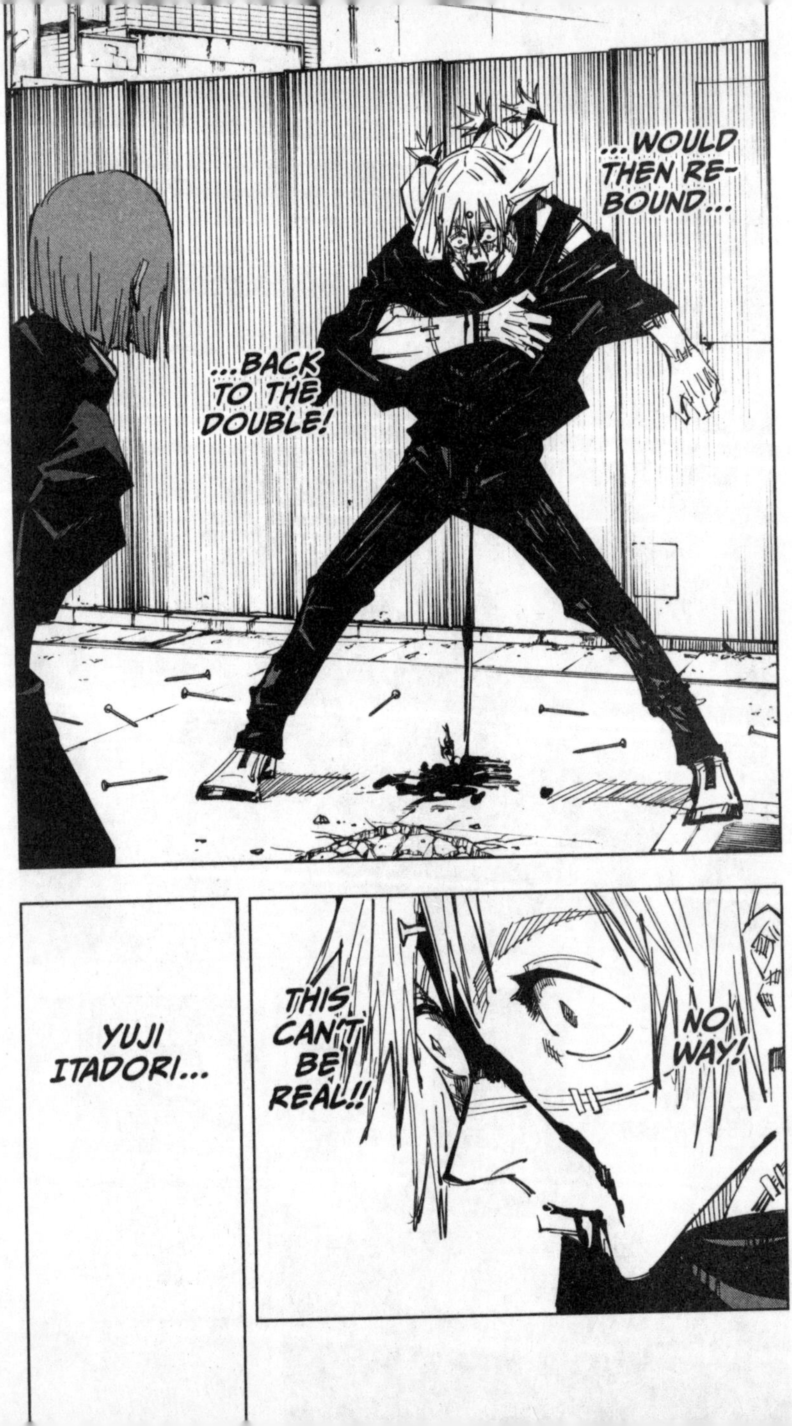
...WOULD THEN RE-BOUND...
...BACK TO THE DOUBLE!
NO WAY!
THIS CAN'T BE REAL!!
YUJI ITADORI...

...ISN'T MY ONLY...

...NATURAL ENEMY!

...DETONATE SOMEWHERE ELSE NEARBY.

I JUST FELT MY CURSED ENERGY...

HM... THAT'S WEIRD.

...YOU COULD'VE JUST GRABBED ME.

AND BACK THEN...

KREE

YOUR CURSED ENERGY ISN'T REALLY ALL THAT STRONG.

HOW DO I PUT THIS...

...SO YOU CAN'T USE YOUR CURSED TECHNIQUE, AM I RIGHT?!

YOU'RE LIKE A DOUBLE OR SOMETHING...

GRCHK

CORRECT...

A Nice Story

• Hiramatsu-san drew this design
of a young Kugisaki for the anime,
and I used it in the manga too.
• When Hiramatsu-san draws
Kugisaki, she's actually cute.

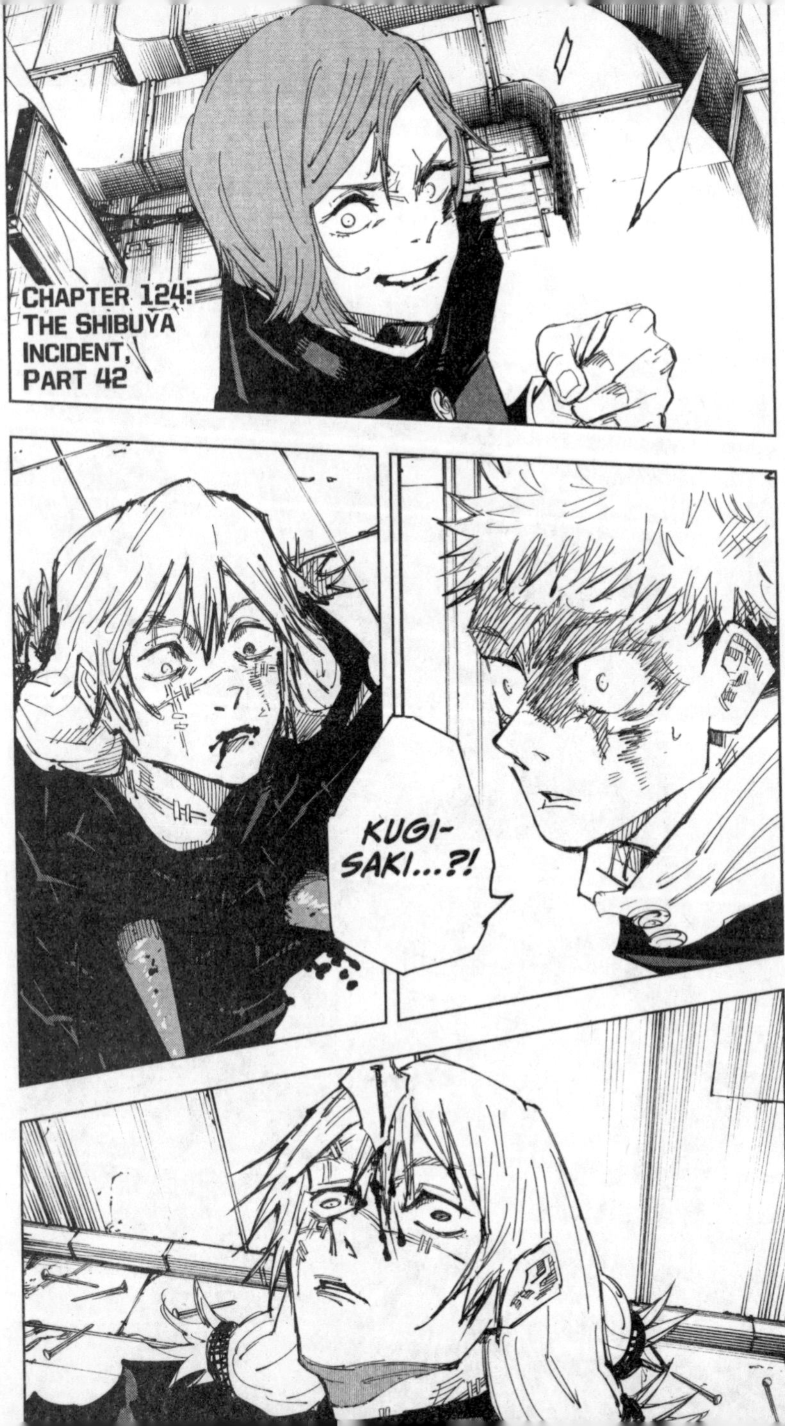
CHAPTER 124: THE SHIBUYA INCIDENT, PART 42
KUGI-SAKI...?!

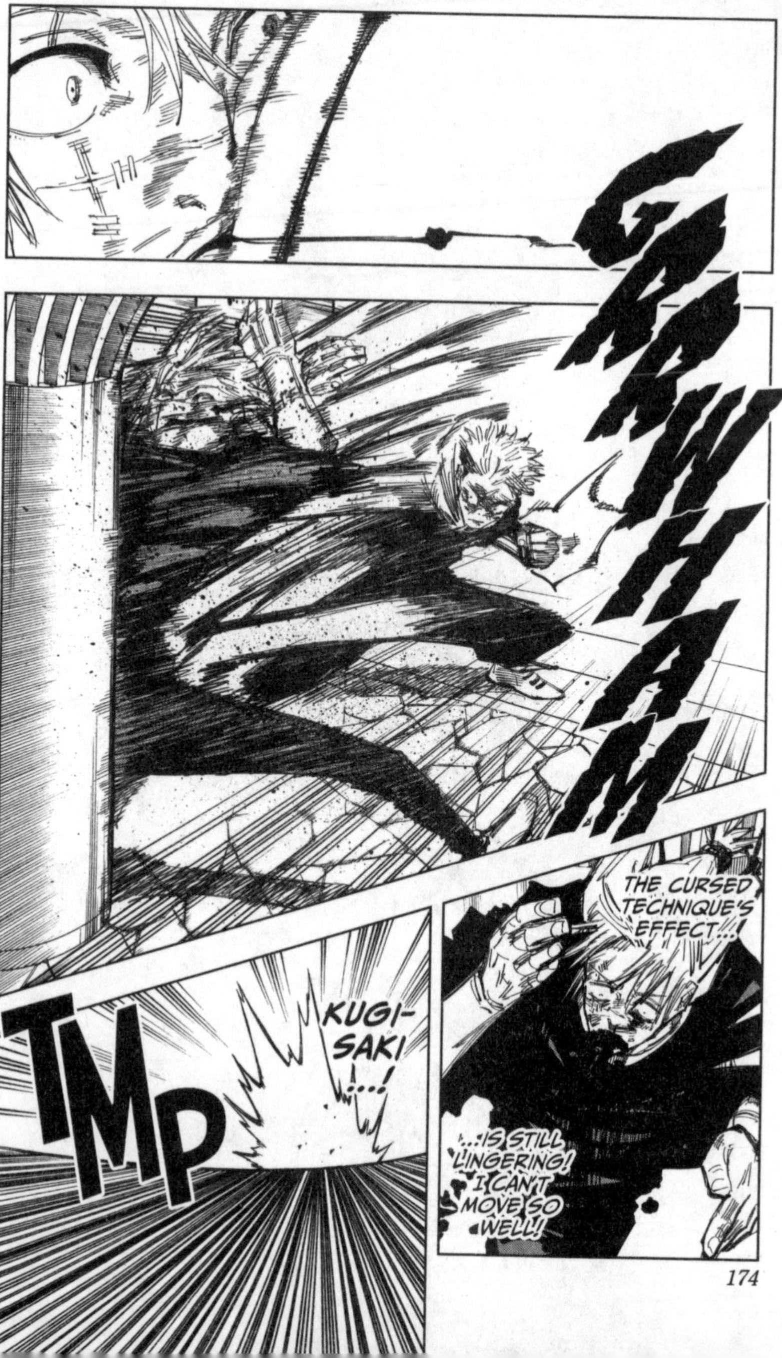
GRWHAM
THE CURSED TECHNIQUE'S EFFECT...
...IS STILL LINGERING! I CAN'T MOVE SO WELL!
KUGI-SAKI...!
TMP

BWAM

THANK
YOU!

I COULDN'T
SAVE ANYONE.

I WASTED
EVERYONE'S
EFFORTS.

GRCH

GRCH

GRCH

BUT...

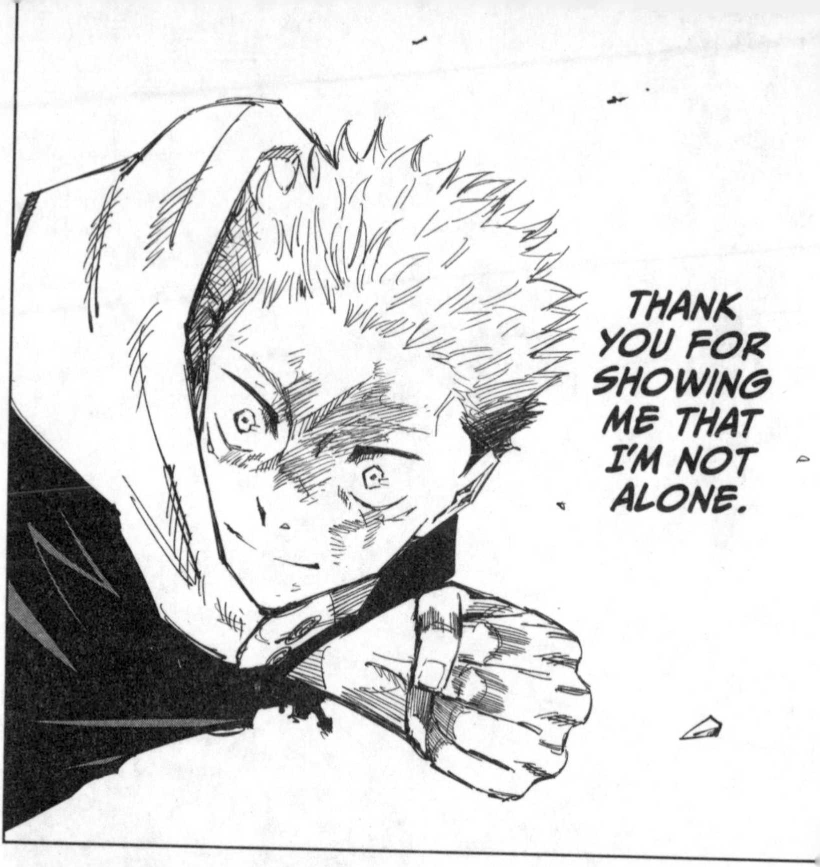
THANK YOU FOR SHOWING ME THAT I'M NOT ALONE.

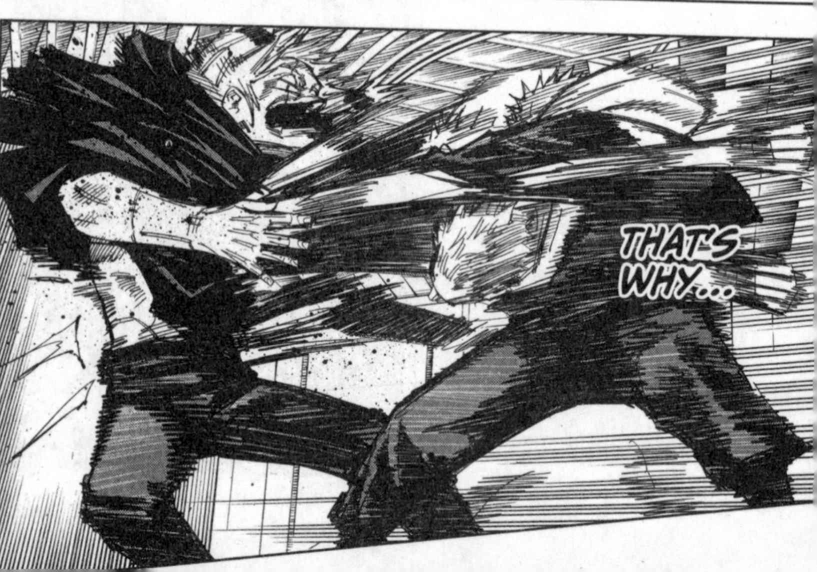
THAT'S WHY...

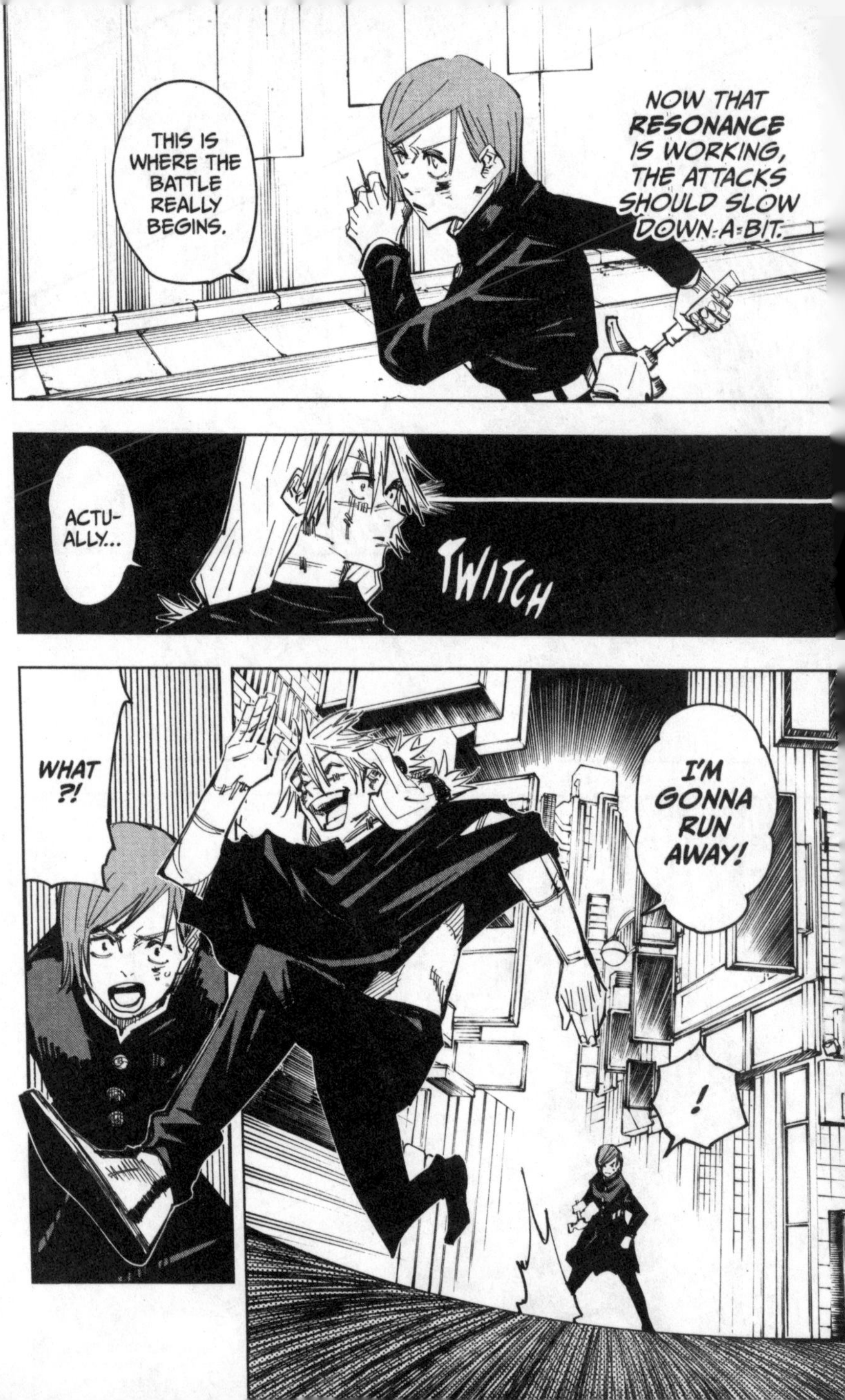
NOW THAT RESONANCE IS WORKING, THE ATTACKS SHOULD SLOW DOWN A BIT.
THIS IS WHERE THE BATTLE REALLY BEGINS.
ACTU-ALLY...
TWITCH
I'M GONNA RUN AWAY!
WHAT ?!
!

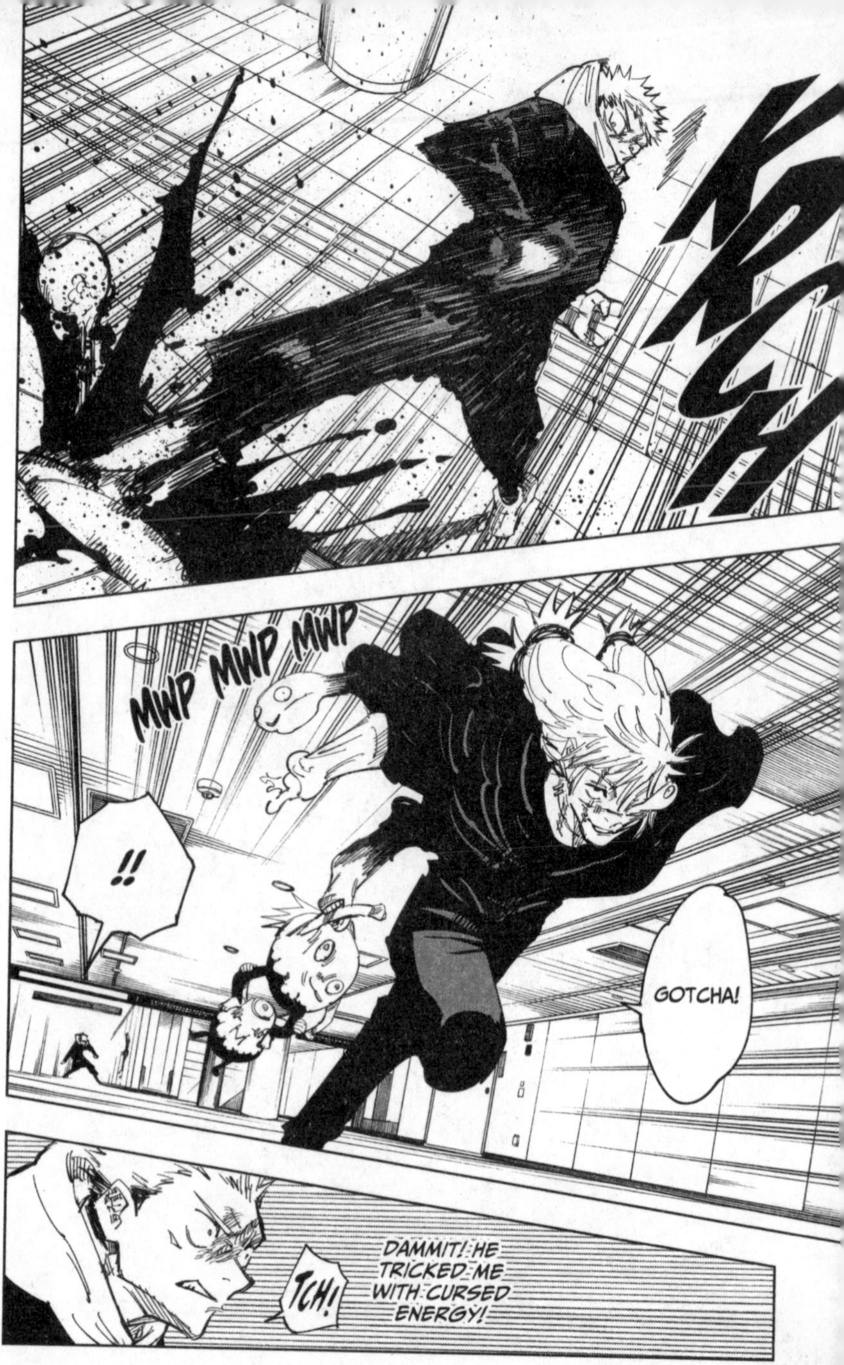
MWP MWP MWP
!!
GOTCHA!
DAMMIT! HE TRICKED ME WITH CURSED ENERGY!
TCH!

VWP

!!

TOMP

TP

TWO MAHITOS?!

DUN DUN DUN DUN DUN

IS HE TRYING TO FUSE BACK TOGETHER TO HEAL?!

WAS THAT DOUBLE SOMEWHERE ELSE BEFORE?!

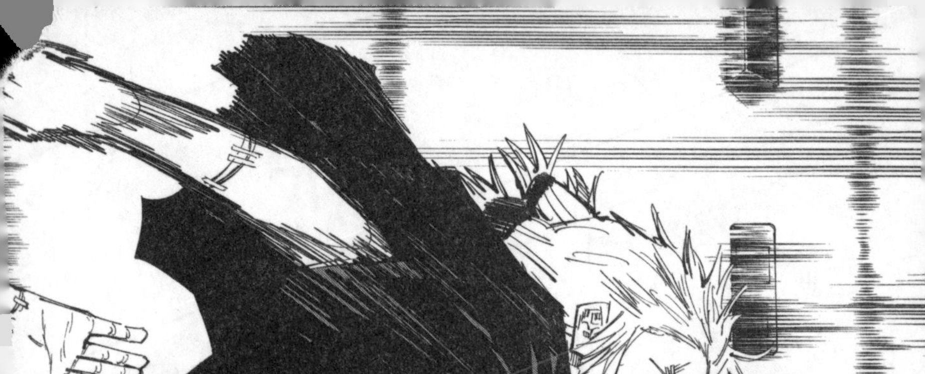

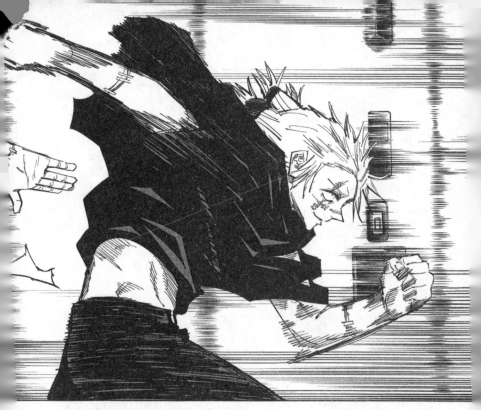

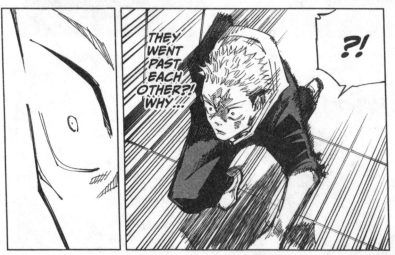

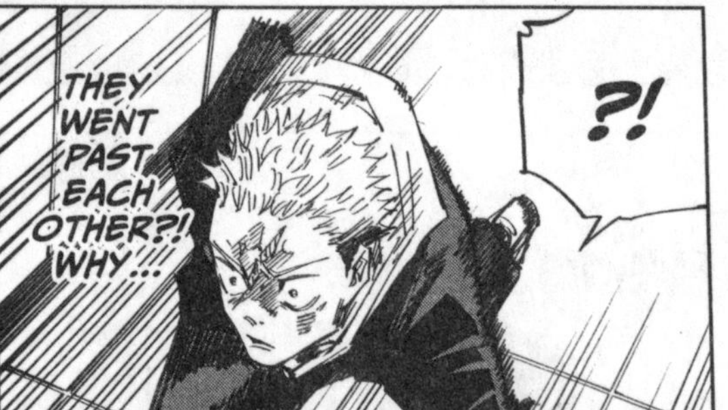
?!
THEY WENT PAST EACH OTHER?! WHY...

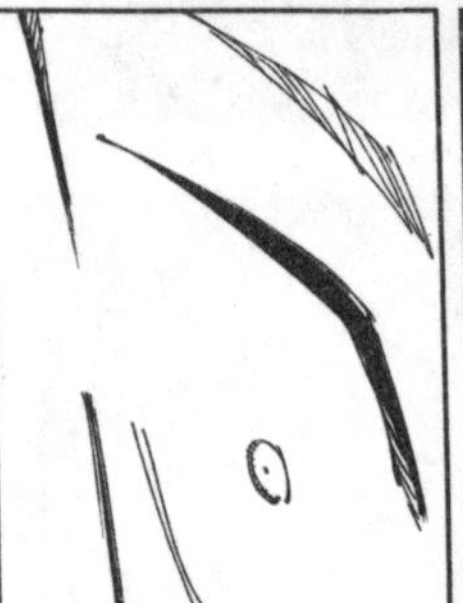

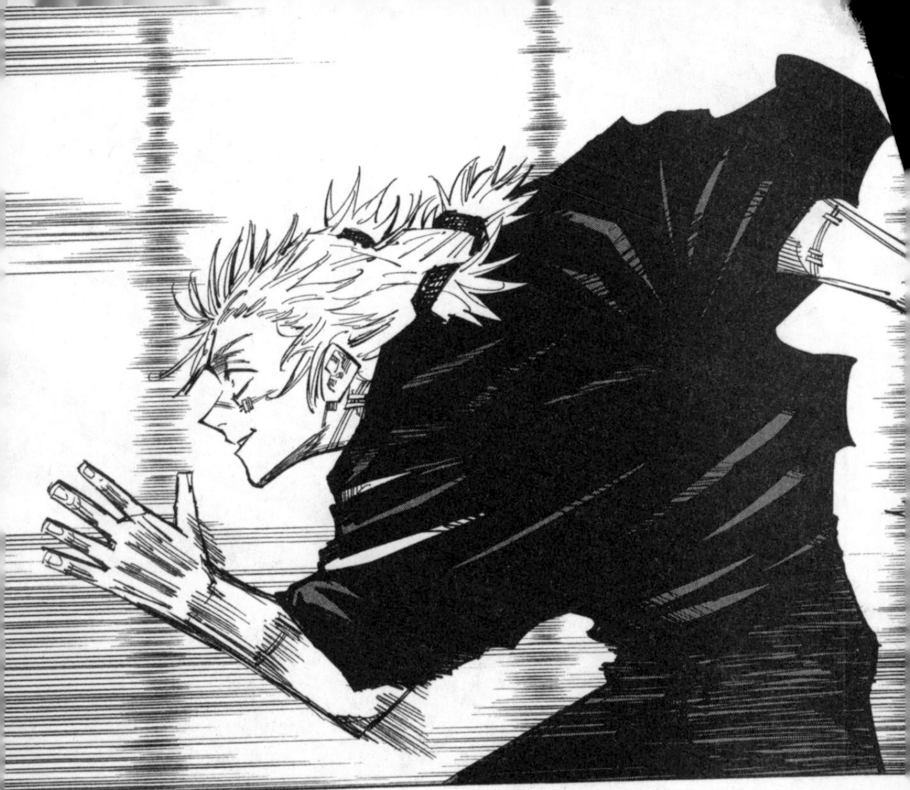
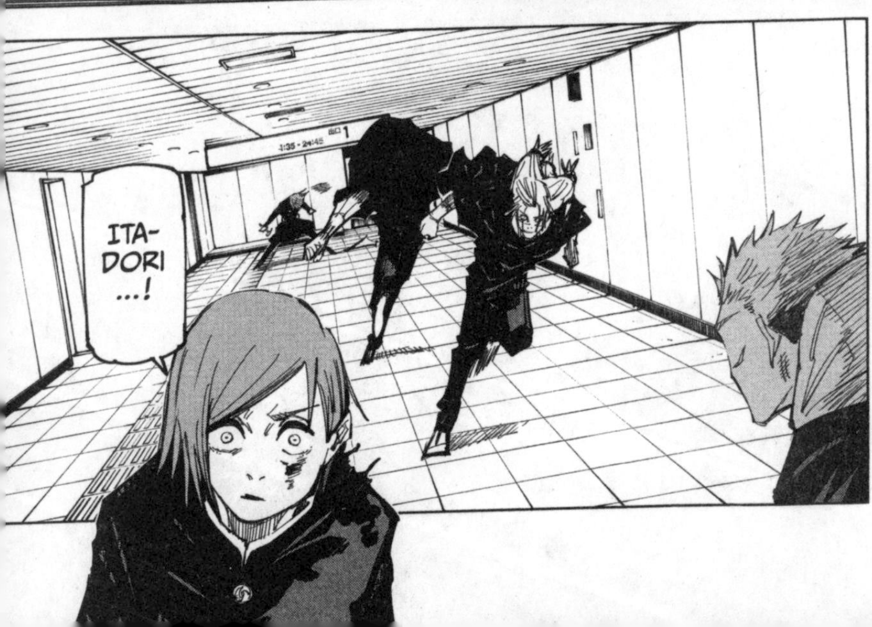
ITA-
DORI
...!

FURTHERMORE, DUE TO HER BATTLE AGAINST THE DOUBLE...

THE REAL BODY ACTED AS A BLIND SPOT SO THAT KUGISAKI WOULD NOT NOTICE THE SWITCH.

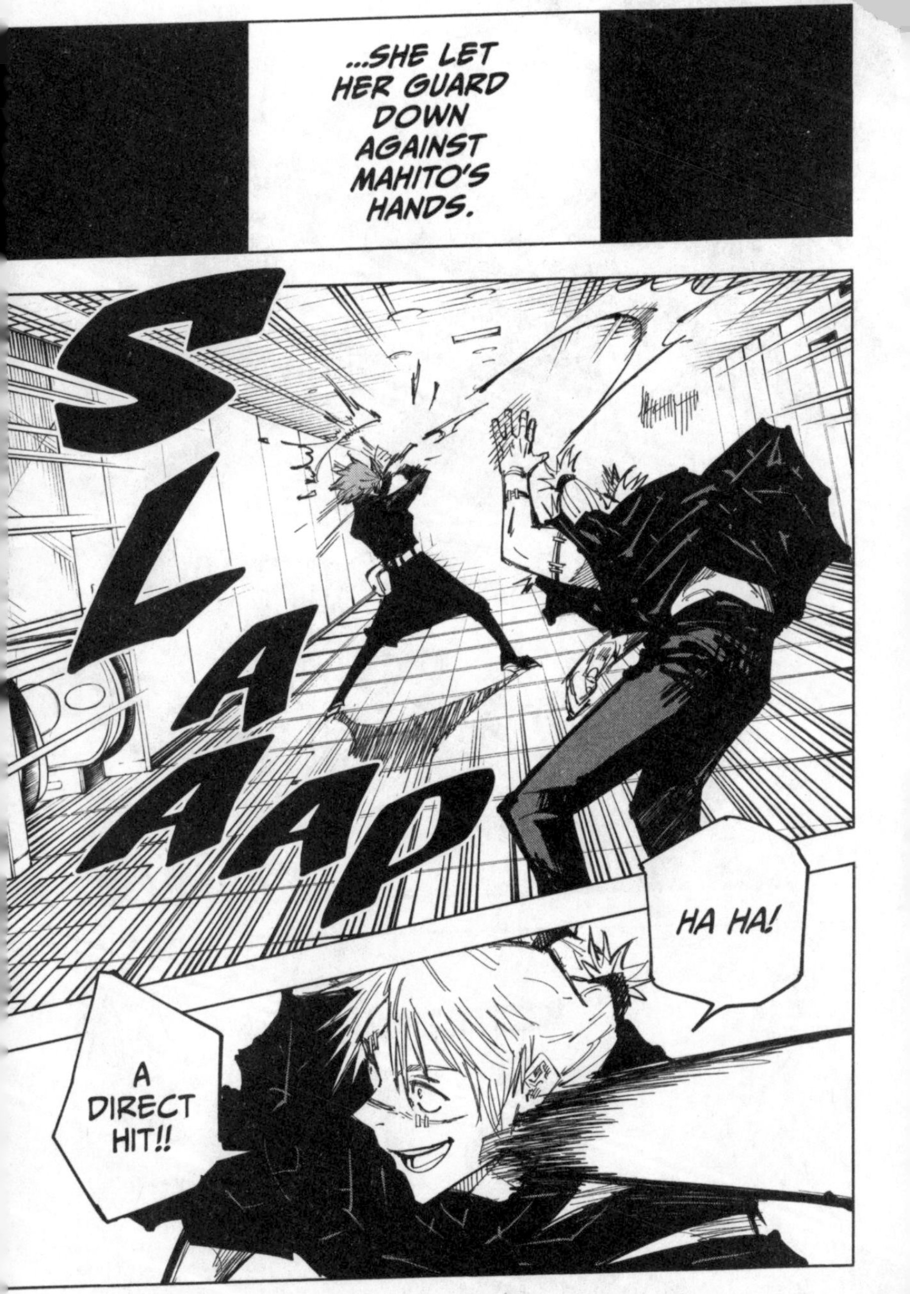
...SHE LET HER GUARD DOWN AGAINST MAHITO'S HANDS.
SLAAAP
HA HA!
A DIRECT HIT!!

188

...WITH ONE TOUCH, BUT...

I COULDN'T KILL THE 7:3 HAIRSTYLE SORCERER...

...HOW ABOUT YOU?

2009...

GRAA-
AHHH!!
DIE!!

NOBARA KUGISAKI
(SIX YEARS OLD)

YOU HAFTA MAKE SURE TO GO FOR THE KILL WHEN THE OPPONENT IS RECOVERING.

MAYBE NEXT TIME, NOBARA.

TO BE CONTINUED

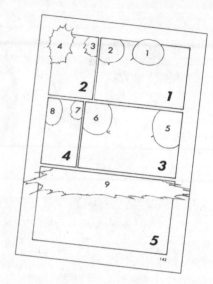

JUJUTSU KAISEN
reads from right to left, starting in the upper-right corner. Japanese is read from right to left, meaning that action, sound effects, and word-balloon order are completely reversed from English order.